100 WALKS
IN NEW SOUTH WALES

100 Walks
in New South Wales

Tyrone T. Thomas

HILL OF CONTENT

MELBOURNE

First Published 1977
by Hill of Content Publishing Company Pty Ltd
86 Bourke Street Melbourne Australia

© Copyright Tyrone T. Thomas

Revised Edition 1980

Printed and bound by Colorcraft Ltd., Hong Kong.

Cover photograph from author's collection

National Library of Australia
Cataloguing-in-Publication data
Thomas, Tyrone T.
  100 Walks in New South Wales.

  ISBN 0 85572 087 5

  1. Hiking—New South Wales.   I. Title.

796.5109944

PUBLISHER'S NOTE
It is imperative that users of this book
check time-tables and transport services
before undertaking any walk suggestion.

CONTENTS

CONTENTS

INTRODUCTION

This book contains information about one hundred walks in New South Wales. It recommends walking areas in the State which are generally frequented by bushwalkers. Population centres are taken into account so that the greatest number of walk suggestions occur in the beautiful places near the biggest cities and the book is organized so that ready reference can be made to those regions. Within each region walks are graded easy, medium and hard. Most routes are circuits of one day's duration, or are planned so that public transport can be used to complete circuits. Seven selected walks are included which are of two days' duration and which the author considers to be the best in the State. They are included for those who want to try camping out.

It is hoped that this book will induce people to go out walking, that it will help them to grow to love the New South Wales bush and to learn to care for it and themselves while walking. Special sections deal with safety, mapping and navigation. The book is designed to suit all grades of walkers and should be a useful addition to *120 Walks in Victoria, 100 Walks in Tasmania and 50 Walks in The Grampians.*

Generally speaking, walk venues in New South Wales are in rugged country, often with sandstone cliffs and therefore distances that can be covered in a day are relatively short. Times taken will vary greatly depending on walker's experience so track notes are listed in terms of distance rather than variable times.

All routes in the Sydney, Newcastle and Armidale

Regions were personally walked by the author during December 1976 and January 1977, except Mount Warning which was previewed in August 1978. All walks in the Wollongong and Canberra Regions were reviewed during April 1979 and all Kosciusko Region walks were reviewed in January and April 1979. Notes were simultaneously compiled or updated, but, naturally, changes will occur in some places with the passing of time.

Every care has been taken in their compilation, but no responsibility will be accepted for any inaccuracies or for any injury or mishap that might arise out of the use of this book. The author and publisher welcome advice of any errors or desirable changes to bring future editions of the book up to date.

Tyrone T. Thomas.

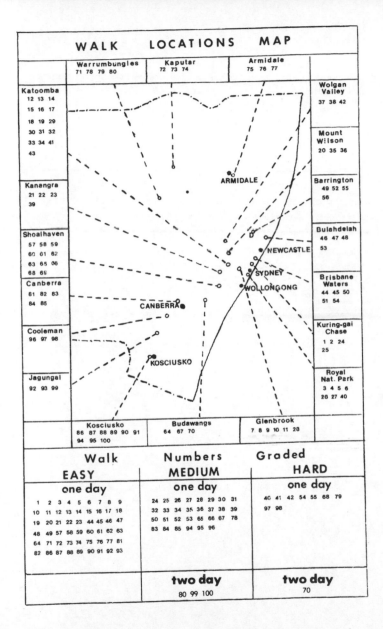

WALK LOCATIONS MAP

Warrumbungles 71 78 79 80	**Kaputar** 72 73 74	**Armidale** 75 76 77

Katoomba
12 13 14
15 16 17
18 19 29
30 31 32
33 34 41
43

Kanangra
21 22 23
39

Shoalhaven
57 58 59
60 61 62
63 65 66
68 69

Canberra
81 82 83
84 85

Cooleman
96 97 98

Jagungal
92 93 99

Wolgan Valley
37 38 42

Mount Wilson
20 35 36

Barrington
49 52 55
56

Bulahdelah
46 47 48
53

Brisbane Waters
44 45 50
51 54

Kuring-gai Chase
1 2 24
25

Royal Nat. Park
3 4 5 6
26 27 40

ARMIDALE

NEWCASTLE
SYDNEY
WOLLONGONG

CANBERRA

KOSCIUSKO

Kosciusko 86 87 88 89 90 91 94 95 100	**Budawangs** 64 67 70	**Glenbrook** 7 8 9 10 11 28

Walk	Numbers	Graded
EASY	**MEDIUM**	**HARD**
one day	**one day**	**one day**
1 2 3 4 5 6 7 8 9 10 11 12 13 14 15 16 17 18 19 20 21 22 23 44 45 46 47 48 49 57 58 59 60 61 62 63 64 71 72 73 74 75 76 77 81 82 86 87 88 89 90 91 92 93	24 25 26 27 28 29 30 31 32 33 34 35 36 37 38 39 50 51 52 53 65 66 67 78 83 84 85 94 95 96	40 41 42 54 55 68 79 97 98
	two day 80 99 100	**two day** 70

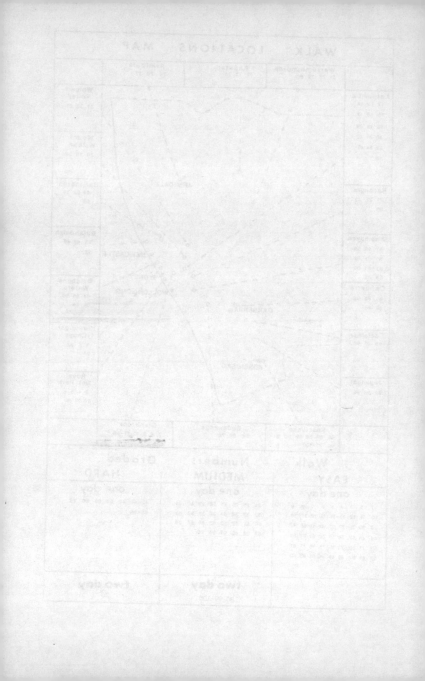

INDEX TO WALK SUGGESTIONS

SYDNEY REGION — Easy Grade

SYDNEY REGION — Medium Grade

1

SYDNEY REGION — Hard Grade

SYDNEY REGION — Overnight Walk

NEWCASTLE REGION — Easy Grade

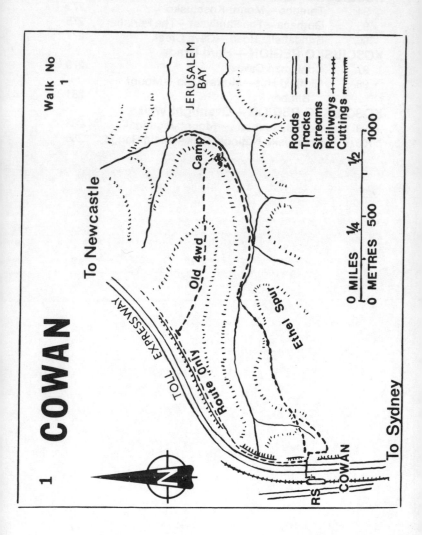

1 COWAN

Walk No 1

To Newcastle

To Sydney

TOLL EXPRESSWAY

Old 4wd

Route Only

Camp

JERUSALEM BAY

Ethel Spur

RS

COWAN

N

Roads
Tracks
Streams
Railways
Cuttings

0 MILES ¼ ½

0 METRES 500 1000

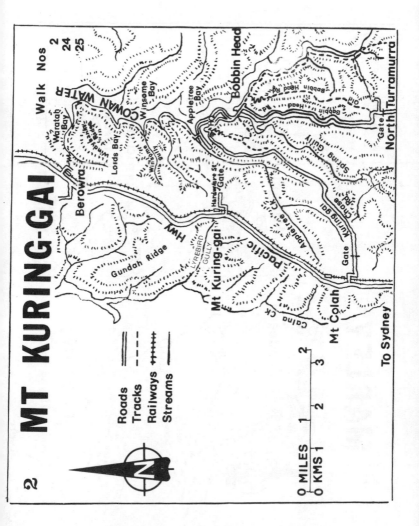

2 MT KURING-GAI

Walk Nos
2
24
25

COWAN WATER

Berowra

Gundah Ridge

BERRA HWH

Mt Kuring-gai

Mt Colah

To Sydney

Waratah Bay
Windy Bay
Windy Hump Bay
Lords Bay
Linwood
King Arbour

Winsome Bay

Appletree Bay

Bobbin Head

Hardware St Gate

LYREBIRD GULLY

Appletree Ck

Caina Ck

PACIFIC

Kuring Gai Chase Rd

Spring Gully

Bobbin Head Rd
Old Bobbin Head Rd

Gate
North Turramurra

Gate

Roads ══════
Tracks ┄┄┄┄┄
Railways ┼┼┼┼┼┼
Streams ─────

N

0 MILES 1   2   3
0 KMS 1   2   3

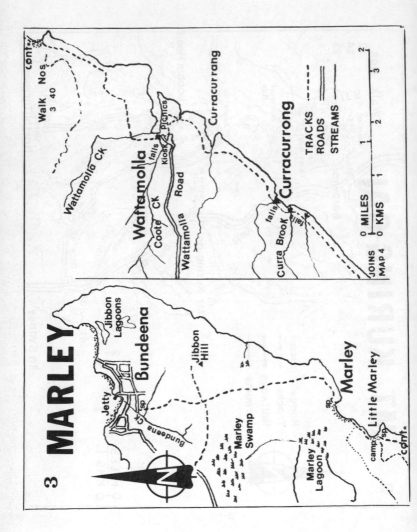

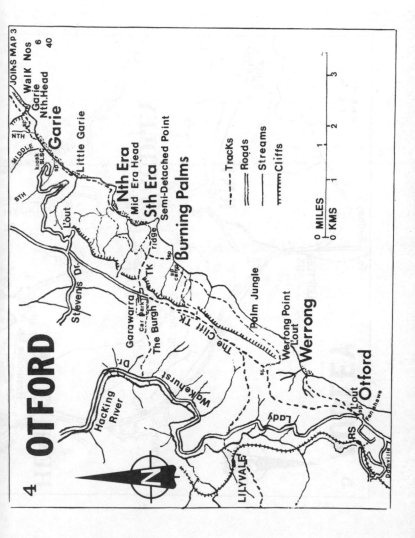

4 OTFORD

Garie

Nth Era
Mid Era Head

Sth Era

Semi-Detached Point

Burning Palms

Little Garie

L'out

kiosk SLSC
NTH
MIDDLE
STH

Stevens Dr.

Garawarra

The Burgh

Car Park

TK

sp camp

ridge

Hacking River

Walkehurst Dr

The Cliff TK

Palm Jungle

Werrong Point
L'out

Werrong

LILYVALE

Lady

RS

Otford
L'out
Fanshawe

Damville

- - - - Tracks
═══ Roads
──── Streams
ᴗᴗᴗ Cliffs

0 MILES	1	1	2	3
0 KMS				

N

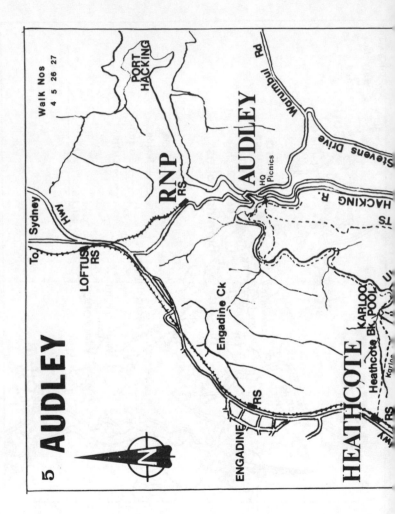

5 AUDLEY

Walk Nos 4 5 26 27

To Sydney

RNP RS

AUDLEY

HQ Picnics

PORT HACKING

Warumbul Rd

Stevens Drive

HACKING R.

TS

LOFTUS RS

HWY

Engadine Ck

ENGADINE RS

HEATHCOTE

Heathcote Bk

KARLOO POOL

Karloo

RS

HWY

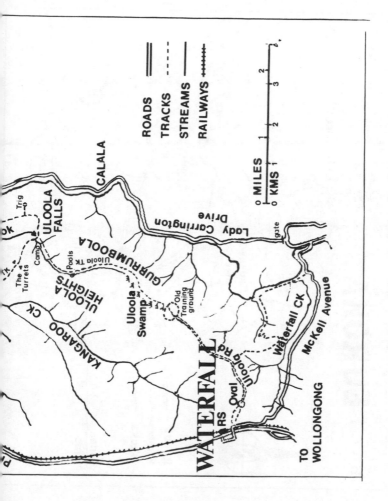

ROADS
TRACKS ------
STREAMS
RAILWAYS ++++++

MILES 0   1   2
KMS 0   1   2   3

CALALA

ULOOLA FALLS

Trig

The Turrets

Camp

Pools

ULOOLA HEIGHTS

KANGAROO CK

Uloola Swamp

GURRUMBOOLA

Uloola TK

Lady Carrington Drive

gate

Old Training ground

WATERFALL

Oval

Uloola Rd

Waterfall CK

McKell Avenue

TO WOLLONGONG

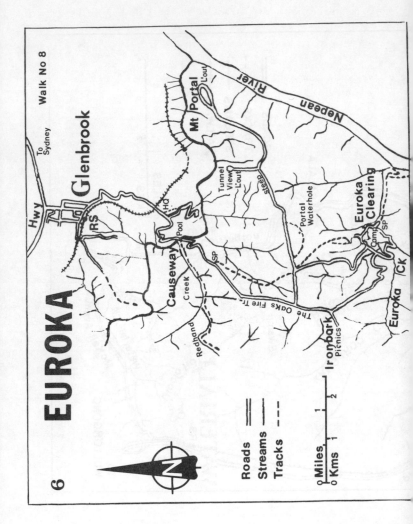

6 EUROKA

Walk No 8

Glenbrook

Hwy

To Sydney

Mt Portal

L'out

Nepean River

Tunnel View L'out

Portal Waterhole

steep

RS

Causeway

HQ

Pool

Creek

SP

Redland

The Oaks Fire Tr.

Ironbark
Picnics

Euroka Clearing

Camp

SP

Euroka Ck

N

Roads ═══
Streams ───
Tracks - - -

Miles 0   1
Kms 0 1 2

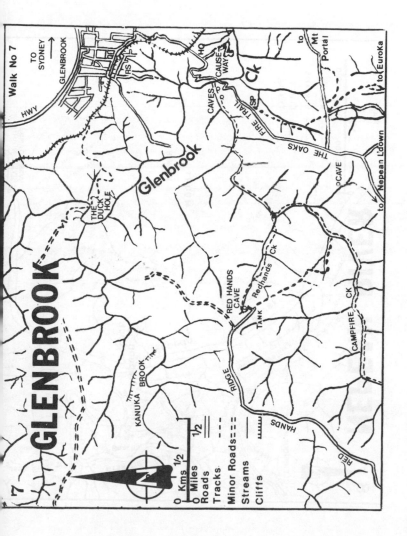

GLENBROOK

7

HWY

THE DUCK HOLE

Glenbrook

KANUKA BROOK

CAVES

CAUSE WAY

HQ

RS

FIRE TRAIL

Ck

CAVE

THE OAKS

to Nepean L'down

to Euroka

to Mt Portal

RED HANDS CAVE

TANK

Redhands Ck

RIDGE

CAMPFIRE CK

RED HANDS

N

0 Kms ½
0 Miles ½

Roads
Tracks
Minor Roads
Streams
Cliffs

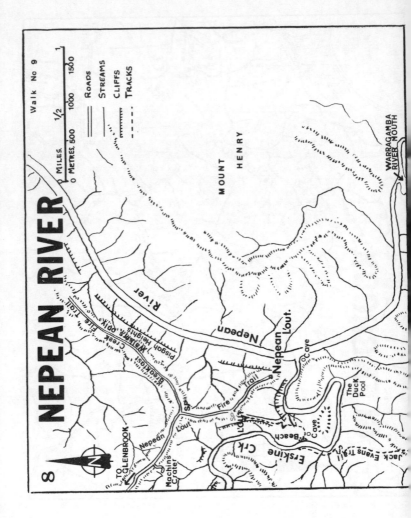

NEPEAN RIVER

8

Walk No 9

MILES. 0   1/2   1

METRES. 0 500 1000 1500

ROADS
STREAMS
CLIFFS
TRACKS

N

TO GLENBROOK

Machins Crater

Nepean L'out.

Blackfeet Creek

Walkers Track

Pigeon Heights

Euroka Trail

Fire Trail

S

L'out.

L'out.

Cove Beach

Erskine Ck

Jack Evans Trail

The Duck Pool

Cave

Nepean L'out.

Nepean River

MOUNT HENRY

River

WARRAGAMBA RIVER MOUTH

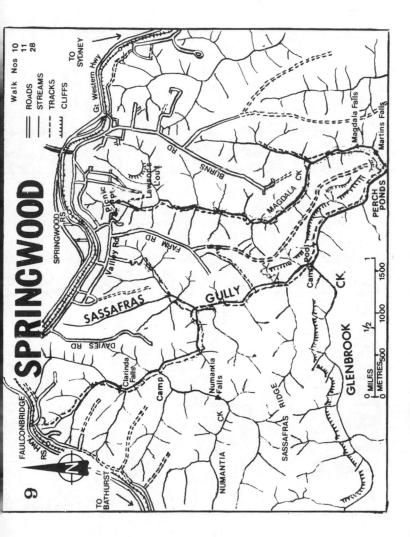

SPRINGWOOD

9

ROADS
STREAMS
TRACKS
CLIFFS

TO SYDNEY

Gt Western Hwy

BURNS RD

Magdala Falls

Martins Falls

MAGDALA CK

PERCH PONDS

Lawsons Lout

Picnic Apt.

SPRINGWOOD RS.

Valley Rd

FARM RD

Camp Pool

SASSAFRAS

GULLY

DAVIES RD

Clarinda Falls

Camp

Numantia Falls

CK

NUMANTIA

SASSAFRAS RIDGE

GLENBROOK CK.

FAULCONBRIDGE

HWY RS

TO BATHURST

N

0 MILES   ½   1
0 METRES 500 1000 1500

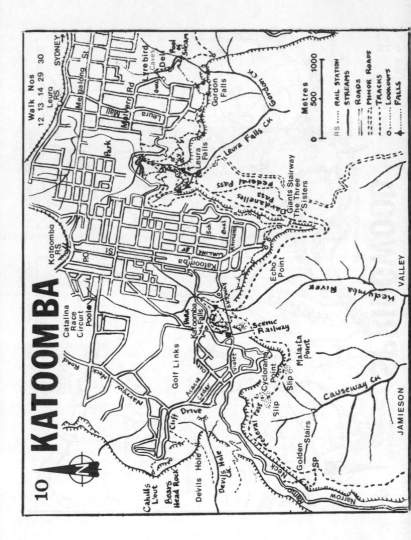

11 KATOOMBA FALLS

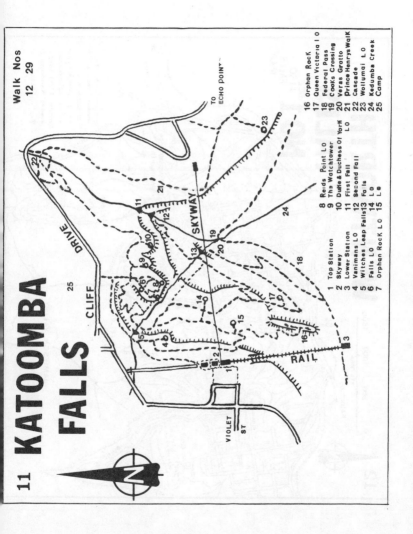

1 Top Station
2 Skyway
3 Lower Station
4 Vanimans LO
5 Witches Leap Falls
6 Falls LO
7 Orphan Rock LO
8 Reds Point LO
9 The Watchtower
10 Duke & Duchess Of York LO
11 First Fall
12 Second Fall
13 Falls
14 LO
15 LO
16 Orphan Rock
17 Queen Victoria l O
18 Federal Pass
19 Cooks Crossing
20 Veras Grotto
21 Prince Henrys Walk
22 Cascade
23 Wollumai LO
24 Kedumba Creek
25 Camp

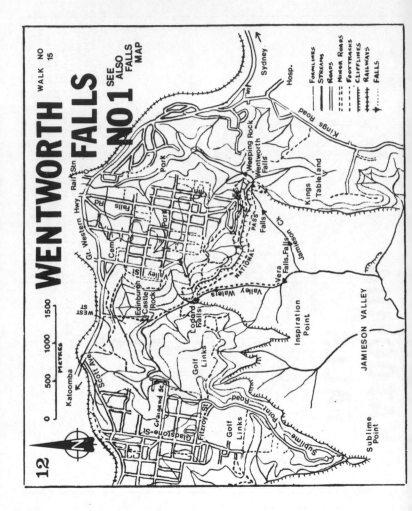

WENTWORTH FALLS NO 1

SEE ALSO FALLS MAP

12

N

METRES
0   500   1000   1500

Katoomba

Legend:
- FORMLINES
- STREAMS
- ROADS
- MINOR ROADS
- FOOTTRACKS
- CLIFFLINES
- RAILWAYS
- FALLS

Hosp.

Sydney

Kings Road

Kings Tableland

Weeping Rock

Wentworth Falls

Rail. Stn.

Park

Gt. Western Hwy.

Falls Rd.

Cem.

Valley St.

Edinburgh St.

Castle Rock

WEST ST

Scott Ave.

Gladstone St.

Craigend St.

Fitzroy St.

Golf Links

Golf Links

Logand Falls

Valley Waters

Vera Falls

Falls Ck.

Jameson Ck.

NATIONAL PASS

Falls

Inspiration Point

JAMIESON VALLEY

Sublime Point Road

Sublime Point

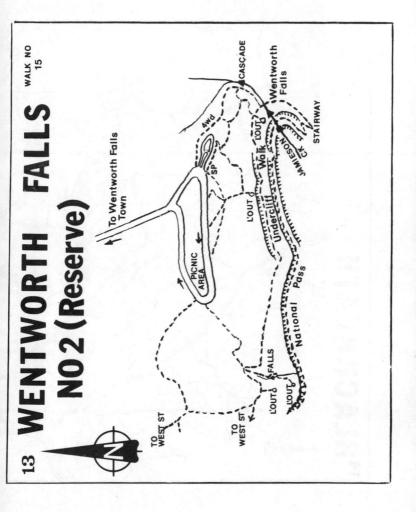

13 **WENTWORTH FALLS NO2 (Reserve)**

To Wentworth Falls Town

CASCADE

4wd

SP

PICNIC AREA

L'OUT

L'OUT

Walk

L'OUT

Undercliff

Wentworth Falls

JAMIESON CK

STAIRWAY

National Pass

L'OUT FALLS

L'OUT

L'OUT

TO WEST ST

TO WEST ST

N

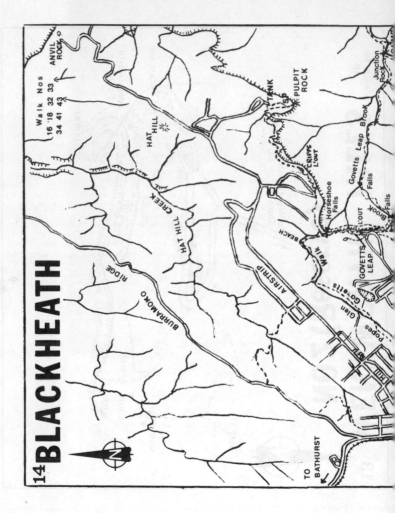

14 BLACKHEATH

N

Walk Nos
16 '18 32 33
34 41 43

ANVIL ROCK

HAT HILL

HAT HILL CREEK

BURRAMOKO RIDGE

PULPIT ROCK

TANK

CRIPPS L'OUT

Junction Rock

Govetts Leap Brook

Horseshoe Falls

Falls

Brook

Falls

BEACH WALK

GOVETTS L'OUT

GOVETTS LEAP

AIRSTRIP

Glen Govetts

Popes Glen

TO BATHURST

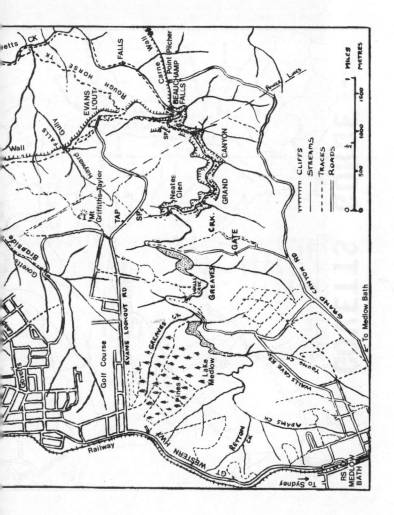

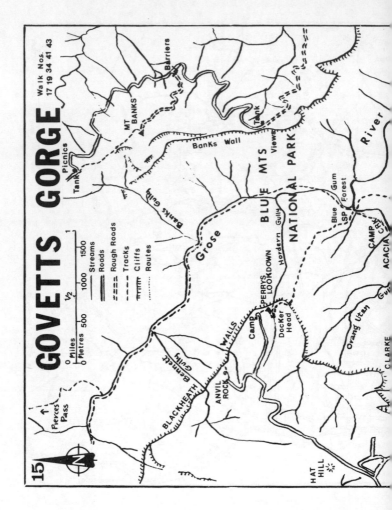

GOVETTS GORGE

Walk Nos. 17 19 34 41 43

15

Scale:
0 Miles ½ 1
0 Metres 500 1000 1500

Streams
Roads
Rough Roads
Tracks
Cliffs
Routes

Perces Pass
Bennett Gully
BLACKHEATH
ANVIL ROCK
WALLS
Camp
PERRYS LOOKDOWN
Docker Head
HAT HILL
Grose
Banks Gully
Picnics
Tank
MT BANKS
Banks Wall
Barriers
Tank
Views
BLUE MTS
NATIONAL PARK
Hordern Gully
Ovang Utan
CLARKE
Blue Gum SP Forest
CAMP
ACACIA
River

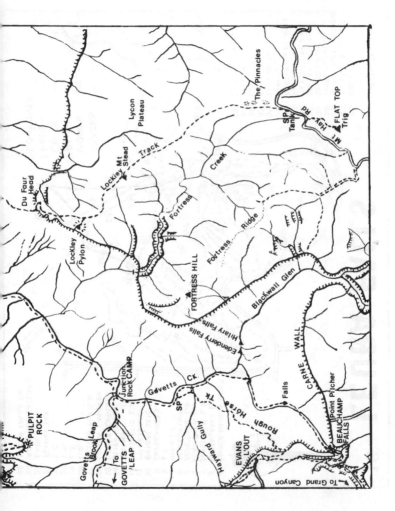

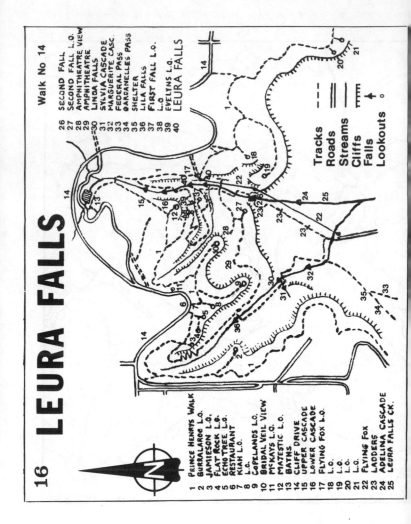

1 PRINCE HENRYS WALK
2 BURRALAROO L.O.
3 JAMIESON L.O.
4 FLAT ROCK L.O.
5 ECHO TREE L.O.
6 RESTAURANT
7 KIAH L.O.
8 L.O.
9 COPELANDS L.O.
10 BRIDAL VEIL VIEW
11 MCKAYS L.Q.
12 MAJESTIC L.O.
13 BATHS
14 CLIFF DRIVE
15 UPPER CASCADE
16 LOWER CASCADE
17 FLYING FOX L.O.
18 L.O.
19 L.O.
20 L.O.
21 L.O.
22 FLYING FOX
23 LADDERS
24 APELINA CASCADE
25 LEURA FALLS CK.

26 SECOND FALL
27 SECOND FALL L.O.
28 AMPHITHEATRE VIEW
29 AMPHITHEATRE
30 LINDA FALLS
31 SYLVIA CASCADE
32 MARGUERITE CASC.
33 FEDERAL PASS
34 DARDANELLES PASS
35 SHELTER
36 LILA FALLS
37 FIRST FALL
38 L.O.
39 EVELYNS L.O.
40 LEURA FALLS

Tracks
Roads
Streams
Cliffs
Falls
Lookouts o

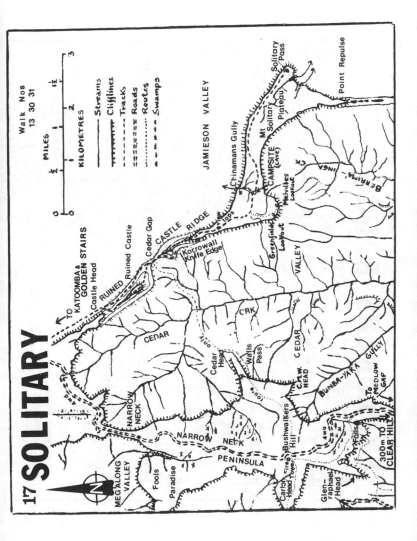

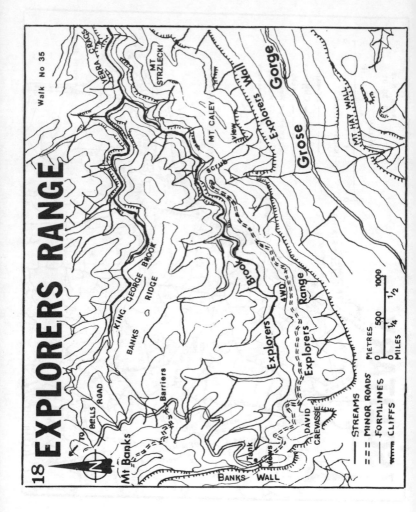

Mt Banks

TO BELLS ROAD

VERRA CRAGS

MT STRZLECKI

MT CALEY

View

Scrub

Explorers Wall

Grose Gorge

Grose

MT HAY WALL

KING GEORGE BROOK

BANKS RIDGE

Brook

Barriers

Explorers Range

4WD

Explorers

DAVID CREVASSE

Tank

Views

BANKS WALL

STREAMS
MINOR ROADS
FORMLINES
CLIFFS

METRES
0   500   1000
MILES
0   ¼   ½

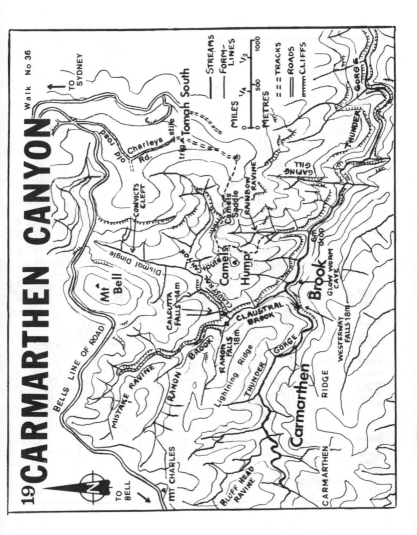

19 CARMARTHEN CANYON

Walk No 36

TO SYDNEY

BELLS LINE OF ROAD

old Bells Rd.

Charleys Rd.

stile

trig Tomah South

CONVICTS CLEFT

Dismal Dingle

Mt Bell

RAINBOW RAVINE

Camels Saddle

GAPING GILL

CALCUTTA FALLS 14m

CLAUSTRAL SPOUTES

Camels Hump

6m drop

GLOW WORM CAVE

CLAUSTRAL BROOK

RANON FALLS 18m

Lightning Ridge

THUNDER GORGE

THUNDER GORGE

Carmarthen Brook

WESTERWAY FALLS 18m

RANON BROOK

MISTAKE RAVINE

mt CHARLES

TO BELL

N

BLUFF HEAD RAVINE

CARMARTHEN RIDGE

CARMARTHEN RIDGE

STREAMS
FORM-LINES
TRACKS
ROADS
CLIFFS

MILES 1/4   1/2
METRES 0 500 1000

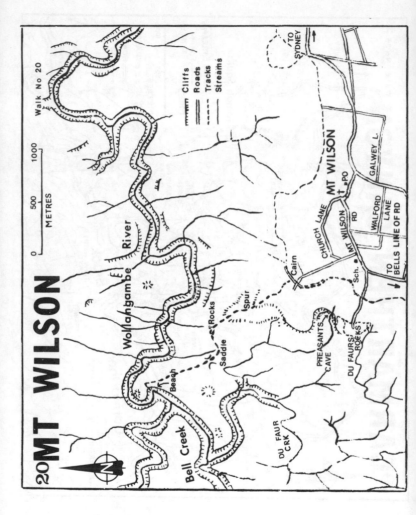

20 MT WILSON

Walk No 20

Bell Creek

Wollahgambe River

METRES
0   500   1000

Cliffs
Roads
Tracks
Streams

Beach

Saddle

Rocks

Spur

Cairn

DU FAUR CRK

PHEASANTS CAVE

DU FAURS ROCKS

Sch.

CHURCH LANE

MT WILSON RD

WALFORD LANE

GALWEY L.

MT WILSON
† PO

TO BELLS LINE OF RD

TO SYDNEY

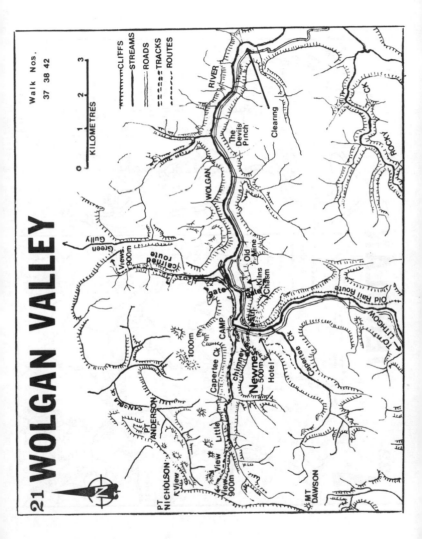

21 WOLGAN VALLEY

Walk Nos.
37 38 42

KILOMETRES
0 1 2 3

CLIFFS
STREAMS
ROADS
TRACKS
ROUTES

N

PT NICHOLSON
View
KANGRA
PT ANDERSON
1000m
Views 900m
Green Gully
Railway route
900m View
Little View
CAMP
Capertee Ck
Chimney
gate
Kilns
Old Mine
gate
Chasm
Newnes 500m
Hotel
Capertee Ck
MT DAWSON
Old Rail Route
LITHGOW
TO LITHGOW →
WOLGAN
The Devils Pinch
Clearing
RIVER
ROCKY CK

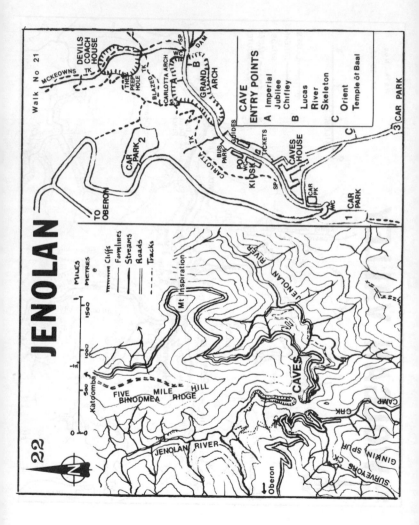

JENOLAN

22

N

MILES
METRES

0   500   1000   1500

——— Cliffs
——— Formlines
——— Streams
——— Roads
- - - Tracks

Katoomba

FIVE MILE HILL
BINOOMEA RIDGE

Mt Inspiration

JENOLAN RIVER

CAVES

JENOLAN RIVER

Oberon

SURVEYORS CK   GINKIN SPUR   CAMP CRK

Walk No 21

MCKEOWNS

DEVILS COACH HOUSE

TK

THE PEEP HOLE

TK

BLAZED

CARLOTTA ARCH

WC

SP

GRAND ARCH

DAM

B

TO OBERON

CAR PARK 2

TK

CARLOTTA

BUS PARK

POLICE

KIOSK WC

TICKETS

GUIDES

SP

CAVES HOUSE

CAR PK

WC

1 CAR PARK

C

3 CAR PARK

CAVE ENTRY POINTS

A Imperial
   Jubilee
   Chifley

B Lucas
   River
   Skeleton

C Orient
   Temple of Baal

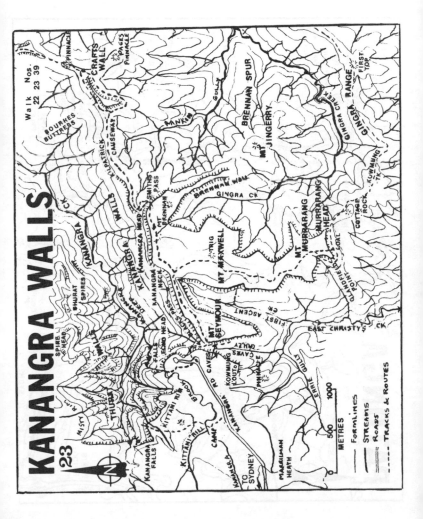

KANANGRA WALLS

23

Walk Nos. 22 23 39

METRES
500 1000

Formlines
Streams
Roads
Tracks & Routes

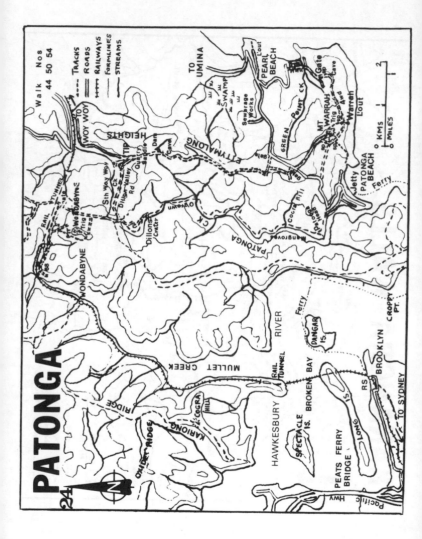

KOOLEWONG

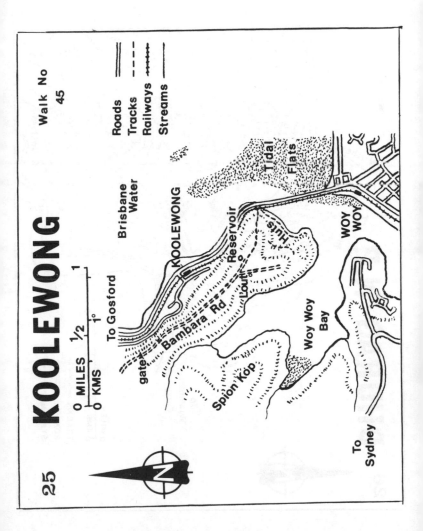

Walk No
45

Roads
Tracks
Railways
Streams

Brisbane
Water

KOOLEWONG

Tidal
Flats

Reservoir

Huts

WOY
WOY

To Gosford

gate

Bambara Rd

Loutit

Woy Woy
Bay

Spion Kop

To
Sydney

N

0 MILES 1/2 1
0 KMS 1

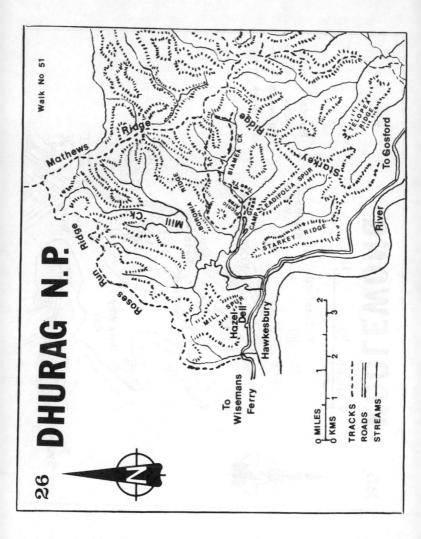

27 PORT STEPHENS

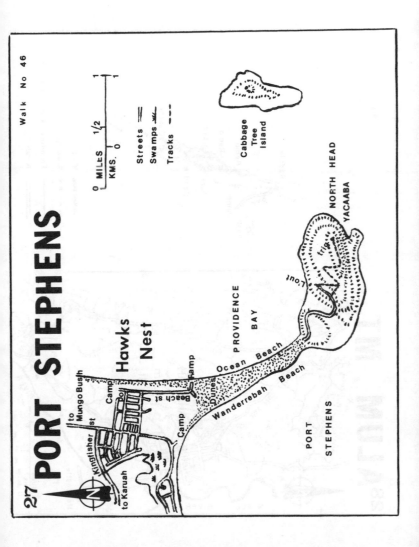

N

to Karuah
to Mungo Bush
Kingfisher St
Camp
Hawks Nest
Beach St
Camp
Dunes
Camp
Ocean Beach
PROVIDENCE BAY
Wanderrebah Beach
PORT STEPHENS
Inlet
NORTH HEAD
YACAABA
Cabbage Tree Island

0 MILES 1/2 1
KMS. 0 1

Streets
Swamps
Tracks

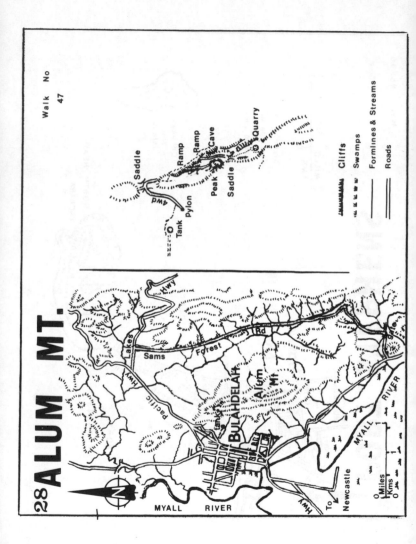

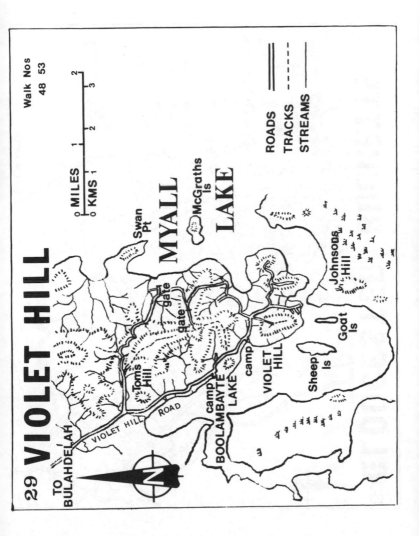

29 VIOLET HILL

TO BULAHDELAH

Walk Nos
48 53

0 MILES 1 2 3
0 KMS 1 2 3

ROADS
TRACKS
STREAMS

Swan Pt

MYALL

McGraths Is

LAKE

VIOLET HILL ROAD

Toms Hill

gate
gate
gate

camp
BOOLAMBAYTE LAKE

camp

VIOLET HILL

Sheep Is

Goat Is

Johnsons Hill

N

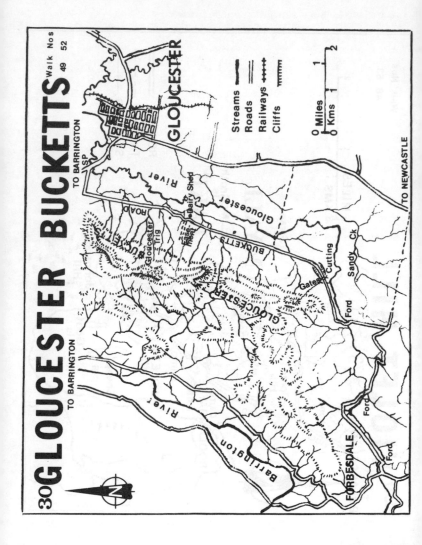

30 GLOUCESTER BUCKETTS Walk Nos 49 52

TO BARRINGTON

N

TO BARRINGTON

GLOUCESTER

TO BARRINGTON SP

Barrington River

Gloucester River

ROAD

Dairy Shed

East Meat

Gloucester Trig

BUCKETTS

GLOUCESTER

Gates

BUCKETTS ROAD

Cutting

Ford

Sandy Ck

Ford

FORBESDALE

Ford

Ford

TO NEWCASTLE

Streams
Roads
Railways
Cliffs

0 Miles   1
0 Kms   1   2

31 BARRINGTON TOPS

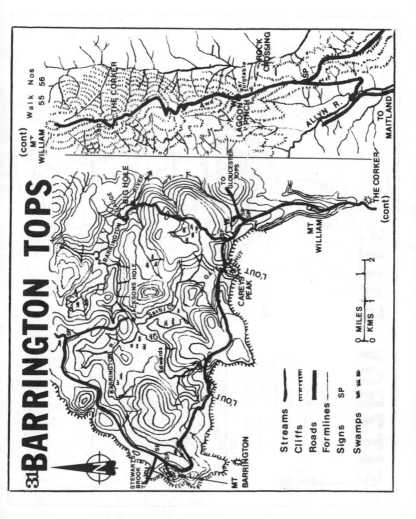

(cont) Walk Nos 55 56 MT WILLIAM

THE CORKER

ROCK CROSSING

SP

LAGOOM PINCH

Potable

ALLYN R.

TO MAITLAND

BARRINGTON COLLEGE BIG HOLE

RIVER

TO GLOUCESTER TOPS

SP

TSONS HOLE

Sax Bk / Ck

GAP HUT

L'OUT

CAREYS PEAK

MT WILLIAM

THE CORKER (cont)

BARRINGTON R.

Edwards

L'OUT

STEWARTS BROOK TK HUT

SP

MT BARRINGTON

Streams

Cliffs

Roads

Formlines

Signs SP

Swamps

MILES 0 1 2
KMS 0 1

N

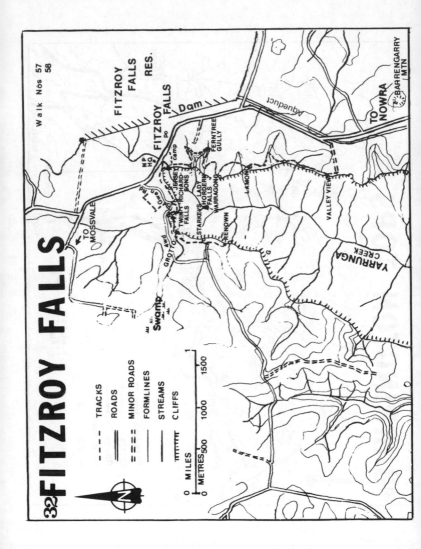

32 FITZROY FALLS

TRACKS
ROADS
MINOR ROADS
FORMLINES
STREAMS
CLIFFS

N

MILES
METRES 500   1000   1500

FITZROY FALLS RES.

FITZROY FALLS

Dam

Aqueduct

TO NOWRA

BARRENGARRY MTN

NP HQ

camp

FERNTREE GULLY

GROTTO Rd

FIRST Rd

TWIN FALLS

RICHARD-SONS

STARKEYS

LADY HORDERN FALLS

WARRAGONG

LAMOND

RENOWN

VALLEY VIEW

YARRUNGA CREEK

TO MOSSVALE

Swamp

33 BERRIMA

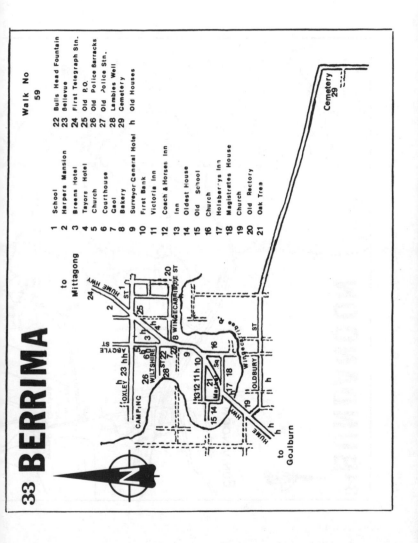

1 School
2 Harpers Mansion
3 Breens Hotel
4 Tayors Hotel
5 Church
6 Courthouse
7 Gaol
8 Bakery
9 Surveyor General Hotel
10 First Bank
11 Victoria Inn
12 Coach & Horses Inn
13 Inn
14 Oldest House
15 Old School
16 Church
17 Holsberrys Inn
18 Magistrates House
19 Church
20 Old Rectory
21 Oak Tree

22 Bulls Head Fountain
23 Bellevue
24 First Telegraph Stn.
25 Old P.O.
26 Old Police Barracks
27 Old Police Stn.
28 Lambies Well
29 Cemetery
h Old Houses

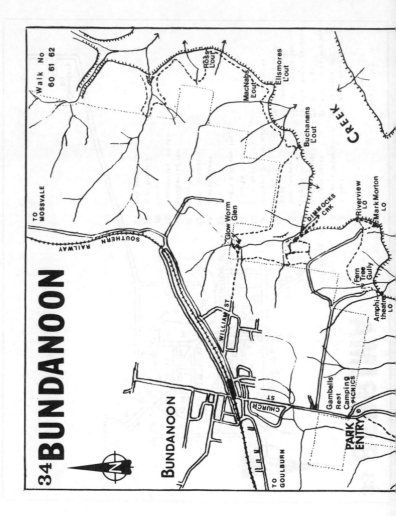

34 BUNDANOON

BUNDANOON

N

TO GOULBURN

TO MOSSVALE

SOUTHERN RAILWAY

Walk No 60 61 62

Ross' L'out

MacNabs L'out

Ellsmores L'out

Buchanans L'out

CREEK

Glow Worm Glen

DIMMOCKS CRK

Riverview LO

Mark Morton LO

Fern Tree Gully

Amphi- theatre LO

WILLIAM ST

CHURCH ST

Gambells Rest Camping PICNICS

PARK ENTRY

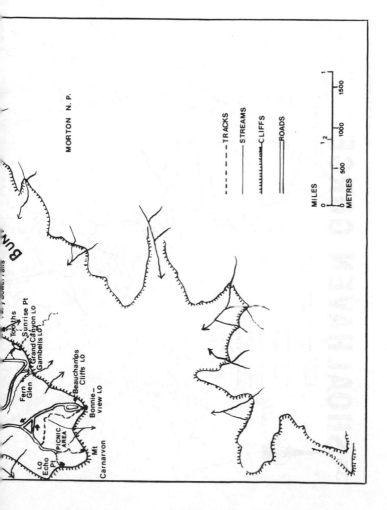

MORTON N. P.

----- TRACKS

———— STREAMS

╨╨╨╨ CLIFFS

════ ROADS

MILES
0   1/4   1/2   1

METRES
0   500   1000   1500

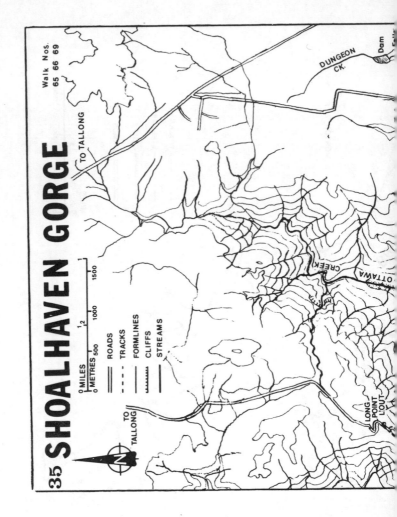

35 SHOALHAVEN GORGE

Walk Nos. 65 66 69

ROADS
TRACKS
FORMLINES
CLIFFS
STREAMS

0 MILES ½
0 METRES 500 1000 1500

N

TO TALLONG

TO TALLONG

DUNGEON CK.

Dam

OTTAWA CREEK

LONG POINT L'OUT

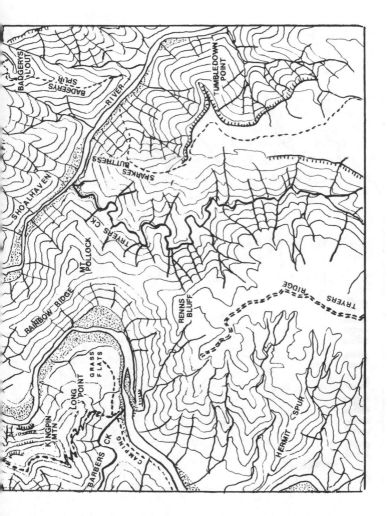

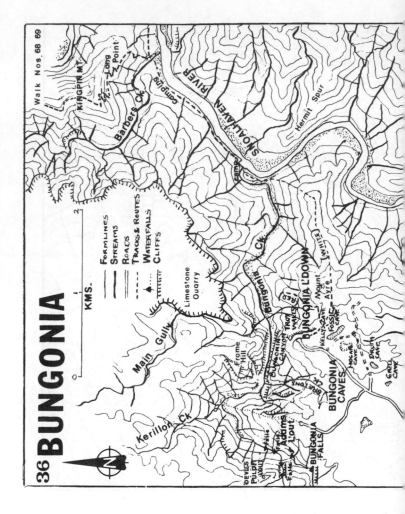

36 BUNGONIA

KMS.

FORMLINES
STREAMS
ROADS
TRACKS & ROUTES
WATERFALLS
CLIFFS

KINGPIN MT.

Long Point

Barbers Ck.

Camp Ing

SHOALHAVEN RIVER

Hermit Spur

Main Gully

Limestone Quarry

Kerillon Ck.

Frome Hill

Bungonia Ck.

BUNGONIA L'DOWN

Mount AVE. [WHITE]

RED AVE.

CLAYMONTS CANYON TRAIL

KELLYS CAVE

FOSSIL CAVE

BUNGONIA CAVES

MOSS CAVE

DRUM CAVE

GRILL CAVE

BREATONS CK.

BUNGONIA FALLS

Adams L'out

DEVILS PULPIT

FANGOLAN

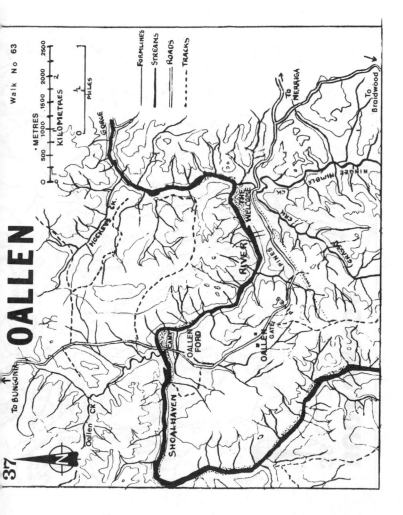

37

To BUNGONIA

OALLEN

Walk No 63

FORMLINES
STREAMS
ROADS
TRACKS

METRES
0 500 1000 1500 2000 2500

KILOMETRES
0 1 2

MILES
0 ½ 1

GORGE

Oallen CK

HICKEYS CK

SHOALHAVEN

OALLEN FORD

CAMP

OALLEN GATE

PINES

RIVER

THE WELCOME

CK

To NERRIGA

NINGEE NIMBLE

CRISONG

To Braidwood

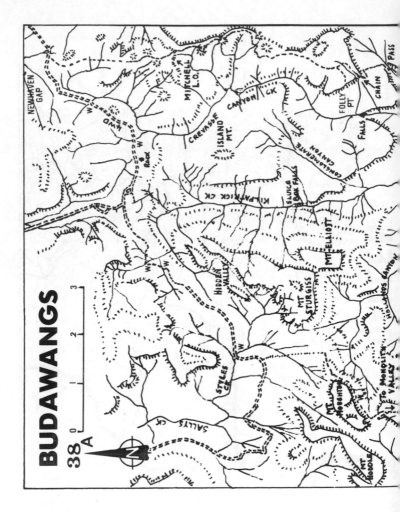

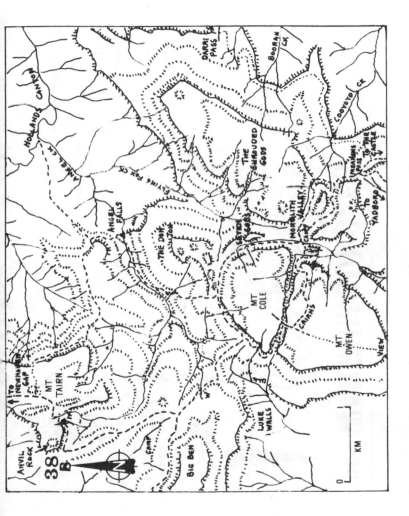

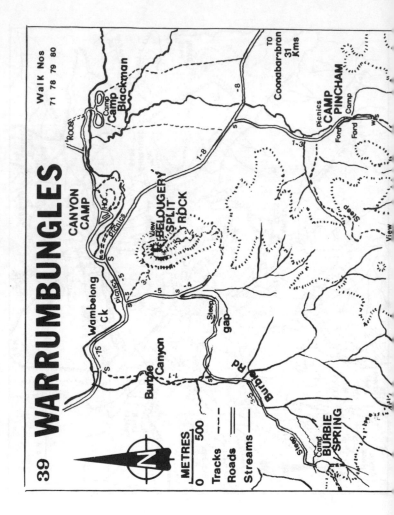

WARRUMBUNGLES

39

METRES
0   500

Tracks ---
Roads ===
Streams —

N

Wambelong Ck

CANYON CAMP

HQ

picnics

-15

-5

.5

3.7

-5

Burbie Canyon

1.1

Steep gap

Burbie Rd

.5

Steep

Camp
BURBIE SPRING

View

BELOUGERY
SPLIT RCK

-5

S -4

1.8

1.3

picnics

Camp
Camp Blackman

'Roost'

TO
Coonabarabran
31 Kms

CAMP PINCHAM

Ford
Ford Camp
WS

-8

Steep

View

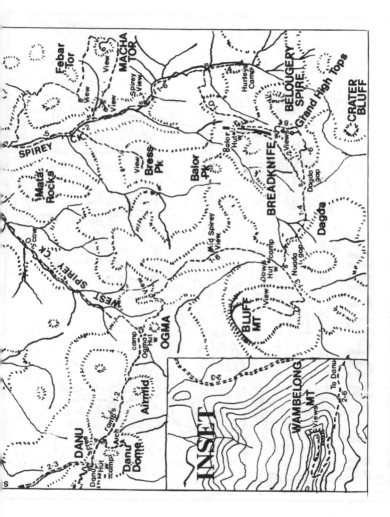

Febar
Tor

View 6

MACHA
TOR

Spirey View

View

s View

View

CK 2

SPIREY

iMata
Rocks

View

Bress
Pk

Balor
Pk

Hurleys
Camp

Balor
Hut

2 Views

BELOUGERY
SPIRE

Grand High Tops

BREADKNIFE

CRATER
BLUFF

Cave

SPIREY CK

WEST SPIREY

Mid Spirey
View

View

Dagda
Gap

Dagda

1-4

OGMA

camp s
Ogma's
Hut

BLUFF
MT

Dows
Hut Camp

View

Nuada
gap

DANU

Danu
Dome

Aimild

Arch

camps 1.2

2.3

Danu
Hut

camps

INSET

WAMBELONG
MT

To Danu

Views

2-6

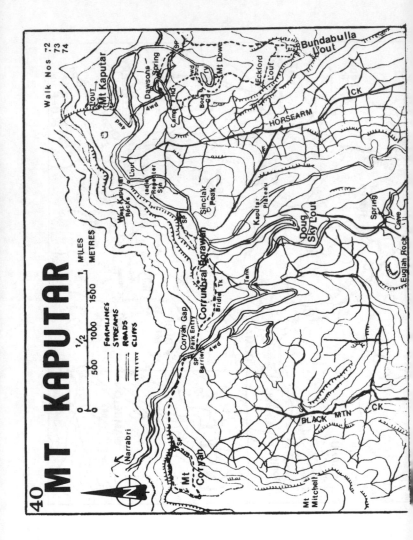

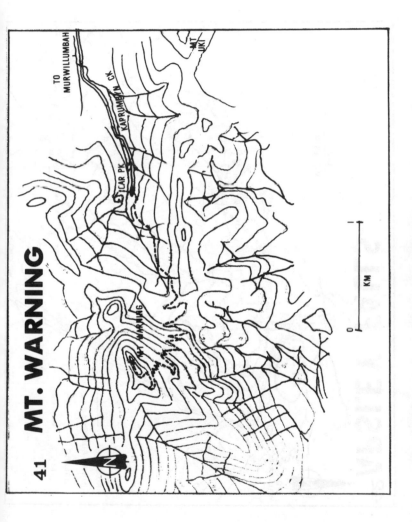

41 MT. WARNING

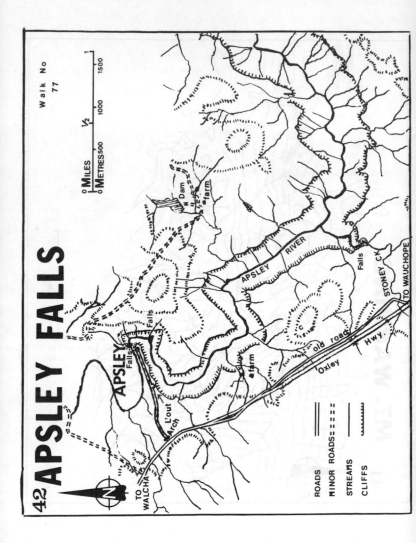

42 APSLEY FALLS

ROADS
MINOR ROADS = = = = =
STREAMS
CLIFFS

N
TO WALCHA

APSLEY
Falls

L'out
Arch

Falls

Dam
farm

APSLEY RIVER

Falls

STONEY CK

TO WAUCHOPE

Oxley   Hwy.

old road

farm

MILES 0   ½   1
METRES 500   1000   1500

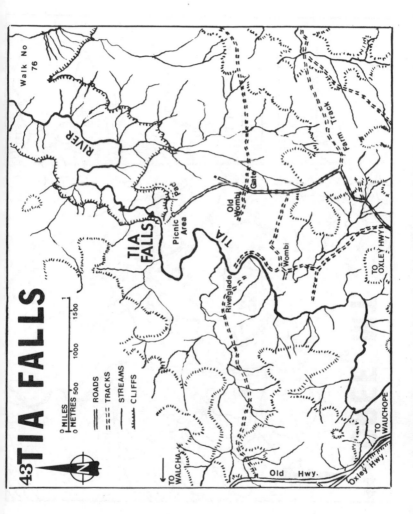

43 TIA FALLS

Walk No 76

RIVER

TIA FALLS

Picnic Area

Old Pad

Old Wombi

Gate

Farm Track

TIA

Wombi

Riverglade

TO WALCHA

Old Hwy.

TO OXLEY HWY

TO WAUCHOPE

Oxley Hwy.

0 MILES
0 METRES 500 1000 1500

— — ROADS
===== TRACKS
~~~ STREAMS
^^^^ CLIFFS

N

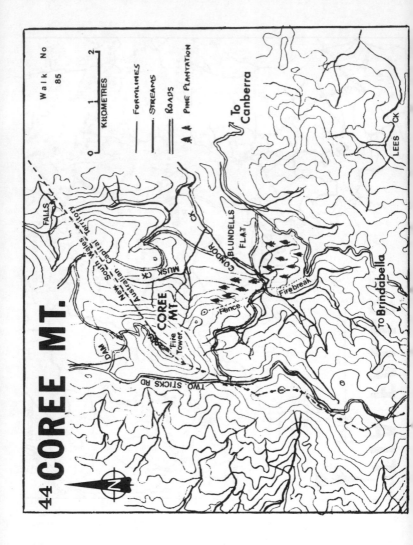

44 COREE MT.

KILOMETRES

FORMLINES
STREAMS
ROADS
▲ ▲ PINE PLANTATION

FALLS

South Wales
New
Australian Capital Territory

DAM

MUSK CK

CONDOR CK

CK

CK

COREE MT.

Fire Tower

TWO STICKS RD

Fence

BLUNDELLS FLAT

Firebreak

To Canberra

To Brindabella

LEES CK

N

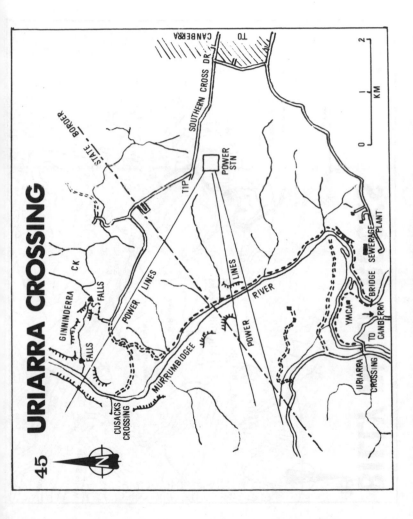

URIARRA CROSSING

45

KM

0 1 2

STATE BORDER

CANBERRA

TO

SOUTHERN CROSS DR

TIP

POWER STN

POWER LINES

LINES

POWER

RIVER

MURRUMBIDGEE

GINNINDERRA CK

FALLS

FALLS

FALLS

CUSACKS CROSSING

YMCA

BRIDGE

SEWERAGE PLANT

URIARRA CROSSING

TO CANBERRA

N

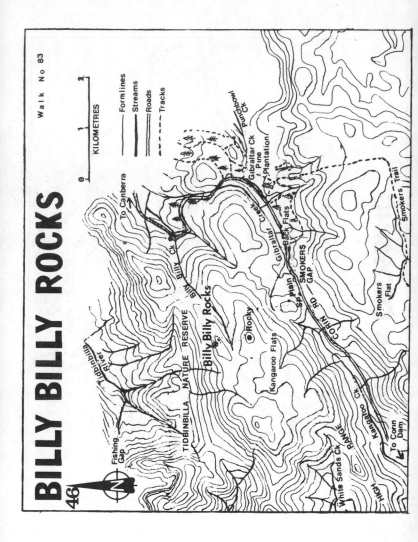

BILLY BILLY ROCKS

46

N

Fishing
Gap

Tidbinbilla
River

To Canberra

Billy Ck

TIDBINBILLA NATURE RESERVE

Billy Billy Rocks

● Rocky

Kangaroo Flats

TIDBINBILLA RANGE

White Sands Ck

HIGH

Kangaroo Ck

To Corin
Dam

SP plain

Gibraltar Creek

Back Flats

Gibraltar Ck
Pine
Plantation

Punchbowl
Ck

SMOKERS GAP

CORIN RD

Smokers
Flat

Smokers Trail

KILOMETRES

0   1   2

———— Formlines
━━━━ Streams
════ Roads
- - - - Tracks

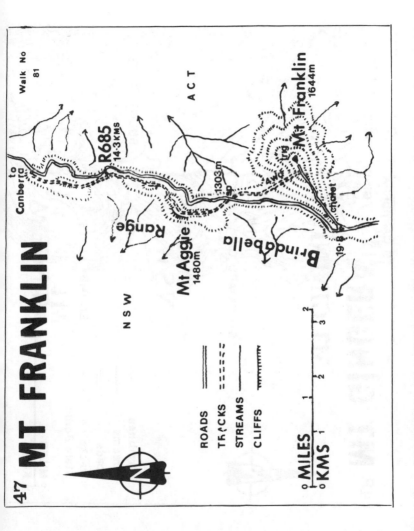

47 **MT FRANKLIN**

to Canberra

R685
14·3 KMS

A C T

Mt Franklin
1644m

Mt Aggie
1480m

Range

Brindabella

NSW

1303m

4WD

chalet

19·8

N

ROADS
TRACKS
STREAMS
CLIFFS

MILES   0   1   2   3
KMS   0   1   2   3

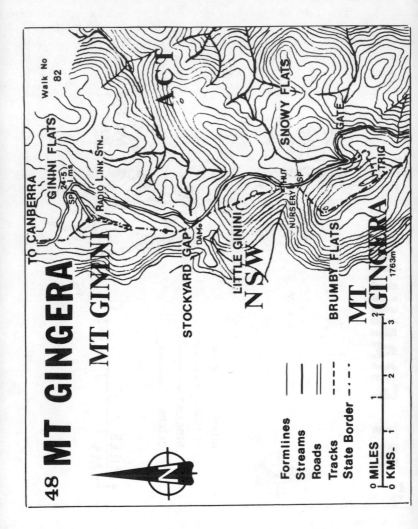

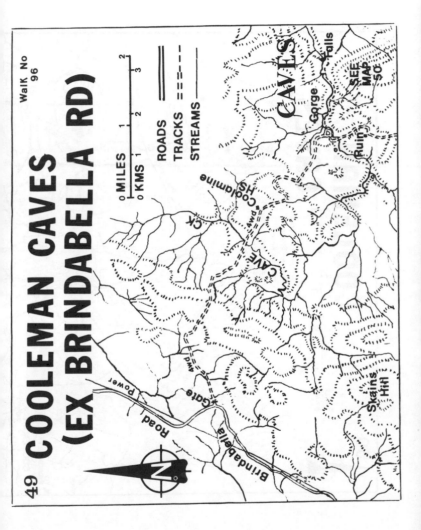

49 COOLEMAN CAVES (EX BRINDABELLA RD)

ROADS
TRACKS
STREAMS

0 MILES 1
0 KMS 1 2 3

CAVES

Gorge
Falls

SEE
MAP
50

Ruin

Coolamine
HS

CAVE CK
4wd

4wd

Gate

Power

Road

Brindabella

Skains
Hill

N

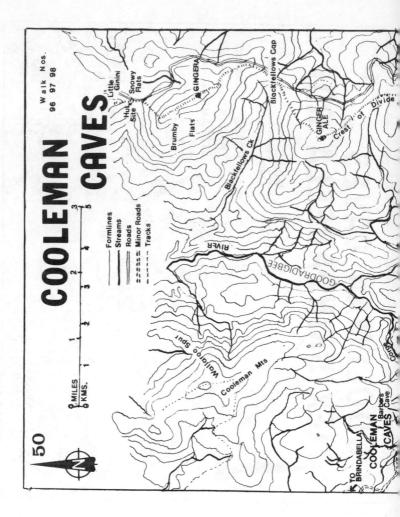

COOLEMAN
CAVES

Walk Nos.
96 97 98

50

Formlines
Streams
Roads
Minor Roads
Tracks

MILES
KMS.

Little
Ginini
Hut
Site
Snowy
Flats
Brumby
Flats
GINGER
Blackfellows Ck
Blackfellows Gap
GINGER
ALE
Crest of Divide

RIVER
GOODRADIGBEE

Wallaroo Spur
Cooleman Mts

TO
BRINDABELLA
COOLEMAN
CAVES
Barbers
Cave
Cave

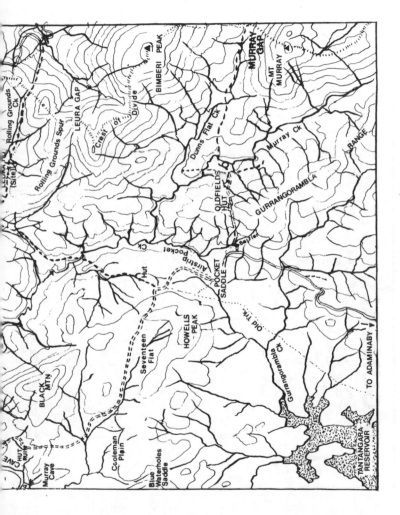

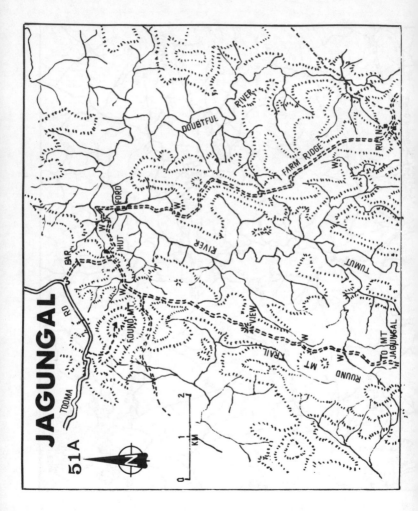

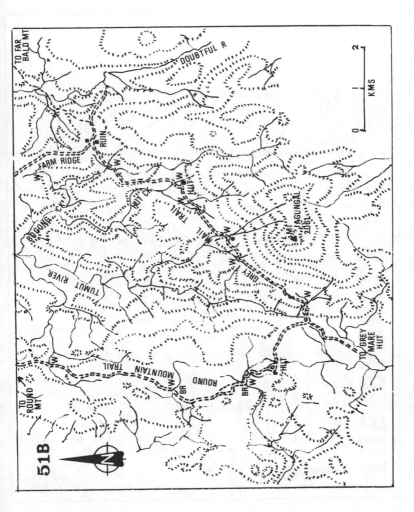

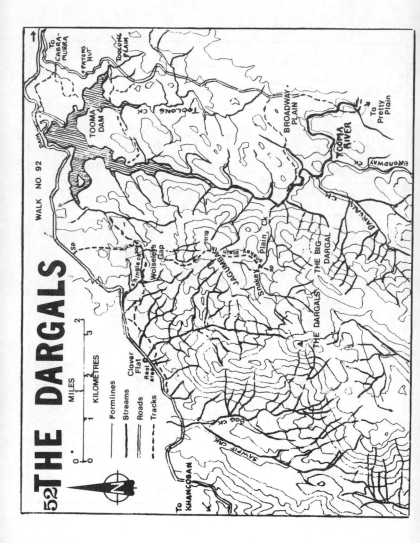

52 THE DARGALS

WALK NO. 92

Legend:
- Formlines
- Streams
- Roads
- Tracks

MILES
0   1   2   3
KILOMETRES
0   1   2   3

N

To CABRA-MURRA

PATONS HUT

TOOLONG PLAIN

TOOMA DAM

TOOLONG CK

BROADWAY PLAIN

To Pretty Plain

TOOMA RIVER

BROADWAY CK

DARGALS CK

SP

Chingle Creek

Wolseley's Gap

Clover Flat

Rest area

trig

JAGUMBA

Snakey Plain Ck

Snakey Plain

SP

THE DARGALS

THE BIG DARGAL

BOG CK

SWAMPY CK

To KHANCOBAN

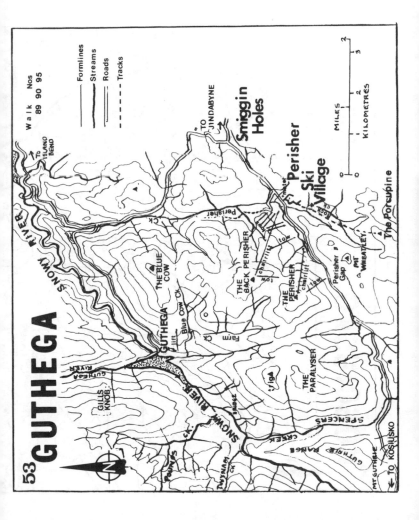

54 KOSCIUSKO

Walk Nos.
87 88 91
94 100

Formlines
CREEKS
ROADS
TRACKS
Snowfields

KILOMETRES
MILES

MT ANDERSON

MAIN RANGE

Gorge Ck

Watsons Crags

Pounds Ck

Twynam Ck

MT TWYNAM ▲2196

Little Twynam

BLUE LAKE

HEDLEY TARN

LAKE

Lake Ck

Club Lake Ck

Club Lake

Club Lake Track

Mt Lee

Carruthers Peak

The Sentinel

LADY NORTHCOTES CANYON

Townsend Spur

Range

▲MT TOWNSEND 2210

LAKE ALBINA

MT GUTHRIE

GUTHRIE RANGE

SPENCERS CK

RIVER

N

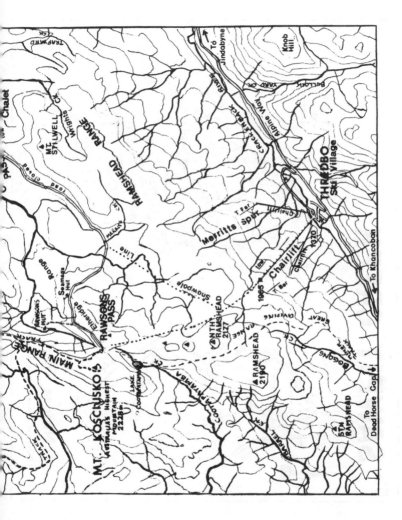

55 SAWPIT CREEK

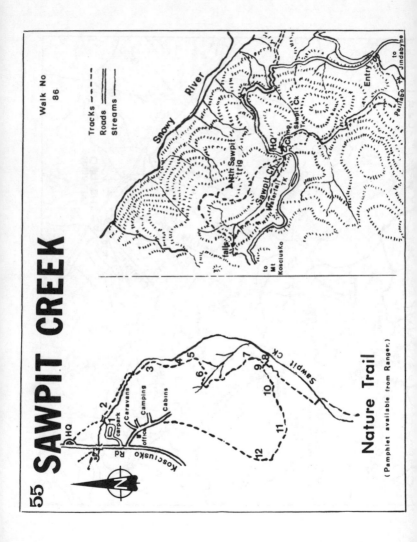

Tracks -----
Roads =====
Streams ———

Snowy River

Nth Sawpit trig

Sawpit Ck
HQ
Waterfall
Camp
Sawpit Ck
TK
falls

to Mt Kosciusko

Entrance

to Perisher
to Jindabyne

Nature Trail

(Pamphlet available from Ranger.)

HQ
Kosciusko Rd
office
Carpark
Caravans
Camping
Cabins

Sawpit Ck

N

1 2 3 4 5 6 7 8 9 10 11 12

SAFETY AND COMMONSENSE
IN THE BUSH

Bushwalking is a very enjoyable recreation, and commonsense safety precautions will keep it that way. Be prepared for any problem that may arise.

First, plan your trip and leave details of your route in writing with some responsible person and report back to them on return. Always carry maps, compass, mirror, first-aid kit, plenty of paper, warm, bright-coloured, waterproof clothing, whistle, matches in a waterproof container, candle, small sharp knife, torch and emergency rations of food. It is of the utmost importance that you should be able to read maps and use a compass.

Second, never try to rush a trip. Think before you act, watch your route on a map and recognize your limitations, especially with distance. A good walker can cover only about five kilometres each hour, and in dense bush perhaps only two kilometres each hour. Always keep together when walking in a group and never walk in a party of less than three.

Third, if lost, STOP! Only move once you have very carefully thought things through. Remember that any movement is best made on ridges and spurs, not in scrub-choked gullies. You should be absolutely sure of directions and should leave a prominent note indicating your intentions and time of leaving. You should put on bright coloured and warm clothing. Once moving, constantly watch the compass, remain on as straight a line as possible and leave notes along the route. If you become tired, stop and rest. Do not over-exert yourself. Remember that severe physical and mental strain, plus cold, means death by exposure. Over the years far too many persons have died unnecessarily, or suffered serious injuries, mainly because they have not understood the seriousness of being caught unprepared in the bush, and then have not been able to cope with the situation. The accepted distress signal is three long whistles, coo-ees, mirror flashes, or any other signal repeated in three every minute. Do not force yourself physically; rather, do things objectively and calmly with plenty of rest.

Fourth, when following suggested walk routes such as are recommended in this book and other publications, ensure that you obtain and use the recommended maps so that the maximum amount of information is available to you. Where more than one map of an area is available, it is advisable to use both. Maps frequently become outdated, especially the Army 1″ to 1 mile series, and this fact must be taken into account. The maps included in this book should be used in conjunction with other maps wherever possible.

Fifth, remember that care of the bushland itself is very important. Many walk routes are in declared National Parks and commonsense regulations must be respected. The bush and the life within it is often in a delicate state of ecological balance and, of necessity, your camp fire must be completely extinguished. Remember the slogan, 'The bigger the fire — the bigger the fool', and on no account light a fire on a high fire danger day.

Sixth, the camp fire is ideal for the disposal of the majority of waste, but silver paper and other foils and cans will not destruct so readily. Wash all cans, remove both ends, flatten them, and carry them, along with any foil or glass, in a plastic bag to the nearest garbage bin. Many walking areas are frequented far more than you may realize and burial of rubbish will eventually create problems. Human waste should always be buried properly away from streams and drinking water. Always wash downstream from the camp site and collect drinking water upstream from the camp site. Remember other people do not appreciate drinking your bath water.

Most walkers like to pitch their tents around a central camp fire but bad weather can drastically change the preference and when this happens an available hut or rock shelter in the sandstone country can provide a welcome shelter in surroundings just as congenial. It is most important that huts used are respected, in return for the generosity of the owners in allowing bushwalkers to use them freely. They should always be left clean and with a good supply of firewood. Walkers who reach a hut or shelter first should not assume that they will be the only occupants for the night. Another party may come along later, probably feeling more tired than you through walking further, so you should move over, sleep on the floor, or do the best possible to share accommodation. It is always wise to carry your tent every trip you intend stopping overnight and not to rely on huts or rock shelters.

Camping in National Parks is frequently confined to certain areas and walkers should ensure that they are aware of those regulations.

Seventh, flooding of streams, even days after heavy rains, can cause delays and even prevent walkers from continuing along their intended route.

Some areas mentioned in these track notes are subject to flooding and walkers' discretion should be used.

Eighth, in the Snowy Mountains, Cooleman Caves and occasionally in other districts suggested as walk venues in this publication, snow falls in winter. The Snowy Mountains, being Australia's highest, become completely snowbound and walks cannot be undertaken for a number of months of the year. This applies to a lesser extent in the Cooleman Caves area.

FIRST AID AT A GLANCE

It is essential that any emergency arising can be dealt with adequately. The St John Ambulance Association *First Aid Book* or an equivalent book should be carried by at least one member of every walking party.

The most likely troubles to be encountered are listed here for rapid reference as in many cases there is no time to do research in a full first aid book. In virtually all serious situations the patient needs to be rested and reassured, often whilst some other person obtains medical assistance. For this reason walk parties should never be less than three in number in any remote place. One person should stay with the patient whilst the other should go for aid.

COMPLAINT	TREATMENT
BLISTERS	Apply an adhesive foam patch, cutting a hole in the foam over the blister so that the surrounding area is raised and pressure is taken off the then uncovered blister. Do not break the blister if possible as infection is a possibility.
HEADACHE	Aspirin and rest.
HEAT EXHAUSTION	Replenish body fluids with plenty of drinks of water or fruit juice and take salt tablets. Rest is essential.

ABDOMINAL DISORDERS, FEVERS	Take Mysteclin V pills and continue the dosage until the trouble is completely corrected. Rest is essential
BURNS	Immediately immerse burn area in cold water to chill. Clean burn thoroughly, despite the pain, and apply a clean bandage. Immobilize the area of the burn.
EXPOSURE TO COLD	Put on warm clothing and get into sleeping bag if possible. Give warm drinks and remove patient to a warmer area by carrying so that he is not further fatigued.
SPRAINS	Immobilize the area and rest it.
SNAKE BITE	Most bites are of a minor nature. The greatest single problem is to reassure the patient as most persons have a disproportionate fear of snakes. Apply a tourniquet for twenty minutes at a time three times interspersed by a couple of minutes. Thoroughly wash the

bite area and completely rest the patient. Identify the snake variety and seek antivenene through a doctor. If patient deteriorates to unconsciousness, apply mouth-to-mouth resuscitation and artificial respiration continually until the necessary medical aid arrives. Cutting the bite and sucking out any poison is now generally regarded as of little or no use and really only upsets the patient, which is the very problem to be overcome.

EQUIPMENT AND FOOD SUGGESTIONS FOR WALKS

SAFETY EQUIPMENT

Maps, compass, small mirror, paper, whistle, matches in a waterproof container, sharp knife, small candle, small torch, textacolour or similar marker, first aid reference book, first aid kit containing bandages, Bandaids, adhesive foam, antiseptic, aspirin, safety pins, Mysteclin V pills, salt tablets and broad rubber tubing for use as a tourniquet, Safety clothing consisting of warm pullover, thick wool socks, bright-coloured shirt or blouse and bright-coloured parka and safety food rations such as nourishing concentrated foods plus a little bulky food such as dried fruits, chocolate, nuts, fruit and seed bars and brown rice.

OTHER EQUIPMENT
Overnight walks: tent, tent pegs, tent guys, good quality sleeping bag, plastic groundsheet, a newspaper, toilet items and a billy.

All Walks: shirt or blouse (wool for winter), shorts, jeans, handkerchief, walking or gym-boots, mug, bowl, cutlery, small towel, lightweight bathers for summer, waterbag (Japara type with zip top), water bottle (aluminium or plastic), can opener and pack.

FOOD
In addition to emergency rations which should be used only in an emergency, the following foods should be carried in quantities dictated by the number of days that the walk will occupy: nuts, dried fruits, chocolate, fruit and seed bars, hard-boiled eggs, packet or cube soups, fruit drink powders, brown rice and rice packet preparations, fresh fruit, honey, wholemeal bread, Vegemite, salami, fruit cake, coffee, tea or other hot drink, bacon, carrot, packet mashed potato and some meusli or porridge. Cans should only be carried by persons accustomed to carrying heavy packs, and empty cans should be washed and carried out of walk areas to garbage disposal bins.

WEIGHT
The most important consideration when carrying an

overnight pack is the combined weight of the contents, and if you carry no more than is stated in this list of equipment and food suggestions then you should not encounter trouble. However, far too many persons include that little extra item or two, or overestimate the quantity of food that they can possibly eat and so suffer the consequences when they have to climb a hill bearing 'a ton of bricks'.

OBTAINING BASIC EQUIPMENT

The purchase of a pack, tent or sleeping bag frequently constitutes a major problem for the newcomer to walking circles. Elementary logic is all that is involved in the decision.

Packs; Comfort, weight and price to be considered; try the pack on in the shop after asking the shop assistant to load it. Generally speaking A-frame packs are not popular but H-frame packs are. Do not buy a pack that feels uncomfortable from the outset. Try to keep the weight down when deciding on the purchase.

Tents; Comfort, weight and price again to be considered. As a general rule nylon tents are wonderfully light but they are so closely woven that condensation inside them is so great that you might just as well be out in the rain! On the other hand Japara and similar type tents are quite heavy and leak if their inside is touched while it is raining.

The logical decision, therefore, is to do one of two things and in both cases the cost of the tent soars. But then you do need to be comfortable.

(1) Buy a nylon tent and a fly which extends well out beyond each end of the tent and also have large

air vents inserted in either end of the tent. Use the fly every night.

(2) Buy a Japara type tent and a fly of nylon to go over it on wet nights only. The fly need not be very big.

Whichever alternative you decide upon, try to keep the weight down.

Sleeping Bags; Comfort, weight and price again to be considered. Far too many people do not think logically when purchasing a bag. They settle for a cheap bag, lie awake in it all night due to the cold, then defeat the whole purpose of their walking trip by being too tired next day to enjoy walking. Remember, you will spend many hours in that bag either blissfully sleeping or lying awake half frozen. The more warmth that you can achieve in a bag the better and as a general rule the more you pay for one, the more warmth. Comfort is therefore the primary consideration in bag choice. Weight and price are secondary.

MAPPING AND NAVIGATION

Two systems of measurement have existed in Australian maps since the metric conversion; consequently, care must be taken not to confuse or misjudge distances, scales and grid references.

The following maps are suggested as the best available to walkers, but numerous other excellent maps are on sale and could usefully supplement these suggestions;

Department of National Mapping Series:
  1 : 100,000 (Planning)
  1 : 50,000

Central Mapping Authority Department of Lands New South Wales

    Topographical Series:
      2" = 1 mile
      1 : 25,000
    Tourist Series:
      Blue Labyrinth
      Hawkesbury River
      Blue Mountains — Burragorang
      Port Hacking & Royal National Park.
    Old Military Series:
      1" to 1 mile
      (Frequently quite dated as regards roads but useful for contours).

These maps are available in the bigger cities at the appropriate Federal or State Government department or at larger bookshops and shops catering for bushwalkers' needs.

Navigation procedures basically can only be learned from experience in the field using map and compass. However, the topic is aptly broached in several excellent publications on sale. One important point with which all walkers should be familiar is that magnetic north is presently 12° east of true north in New South Wales.

Usually, excellent opportunities exist to learn navigation when walking with a bushwalking club. There are in fact, numerous bushwalking clubs which newcomers to walking and others can join, and thus gain the safety, advice, experience and companionship that comes from walking with a club-organized walk under a leader and usually with transport arranged.

Enquiries of a general nature and concerning the

various clubs can best be made through the Federation of Walking Clubs.

This publication provides a map covering the area of every walk route suggested and to some extent these maps should be sufficient for navigation requirements. However, it would be impracticable to provide maps covering a larger area surrounding the walk spots and therefore to rely upon these maps entirely would be unwise. (For example, if the walker became lost and walked off the map coverage.) It is strongly recommended that every endeavour be made to purchase Government or other maps before setting out on these trips.

Walk number	Recommended Additional Maps
1	Lands Dept Hawkesbury River 1″ to 1 mile
2	Lands Dept Hawkesbury River 1″ to 1 mile
3	Lands Dept Tourist map of the Port Hacking District
4	Lands Dept Tourist map of the Port Hacking District
5	Lands Dept Tourist map of the Port Hacking District
6	Lands Dept Tourist map of the Port Hacking District
7	Lands Dept Blue Labyrinth 2″ to 1 mile
8	Lands Dept Blue Labyrinth 2″ to 1 mile
9	Lands Dept Blue Labyrinth 2″ to 1 mile
10	Lands Dept Springwood Standard 2″ to 1 mile
11	Lands Dept Springwood Standard 2″ to 1 mile
12	Lands Dept Katoomba Standard 2″ to 1 mile
13	Lands Dept Katoomba Standard 2″ to 1 mile
	Lands Dept Jamieson Standard 2″ to 1 mile
14	Lands Dept Katoomba Standard 2″ to 1 mile
15	Lands Dept Katoomba Standard 2″ to 1 mile
16	Lands Dept Kaotomba Standard 2″ to 1 mile
17	Lands Dept Mount Wilson Standard 2″ to 1 mile
18	Lands Dept Katoomba Standard 2″ to 1 mile
19	Lands Dept Katoomba Standard 2″ to 1 mile
20	Lands Dept Mount Wilson Standard 2″ to 1 mile

Lands Dept Wollangambe 1 : 25,000
21 Lands Dept Jenolan Standard 2″ to 1 mile
22 Myles J. Dunphy Kanangra Tourist Resort
23 Myles J. Dunphy Kanangra Tourist Resort.
24 Lands Dept Hawkesbury River 1″ to 1 mile
25 Lands Dept Hawkesbury River 1″ to 1 mile
26 Lands Dept Tourist map of the Port Hacking District
27 Lands Dept Tourist map of the Port Hacking District
28 Lands Dept Springwood Standard 2″ to 1 mile
29 Lands Dept Katoomba Standard 2″ to 1 mile
30 Lands Dept Katoomba Standard 2″ to 1 mile
   Lands Dept Jamieson Standard 2″ to 1 mile
31 Lands Dept Jamieson Standard 2″ to 1 mile
   Lands Dept Katoomba Standard 2″ to 1 mile
32 Lands Dept Katoomba Standard 2″ to 1 mile
33 Lands Dept Katoomba Standard 2″ to 1 mile
34 Lands Dept Katoomba Standard 2″ to 1 mile
35 Lands Dept Mount Wilson Standard 2″ to 1 mile
36 Lands Dept Mount Wilson Standard 2″ to 1 mile
37 Dept National Mapping Glen Alice 1 : 50,000
   Dept National Mapping Glen Davis 1 : 50,000
38 Dept National Mapping Glen Davis 1 : 50,000
   Dept National Mapping Glen Alice 1 : 50,000
39 Myles J. Dunphy Kanangra Tourist Resort
40 Lands Dept Tourist map of the Port Hacking District
41 Lands Dept Mount Wilson Standard 2″ to 1 mile
42 Dept National Mapping Glen Alice 1 : 50,000
   Dept National Mapping Glen Davis 1 : 50,000
43 Lands Dept Katoomba Standard 2″ to 1 mile
   Lands Dept Mount Wilson Standard 2″ to 1 mile
   Lands Dept Mount Wilson Standard 2″ to 1 mile
44 Myles J. Dunphy Patonga—Kariong Section Brisbane
      Waters N.P.
45 Myles J. Dunphy Patonga—Kariong Section Brisbane
      Waters N.P.
46 Army Port Stephens 1″ to 1 mile
47 Army Bulahdelah 1″ to 1 mile
48 Army Bulahdelah 1″ to 1 mile
49 Army Gloucester 1″ to 1 mile
50 Myles J. Dunphy Patonga—Kariong Section
      Brisbane Waters N.P.

51 Lands Dept Hawkesbury River 1" to 1 mile
52 Army Gloucester 1" to 1 mile
53 Army Bulahdelah 1" to 1 mile
54 Myles J. Dunphy Patonga—Kariong Section
    Brisbane Waters N.P.
55 Army Woolooma 1" to 1 mile
56 Army Woolooma 1" to 1 mile
57 Lands Dept Bundanoon Standard 2" to 1 mile
58 Lands Dept Bundanoon Standard 2" to 1 mile
59 Nil
60 Lands Dept Bundanoon Standard 2" to 1 mile
61 Lands Dept Bundanoon Standard 2" to 1 mile
62 Lands Dept Bundanoon Standard 2" to 1 mile
63 Dept National Mapping Oallen 1 : 50,000
64 Lands Dept Endrick 1: 25,000
65 Lands Dept Caoura Standard 2" to 1 mile
66 Lands Dept Caoura Standard 2" to 1 mile
67 Lands Dept Endrick 1 : 25,000
68 Lands Dept Caoura Standard 2" to 1 mile
69 Lands Dept Caoura Standard 2" to 1 mile
70 Lands Dept Endrick 1: 25,000
    Lands Dept Corang 2" to 1 mile
71 J. R. Whitehead Warrumbungle Nat Park Central
    area 1 : 10,000
72 Lands Dept Kaputar Standard 2" to 1 mile
73 Lands Dept Kaputar Standard 2" to 1 mile
74 Lands Dept Kaputar Standard 2" to 1 mile
75 Dept National Mapping Tweed Heads 1 : 250,000
76 Lands Dept Tia Standard 2" to 1 mile
77 Lands Dept Apsley Standard 2" to 1 mile
78 J. R. Whitehead Warrumbungle National Park Cent.
    area 1 : 10,000
79 J. R. Whitehead Warrumbungle National Park Cent.
    area 1 : 10,000
80 J. R. Whitehead Warrumbungle National Park Cent.
    area 1 : 10,000
81 Dept National Mapping Cotter 1 : 50,000
82 Dept National Mapping Bimberi 1 : 50,000
83 Dept National Mapping Bimberi 1 : 50,000
84 Dept National Mapping Umburra 1 : 50,000

1 COWAN — JERUSALEM BAY

Jerusalem Bay is a secluded little arm of Cowan Creek which is part of the Hawkesbury Estuary. The bay is ideal for fishing, swimming and relaxing in the bush. It is also suited to bush camping. Apart from the few watercraft which venture up the bay, the only access is by walking.

Go to Cowan railway station, cross to the east side platform and halfway along the platform, descend some steps then turn left (north) and walk 75 metres past the end of the platform. Turn right (east) down a fenced off easement, cross the Sydney-Newcastle Tollway on a concrete bridge then at a 'T' junction turn left up hill a little and then follow this foot track down into the beautiful forest of Kuring-gai Chase. The track is shortly joined by another lesser track which leads from the right hand fork back at the 'T' junction. The forest is fairly dense for Hawkesbury sandstone country and the variety of trees and shrubs is surprisingly large. Within about a kilometre the track crosses a stream in the valley and thereafter skirts the northern bank of the stream which widens into an inlet. Only 2.0 kilometres from Cowan station you should be at Jerusalem Bay. The most interesting part is that part furthest along the track where the track is heading north before ending in dense bush and amid rocky bluffs at a creek entry from the north-west into the bay. Lunch and a long break is suggested before you retrace your outward route back up the 250 metres of elevation. Other return routes are possible but the alignment of the Tollway spoils the latter part of them.

MAP REF: *Cowan map provided with this publication.*
Map 1.
WALK DISTANCE: 5 km.
GRADING: One day, easy.

2   NORTH TURRAMURA—BOBBIN HEAD

Catch a Bobbin Head bus from Turramura station and alight at the Kuring-gai Chase entrance or drive to the entrance to start this walk, which features the upper reaches of Cowan Water and the boating centre of Bobbin Head. There would be plenty of time for swimming if the weather is warm and lunch could be an extended break at Bobbin Head where there are all facilities including both a kiosk and a shop selling most supplies.

Just inside the park entrance, a bitumen road leads off to the east to The Sphinx, a small replica of the Egyptian version. A tablet at the site informs visitors of its origin connected with war service in Egypt. Next, walk down a track to the north of The Sphinx for only 20 metres, turn right at a gravelled vehicular track, then immediately left again down a rough disused jeep track which leads down to Cowan Creek. A foot track then follows the western bank of Cowan Creek (or Cowan Water as it is known further down stream where it broadens into an estuary) to Bobbin Head boating centre. The distance is 6.5 kilometres. A number of points exist along Cowan Water where you could swim if you wish. Mangroves grow at several points too.

Spend some time at Bobbin Head then retrace 400 metres from the bridge over the Cockle Creek arm of Cowan Water, along behind the boat works area to the signposted track to North Turramurra via the

Old Bobbin Head Road (3.25 kilometres). There is only a foot track up from the water's edge initially, but it soon joins the old road as it zig-zags up the spur then flattens out along a ridge southwards back to the park entrance where the walk started. The zig-zag section of the old road provides excellent views of Bobbin Head and Cowan Water generally and once on the tops you will most likely notice the large variety of wildflowers, especially during the months July to October.

MAP REF: *Mt. Kuring-gai map provided with this publication.* Map 2.

WALK DISTANCE: 10 km.

GRADING: One day, easy.

3 BUNDEENA—LITTLE MARLEY BEACH

There are very few beaches close to Sydney which are not crowded at weekends and on public holidays. Little Marley Beach is almost on the suburban doorstep. It is a beautiful, safe beach reached by a short ferry trip from Cronulla to Bundeena and a 5.0 kilometre walk through the Royal National Park. The beach at Bundeena and Marley Beach are passed on the way. Marley Beach surf is dangerous when rough, however, so you should continue the short extra distance to Little Marley with its grassy slopes, bush camping area and, of course, swimming and body surfing.

Ferries operate fairly regularly from Cronulla station jetty but check their times first. It takes only about thirty minutes to cross Port Hacking to Bundeena.

From Bundeena jetty, walk straight south up Brighton Street past the few shops and at the top of the rise turn right (west) down Scarborough Street.

(Second street on the right from the jetty.) Down on the flat part of Scarborough Street there is a sign next to a fence line on the south side. The sign reads 'Marley' and a minor foot track leads along the fence line. Where the fence stops, diverge slightly right across a swampy creek crossing then diverge left up hill on a very rough jeep track which almost immediately becomes a good foot track. The area was burned out in late 1976, and the track, therefore, will change character very quickly. About 1.5 kilometres from Bundeena jetty, and after you have arrived on the flat plateau supporting many grass trees, a jeep track crosses your path and within another kilometre views of the south coast start to emerge as you leave the burned out area. Views include your destination, Little Marley Beach. The track's condition after entering the National Park is very good and is actually a jeep track. The terrain is mostly flat and vegetation is seldom more than 1.5 metres tall, so there are expansive views most of the time. Soon the track starts to turn south-westwards as it nears the cliff line north-east of Marley Beach. It then tends to split into many tracks and it is hard to follow any one main route. It is best to stay near the cliff rim. As you approach Marley Beach a sign warns of the dangerous surf and also points the way back to Bundeena for your later return trip. Walk to the south end of Marley Beach then follow a track through the scrub just above the rocky shoreline until you emerge on beautiful Little Marley Beach. Its southern end is grassy and sheltered. The sea is usually ideal for swimming, but drinking water is sometimes a problem. Have your lunch and a long break before retracing the same tracks back to the Bundeena Ferry.

MAP REF: *Marley map provided with this publication.*
  Map 3.
WALK DISTANCE: 10 km.
GRADING: One day, easy.

4 HEATHCOTE—KARLOO POOL—AUDLEY

Few people would argue against any suggestion to wander along a stream on a hot day, swim in its many rock pools and to lie on its sandy beaches. Kangaroo Creek in Royal National Park is one stream which is superb for these purposes. Like the rest of the park, the area is sandstone and supports a large number of wildflowers especially in the months from August to November.

Start this walk suggestion at Heathcote station so that, initially, the walk is down hill along what is known as the Karloo Track. Opposite the east side of the rail station is a firefighting equipment yard and on each side of the yard is a track. Follow either track; at the rear of the yard they join and a signpost points the way to Karloo Pool 2.3 kilometres and to Audley 10.5 kilometres. There is a small area of lawns and trees at the spot which makes the park entry rather pleasant. Follow the track eastwards across Heathcote Brook then sidle up on to Goondera Ridge and descend the spur off the ridge end directly to Karloo Pool which is a large deep rock pool in the sandstone bed of Kangaroo Creek at its confluence with Heathcote Brook. Have lunch at this delightful spot which is also ideal for swimming and bush camping.

A track leads off up hill south-west for 2.2 kilometres to Uloola Falls but this should be ignored in favour of following Kangaroo Creek downstream to Audley. There are tracks along the creek bank at all points where you can't simply walk across the sandstone beds. At a number of points rocky outcrops and scrub will slow your progress but, if you take your time and stop frequently to enjoy the beauty all around you and to swim if the weather permits, then the route will seem reasonably easy. West of Audley, where Kangaroo Creek is joined by Engadine Creek, you should make sure you cross to the south bank of Kangaroo Creek as a long deep stretch of river follows. Also at this point there are two routes to Audley. One is up and over Gurrumboola Heights, the other follows the south bank. Both ways are difficult but perhaps the river walk is more beautiful, especially if there are many little hire boats about. However one or two awkward spots exist and the grass is long at times. Once in view of the lawns at Audley, you must climb slightly up to avoid cliffs then descend to the bridge over the Hacking River. You will then be in the middle of the main tourist area where there is a National Park visitors' centre and all amenities including a kiosk. Lastly follow the bitumen road across the causeway and up north to Royal National Park railway station and the end of the walk.

MAP REF: *Audley map provided with this publication.* Map 5.

WALK DISTANCE: 11 km.

GRADING: One day, easy.

5 HEATHCOTE—KARLOO POOL—ULOOLA FALLS—WATERFALL

This walk recommendation is through areas in the Royal National Park renowned for wildflowers which are at their best between August and November. It is a walk which starts and ends at railway stations with trains used to complete a circuit. It includes two really beautiful spots, both of which are also bush camping places and have good water supplies and therefore would be ideal for lunch. The two places are Karloo Pool and Uloola Falls.

Opposite the east side of Heathcote railway station is a firefighting equipment yard and there are foot tracks along both sides of the yard which join to the east and rear of the yard. Take either track and at their junction there is a signpost and a small lawn. Follow the named Karloo Track eastwards across Heathcote Brook, sidle up on to Goondera Ridge then descend down the end of the ridge directly to Karloo Pool only 2.3 kilometres from Heathcote Station. The pool is a large swimming hole in the sandstone bed of Kangaroo Creek at the confluence of Heathcote Brook.

Next, follow a foot track up hill south at first from the pool. There is no signpost but the track is fairly easy to see. It divides and rejoins as it climbs on to Uloola Heights and then swings south-east, crosses the ridge and leads past two sandstone stacks known as The Turrets. There is one stack on either side of the track and a few pencil pines exist beside the rocks. Only 2.2 kilometres from Karloo Pool you should arrive at Uloola Falls, a 20-metre-high set of falls which cascade in three steps. The area has a lot of bare sandstone about so is interesting and open. There is a track leading off to Audley at the falls but it should be ignored in favour of the Waterfall Track which leads up the east bank of Uloola Brook. Several small cascades exist upstream from the main falls and about a kilometre south The Blue Pools should be met. They are small, but lovely, rock pools. Masses of white heath and white hakea flowers bloom in the area in

December-January. A kilometre further south you should approach Uloola Swamp after having continued to follow the track close to Uloola Brook. The track then skirts the eastern edge of the swamp and heads south-westwards. At the south end of the swamp the remains of an old training track should be crossed and by this time the foot track has become a jeep track. It winds across dry country to the signposted junction of the Couranga Track which leads off south-east. Finally you should walk 500 metres west to arrive at the Waterfall Football Ground. Keep to the north side of the oval and a foot track should be noted. Follow it north-west directly up across a grassed area and past a signpost at the north side of the local Fire Station to the south end of Waterfall Railway Station.

MAP REF: *Audley map provided with this publication.* Map 5.

WALK DISTANCE: 10.5 km.

GRADING: One day, easy.

6 OTFORD—BURNING PALMS—GARAWARRA—OTFORD

Burning Palms is a small beach locality in the southern part of the Royal National Park south of Sydney. It is a pleasant, remote beach which cannot be reached by car. To reach it the walker must either descend what is known as The Burgh Ridge or sidle down through Palm Jungle. This walk suggestion includes both these access routes and permits the walker to see wonderful beaches, views, palms and jungle.

Travel by car to Otford Gap or catch a train to Otford. Check train times though, as few stops are made at this little station. Once at the station's south end climb up a foot track to the east. Shortly the track forms a 'T' shape with an earth road. Turn left and follow the road uphill until it emerges via Fanshawe Road on to Lady Wakehurst Drive at Otford Gap. The gap provides superb views south to Wollongong and beyond and from it a foot track leads north up a grassy spur. Soon the track sidles up the western slopes as the spur becomes narrower and leads to a high rocky ridge. There are reasonable views to both east and west and after about 800 metres the hilltop is reached. It is then a kilometre north then east along a foot track, then a jeep track to a signposted junction where you should fork right. This foot track to Burning Palms via Palm Jungle initially follows near the top of a cliff line then emerges at spectacular Werrong Point, a rock outcrop which gives views down over Werrong Beach and right along the coast to the south. From this point the track descends round the southern slopes of a bluff then sidles down the east side of the coastal cliff lines through Palm Jungle which is very beautiful and shady. There is no plant understorey in much of the jungle and consequently the track is quite open and easy to follow. There are aluminium can lids used as markers, too. The palms, vines and jungle, generally, are fascinating and extend for about 2.0 kilometres. You should then arrive on steep, open slopes which provide good views along the coast. Soon the track enters grassed areas, passes a Ranger's hut (with tank water supply at the rear of the hut) then descends some steps on to the south end of Burning Palms Beach. At this point you are about 5.8 kilometres from Otford Gap. The beach is only small but is quite picturesque and swimming and lunch are recommended.

There are a number of huts up the slopes from the beach and a signposted foot track at beach level reads "Garawarra'. The track leads between the huts steeply up a gully to a saddle 600 metres due north on The Burgh Ridge which heads up westwards. Once at this grassy saddle, turn left (west) uphill on a well-defined foot track through forest. You should arrive at Garawarra Picnic Ground and a carpark on the hilltop, 900 metres away.

Next turn south-south-west along the signposted Cliff Track and follow it for 2.5 kilometres to rejoin your outward route. The Cliff Track is a jeep track and offers fast walking close to the coastal cliff line, so you get some views out to sea but generally the route is forested. Avoid the minor foot tracks off east sharply down hill to Burning Palms via Lookout Squeeze and the slanting jeep track veering off right to Lilyvale. Neither of these tracks is signposted. However, when you reach the junction where you turned off to Palm Jungle on your outward route you should see a sign informing you that it is 4.0 kilometres to Otford and 4.0 kilometres to Garawarra. Both these distances seem to be overstated by at least a kilometre.

MAP REF: *Otford map provided with this publication.* Map 4.

WALK DISTANCE: 12 km from Otford Gap, 13.5 km from Otford Station.

GRADING: One day, easy.

7   GLENBROOK CROSSING — REDHAND CAVE

Perhaps the closest walk venue to Sydney in the Blue Mountains is the Redhand Cave circuit. It is also quite beautiful and serene. Redhand Cave is a sandstone overhang with Aboriginal hand markings on it and the cave is the focus of the walk, but other features are the cool, sassafras-filled gully and pools surrounded by ferns.

Travel to Glenbrook and enter the Blue Mountains National Park, then descend to Glenbrook Creek car park where there is a concrete causeway and the start of this walk route. A sign on the south side of the causeway near a rock outcrop shows the start. For 2.0 kilometres the track follows the south bank of Camp Fire Creek, then for a further kilometre it follows the south bank of Redhand Creek to the cave. The only turnoff along the way is your return route track which enters from the south-east along Campfire Creek.

Have a good look at the Aboriginal markings; it is believed that they acted as some form of signature. Next, climb to the right, up and on to the top of the cave's outcrop where a 250-metre-long track should be followed south to tank water, a carpark and the suggested lunch place. From this point a minor foot track should be followed south-east along the ridge top through dry scrub and trees. The track then sidles east, then south, then down into Campfire Creek which is beautiful, cool and ferny. Cross to its east bank and walk a kilometre north, to rejoin the outward route. It is then 2.0 kilometres back to the end of the walk. Just 100 metres short of the Causeway, there is an interesting sandstone overhang. Perhaps a swim at the Causeway pool to cool off may be welcome.

MAP REF: **Glenbrook map provided with this publication.** Map 7.

WALK DISTANCE: 8 km.

GRADING: One day, easy.

8 GLENBROOK CAUSEWAY—EUROKA CLEARING—NEPEAN RIVER

If it looks like being a hot day and you would like to walk just a short distance to a swimming place on a river near Sydney, try this route. It starts and finishes at Glenbrook Causeway, just inside the Blue Mountains National Park, south of Glenbrook. The causeway itself has a swimming hole adjacent to it on Glenbrook Creek.

Walk up the bitumen road southwards from the causeway via hairpin bends. It soon becomes a gravelled road and, 600 metres from the causeway, a foot track diverges left at a signpost pointing the way to Euroka Clearing. Follow the trail for 1.3 kilometres to emerge at a minor road junction on a broad ridge. The bush is rather dry and uninteresting at this point, but wildflowers are good in spring. Continue on the trail south-east for 1.2 kilometres downhill to Euroka Clearing, a large grassed basin which was apparently once the vent of a volcano, but now is a picnic and bush camping area. Head 200 metres to the north-east corner of the clearing from where a good foot track leads east 1.2 kilometres along the banks of Euroka Creek to the Nepean River. There is a signpost at the start of the track and just as you descend the last steep pinch to the river you should fork left.

Swimming and lunch by the river should be most pleasant at this scenic spot. The river is wide and flows through a gorge and a number of shady places exist. Simply retrace the outward route when you are ready to return.

MAP REF: *Euroka map provided with this publication.*
Map 6.
WALK DISTANCE: 9 km.
GRADING: One day, easy.

9   NEPEAN LOOKDOWN — ERSKINE CREEK

The Blue Mountains National Park has some quite remote sections where the walker can be far removed from life's rush and bustle. Surprisingly, one of the closest parts of the park to Sydney is one of the most isolated. It is the Nepean Lookdown area and is ideally suited to walking in hot weather, as the route is along a creek side with white sand beaches, rock swimming pools and shady trees abounding.

Travel to Glenbrook and turn south into the National Park where there is a visitors' centre. Go on down the hill across pretty Glenbrook Creek Causeway and drive on 11.5 kilometres via the gravelled Oaks Firetrail to Nepean Lookdown. There are several forks in the road on the way but the area is well signposted.

Have a look at the Nepean River far below then walk back 600 metres to a carpark and signpost indicating the way to Erskine Creek via Jack Evans Trail. Walk south along this good trail and, within 100 metres, turn right to a superb view down on to Erskine Creek from a rock ledge known as Erskine Lookdown. Return the 20 metres to the main track and descend via steps and the well-graded track to a saddle then fork right (west) down to the creekside beach. The left fork at the saddle is a little indistinct but it is the return route and should be noted. The total distance from the carpark to Erskine Creek is only a kilometre. The creek forms a loop southwards called Platypus

Loops so it is best to wander south then east, following the stream bank and wading where necessary until you choose a sandy beach for lunch. Take your time walking as rock scrambling is required and it can be rather tiring if you rush. Perhaps some sun basking and swimming would be good, too. Just to sit and listen to the myriad birds, or to gaze up at the towering cliffs would be enjoyable.

The walk continues on downstream swinging north-west then east again until the junction of the Nepean River is reached. Have a rest by the river then retrace 600 metres back to where Erskine Creek bends south. At this spot a small foot track leads west directly up to a saddle only 250 metres from the stream. Head up this small track, then turn north back up the well-grated, short track to the carpark. Finally, retrace the 600 metres along the road to Nepean Lookdown for another look down on where you have been.

MAP REF: **Nepean River map provided with this publication.** Map 8.

WALK DISTANCE: 6 km.

GRADING: One day, easy.

10   SPRINGWOOD — MAGDALA CREEK — SASSAFRAS CREEK

Much of the walking in the Blue Mountains becomes difficult once you try to descend into the magnificent forested areas of the valleys and gorges. The structure of the mountains is such that the further west you go towards the Blackheath area, the more rugged the sandstone country. At Springwood you are still well east and any walking is relatively easy, yet you can see gullies equally as beautiful, shaded and ferny.

Magdala Creek, south of the town, is especially good and cascades over two pleasant waterfalls also.

Start and finish this walk at Springwood Railway Station. First, walk south-west along the south side of the railway line in Macquarie Road and turn into Homedale Street. Where it turns west and becomes Valley Road, turn east down 150 metres into the Picnic Point Reserve where a trail commences and where tank water is available. It is only about 600 metres from Springwood station.

Follow the track north-east into the gully for 100 metres, cross a bridge and turn south down the headwaters of Magdala Creek. In 200 metres veer right rather than take the signposted Lawsons Lookout track. Cross from one side of the creek to the other a number of times as you descend south through ferns and fine forest. Trigger plants are quite common too. After 2.0 kilometres, rock outcrops become bold and, 500 metres later, a very minor track joins in from the north as you cross to the east bank after having swung east for a few hundred metres. It is then a 600 metre walk south down to Magdala Falls and Blue Pool. The trail crosses to the west bank midway to the 10-metre-high falls. A small gorge is in the area downstream from the falls and ferns, rock overhangs and cascades make a perfect setting for a lunch break. It is only about 400 metres south down to Martins Falls also of about 10 metres drop and equally pretty. A further 500 metres walk brings you to the junction of Magdala Creek and Glenbrook Creek at a place known as Perch Ponds. A signpost indicates the route alternatives. One track branches off south-east to Martins Lookout and should be ignored. Instead, turn north-west and follow the north-east slopes of Glenbrook Creek for 1.5 kilometres to the confluence of Sassafras Creek and Glenbrook Creek, where there is a lovely pool, a bush camping area, and the track crosses to the west bank of Sassafras Creek. Follow it northwards 750 metres to the signposted junction of the track via Bee Farm Road to Springwood where you should stay on the west bank of Sassafras Creek and continue north. In 350 metres you must cross to the east bank and in a further 400 metres meet a further track junction where there are no signposted directions. The left fork leads to Faulconbridge, but you should head north-east up a side gully. The whole of this area is wonderfully green and shady and, at many points along the way, pools suited to swimming will have been passed.

Follow the gully north-east then head up a well-trodden track around and onto a spur which leads up to Sassafras Gully Road, Springwood, about 1.5 kilometres from Sassafras Creek. Finally, walk north 200 metres along the road, turn right into Valley Road, walk 400 metres east, turn north back up Homedale Street then north-east into Macquarie Road to Springwood station.

MAP REF: *Springwood map provided with this publication.* Map 9.

WALK DISTANCE: 11 km.

GRADING: One day, easy.

11 SPRINGWOOD—SASSAFRAS GULLY—FAULCONBRIDGE

Sassafras Creek, near Springwood in the Blue Mountains, must surely rate high as one of the most beautiful, shady and ferny gullies within reasonable proximity of Sydney. At the same time, walking through the gullies is not difficult. Sassafras, a plant which grows only in cool damp conditions grows in abundance.

Travel to Springwood station then follow Macquarie Road south-west along the south side of the railway line for 300 metres, turn south-east into Homedale Street then west into Valley Road and south along Bee Farm Road until you reach Yondell Road about 1.8 kilometres from the station. Walk along gravelled Yondell Road 250 metres to where a signpost on the west side points down a foot track to Sassafras Creek. It is the Wiggins Track which descends a small creek valley for 850 metres to put you in the midst of magnificent forest and fern gullies. There is a sign at a track junction on the south bank of Sassafras Creek at this point. You should follow the right fork north-west for 350 metres then cross to the east bank for a further 400 metres to where another track junction should be met. There are many lovely rock pools along Sassafras Creek and one of the best is near this junction. Fork left westwards along the north bank towards Faulconbridge but there is no signpost to indicate the way. Just 250 metres later you should cross to the south bank then stay on that side of the creek as the trail climbs up the slopes through rainforest for a kilometre. There are views across the valley to the high cliffs opposite. The track then descends slightly to the confluence of Numantia Creek where there is a small area suited to bush camping and lunch is suggested on this grassy space.

After lunch, you should follow the west bank of Sassafras Creek north-west through further dense and shaded bushland. Ground ferns, sassafras and sturdy eucalypts predominate. After a kilometre you should arrive at the tiny Clarinda Falls which are only about five metres high. You must then zig-zag up to, and above, some cliffs into open forest which is in strange contrast to the damp forest traversed so far. Next cross to the east bank 400 metres upstream from the falls and you should then approach some rock overhangs and start a steep climb up through rocky outcrops surrounding the headwaters of the creek. The track rises above the bluffs on to a bitumen road just 40 metres south of a railway level crossing. At the crossing, turn left along either the north or south side of the line and in 300 metres arrive at Faulconbridge station.

MAP REF: *Springwood map provided with this publication.* Map 9.

WALK DISTANCE: 8 km.

GRADING: One day, easy.

12 KATOOMBA FALLS—ECHO POINT—THE THREE SISTERS.

Katoomba must surely rate as the most famous of Australian mountain resorts. Before people used cars so much, walking was one of the more popular leisure activities and facilities for walkers around Katoomba were accordingly installed on a grand scale. It is a pity that tracks, signs, seats, handrails and other facilities have been allowed to fall into disrepair but the general decay of Katoomba's walking facilities must reflect society's priorities to some extent. Nevertheless, what remains is good and such magnificent places as Katoomba Falls, Echo Point and The Three Sisters are well serviced.

It is possible to spend a whole day ambling around on the numerous old tracks as well as the three main points of interest, and yet be no more than 2.0 kilometres from Echo Point at any one time. The Scenic Railway, said to be the steepest incline railway in the world, can be used to regain the 250 metres altitude which you would have descended during the day. The railway, incidentally, rises at an incline of up to 52° and it passes through a 75-metre-long tunnel. The last car leaves at 4.55 p.m.

Start this walk suggestion at the top station of the railway and follow the map in this book very closely. There are so many tracks that it is easy to go wrong if you do not watch the map closely. Many errors exist in other maps available. Walk north around the railway winding-gear sheds, where you should find a good foot track. The sheds are just north of the station, kiosk and restaurant. Follow the track as it contours then turn right at the first junction. This trail leads directly south-east to Vanimans Lookout for a good general view. Next, retrace a few metres and turn left down the continuation of the track which descends to a point due east of the Scenic Railway's top station. At this point the track to Orphan Rock is passed. Next pass through a narrow gap where there is another small lookout to your right. Continue on downhill and take the first turn right straight east down a track labelled Federal Pass. In a few metres you should turn south at another intersection and descend via Juliets Balcony and Furbers Steps to another junction beside a creek and bridge. Cross the bridge and walk generally north-east to the foot of the Second Katoomba Fall. This is a magnificent place for a pause. Rainforest and ferns predominate in the area and there is little undergrowth.

Next, retrace your route back across the bridge and

up past Juliets Balcony to the junction where the Federal Pass sign exists. At this point turn right (north) and walk up to the base of Witches Leap Falls. These falls have a 20 metre drop only but are quite beautiful. Follow the trail uphill more steeply and within about 250 metres you should emerge at the steps on to Reids Point. There are some four trails joining at the steps. The north track leads to a little kiosk nearby should you want a short break for a few minutes. To the south, Reids Point provides good views of Witches Leap Falls, Orphan Rock, a general view, and a view of Katoomba Falls as you walk anti-clockwise around the oval-shaped track which returns you to the steps. The track should next be taken east 100 metres past the Watchtower Lookout and on 100 more metres to the Duke and Duchess of York Lookout. It gives good views southwards over Katoomba Falls area. Next, head north along the west bank of Kedumba Creek to some cascades just near Cliff Drive. Cross the creek at the cascades and follow the trail back south on the eastern slopes of Kedumba Creek. The trail, incidentally, is called Prince Henrys Walk. It leads underneath the Katoomba Skyway cables where there is a good view south then it heads east round the cliff rim, under small rock overhangs and past two minor lookouts to Lady Darleys Lookout at the south end of Katoomba Street (Katoomba's main street). Continue south-east and very shortly you should arrive at Echo Point where all facilities exist and where there is of course the famous broad view of the Jamieson Valley, Mount Solitary and the Three Sisters. Perhaps this lookout is the most famous in Australia.

Two concreted paths initially lead from Echo Point

towards the north end of The Three Sisters. Take the one which keeps closest to the cliff rim, as it gives better views. The two paths rejoïn and then an arch should be met. Go under the arch and out on to The Three Sisters Lookout then turn down the Giants Staircase. It leads to Honeymoon Point (which is actually on one of The Three Sisters) then past Eves Lookout and down numerous steps to join a contouring trail called The Dardanelles Pass. Turn right (south) and follow the track as it contours around below The Three Sisters and is joined by the Federal Pass Track from your left as you turn north. Keep walking roughly north-west through magnificent forests to cross Kedumba Creek again, then swing south-west and climb slightly past a track coming in from the right then in 200 metres arrive at the foot of the Scenic Railway. A hair-raising ride finishes the interesting day. Lunch could be enjoyed just about anywhere along the way but it is best to carry your water as the water, below the cliff line especially, is badly polluted.

MAP REF: *Katoomba Falls area and Katoomba maps provided with this publication.* Maps 10 and 11.

WALK DISTANCE: 7 km.

GRADING: One day, easy.

13   KATOOMBA SCENIC RAILWAY—RUINED CASTLE

There are a number of cliff rim and undercliff walks close to Katoomba and a favourite practice is to walk along the cliff tops, descend them, walk along the cliff base, then use the Scenic Railway to ascend back to the tops. One walk of this nature with a lot of geological interest is the route out to the Ruined Castle. The Blue Mountains consist largely of bedded sandstones of enormous depth indicating that they were laid down under the sea over a vast period. Hundreds of metres down the cliffs, coal seams exist and the Federal Pass Track passes along the level of the coal bedding. A number of disused tunnels can still be seen. The Scenic Railway was originally installed to get coal up to the cliff tops and, in those days, walkers used to sit on top of the coal to get a ride up. The very fact coal exists at such levels shows that once the surface was at that level as coal is the result of forests being compressed.

Start walking from the top of the Scenic Railway and head west up Violet Street. Where the street bends north-west, follow a very rough road southwest up over a ridge. This is called Short Street but there are no signs and it doesn't really look like a street. In 100 metres you should arrive at the intersection of Cliff Drive and Narrow Neck Road. Follow Narrow Neck Road for 2.0 kilometres roughly southwest. It is a dusty, gravelled road but there are magnificent views on both sides of the road as it crosses an 'isthmus'. As you approach a steep incline in the road which has guard railing along its side, you should look for a post on the left side of the road. It marks the top of the Golden Stairs Track. The post obviously once carried a sign and is about 100 metres north of a sign advising motorists that the incline section of Narrow Neck Road and beyond is suited to four-wheel-drive vehicles only.

Descend the Golden Stairs which are quite steep; they have two short steel ladders but there are formed steps to make the descent easier. At the bottom a sign points your way south to the Ruined Castle via a contouring trail. This is the Federal Pass Track and it leads south about 2.5 kilometres to another sign-posted track off uphill to the right on to a saddle. From the saddle, the track rises along the ridge for 500 metres to the summit of the Ruined Castle. Make sure you scramble up the rock stacks for good views; perhaps lunch on the top would be pleasant but there is no water supply in the immediate vicinity.

The return journey for the first 3.2 kilometres is a retrace of the outward route back to the base of the Golden Stairs through the rainforest. You should then continue to follow the Federal Pass Track as it contours round through more ferns and rainforest. Next, cross the scree slopes below the mighty rock slip at Cyclorama Point and head past the entrances to a number of old coal mines to the base of the Scenic Railway. It is about 2.75 kilometres from the foot of the Golden Stairs to the foot of the railway but every section of the route is packed with interest, including distant views, cliff views, dense forests, ferns and cascades. The last car of the railway leaves at 4.55 p.m. and there is a kiosk at the top for refreshments. Should you miss the last car there is a trail to the tops. It leads off east of the lower station.

MAP REF: **Katoomba and Solitary maps provided with this publication.** Maps 10 and 17.

WALK DISTANCE: 12.5 km.

GRADING: One day, easy.

14   LEURA CLIFFS—LYREBIRD DELL

The Leura Falls area has a multitude of foot tracks mostly installed in the days before cars were used so extensively and when walking was much more popular. There are, of course, so many interesting little glens, falls, overhangs and other features to see that the number of tracks is indeed necessary. Sometimes it is rather pleasant just to wander round every little track seeing the attractions along each, but regrettably it is most difficult to get a map that correctly shows all routes and so one can easily be confused and have to retrace walks. This suggestion however is based upon the Leura Falls map included in this book and the map should assist greatly. In order to make the trip one which involves a day's activity rather than an hour or two, the adjoining Leura cliffline walk is included.

Start the walk at the intersection of Leura Mall and Malvern Road, Leura. Leura Mall is the town's main street and Malvern Road is the fourth east-west cross street southwards from the railway line. First, walk west to the end of Malvern Road, turn south for 50 metres then veer right down a foot track which joins Cliff Drive in just 300 metres. There are shelter sheds, baths and a picnic area just west of the spot. Also Leura Falls Creek flows through southwards and a trail leads down its west bank. Follow this track, then diverge right rather than cross a bridge and continue to Majestic Lookout. It provides a reasonable view of the valley. Next walk west and at the next junction keep going west along the signposted kiosk track. (Incidentally, the kiosk is now a restaurant.) Cross the head of a stream, turn south and pass a rock overhang amid beautiful ferns, then at the next fork, shortly afterwards, take a minor side trip to lovely Bridal Veil View. It is perhaps the best view in the area. Return to the main track, bypass the signposted Copeland Lookout track (the sign is high up on a tree), then climb a few steps north to the restaurant at Kiah Lookout on Cliff Drive. Next, walk just a few metres west on Cliff Drive and join another signposted trail indicating an alternative route to Federal Pass via Leila Falls. Just 10 metres south, turn west and walk to Jamieson Lookout. Have a look at the view, then fork left and start the descent through a magnificent gully down many steps along the east bank of the gully. Soon you should arrive at Leila Falls. The falls are only small but are pretty. Stay on the east bank rather than cross at the falls base, then walk round below the cliff line through The Amphitheatre with its magnificent ferns and overhang, take a very short side trip to the right to the lookout overlooking the second Leura Fall, then continue to the intersection of four trails at Leura Falls Creek just at the base of Weeping Rock. Turn north uphill to the base of First Leura Fall (or Bridal Veil) which from this position is very pleasing, then swing back west then east up many steps until you arrive near the top of First Leura Falls. On the way, ignore a turnoff to the left and stop for a look at the fine views at each of the two lookouts. Once above the falls, walk north along the stream's east bank past pleasant little cascades and a swimming hole. Not far upstream Prince Henry's Cliff Walk doubles back to your right and contours southwards. Follow it past Flying Fox Lookout and another un-named lookout soon after, a rock overhang with a seat under it, and past the turnoff to Bridal Veil View Lookout on your right. The cliff walk then turns north-east temporarily then continues on past interesting Tarpeian Rock with its strange sandstone bedding ridges, past Fernery Cave, Olympian Rock, Buttenshaw Bridge, and Elysian Rock to Gordon Falls Lookout carpark. Walk down the side track just a few metres to view Gordon Falls; there is no point in going all the way down as trees block the falls view. Return to the carpark where there is drinking water and picnic facilities. It would be a good place for lunch before continuing on down a trail to the Pool of Siloam, a lovely, cool swimming hole on Gordon Creek. The pool is just 10 metres east of the main Lyrebird Dell Track, which should next be followed north. There are some remarkable rock over-hangs and a waterfall along Lyrebird Dell. The trail then swings west up to a gravelled road. Turn right (north) and walk up the road out through the reserve entrance back into Malvern Road. It is then only two blocks back west to the walk starting point. Those persons without transport could easily start and finish this walk at Leura station and simply add the short distance along Leura Mall.

MAP REF: *Katoomba and Leura Falls maps provided with this publication.* Maps 10 and 16.

WALK DISTANCE: 6 km.

GRADING: One day, easy.

15 VALLEY OF THE WATERS—NATIONAL PASS—UNDERCLIFF WALK

The cliffline walks at Katoomba in the Blue Mountains are both popular and scenic but, nearby at Wentworth Falls, scenery is even better and goes largely un-noticed. At Katoomba, the trails are at the top and at the base of the cliffs, but at Wentworth Falls the trails are cut into the cliffs halfway up them so that views are uninterrupted and really spectacular and cliff overhangs are seen to their fullest advantage. So, next time you visit the Blue Mountains area, travel along the Great Western Highway to a point 400 metres west of the 100 kilometre peg from Sydney. There are some big pine trees at the corner of West Street at the spot. It is the suggested starting point for walking.

First, walk 100 metres south on West Street then where the road turns west walk to the road edge and you should see a sign: 'Nature Trail to Conservation Hut'. The trail leads downhill south beside the sign. Do not take the jeep track diverging to the right. Follow the Nature Trail down across a small gully and up onto Edinburgh Castle Rock, then descend round the rock's western edge, below its cliffs and on down into the Valley of the Waters gully where there is eventually a bridge to the west bank and a sign pointing the way to a golf course. You should however remain on the east bank and very shortly you will be amid beautiful ferns and at the intersection of four tracks. Follow the National Pass track which is the one leading down the valley. It leads straight to the top of lovely Lodard Falls then descends to their base via magnificent rock swimming holes and ferny glades. Just below the falls take the left fork trail rather than the right fork to Vera Falls. National Pass Track, the one you should follow, then continues for nearly 2.0 kilometres on what surely is the most spectacular cliff walk in Australia and about the best overall walk in the Blue Mountains. The sandstone cliffs are in horizontal beds and this remarkable track follows round the contour of the bedding in a tiny ledge. In places the cliffs have been carved out to permit a through walk, and for most of the way you are under cliff overhangs and even walking behind waterfalls. The views of the Jamieson Valley are spectacular as there is little foreground vegetation to block the view. There are, however, wonderful displays of bottlebrush flowers in summer. Eventually you should arrive at the Wentworth Falls which descend in two stages and National Pass crosses the stream amidst spray between the two drops. (If there have recently been heavy rains a raincoat would be advisable.) The trail then climbs up man-made stairs cut out of the sandstone to the head of the upper fall. Lunch here is suggested.

At this point there are a number of foot tracks beginning, as the area is a picnic reserve. Remain as close to the cliff rim as possible diverging left at each junction. The aim is to follow the Undercliff Walking Track which, like National Pass, follows crevasses along sandstone bedding, but high above National Pass. Keep on heading west and at two points tracks lead off left. In the first instance the side route leads to a small waterfall and then on to a lookout, and in the second case the side route leads to a minor lookout. Take both these side trips. Some six tracks lead off to the right from Undercliff Walk and all should be ignored in favour of the cliff edge route. Always diverge left at each junction. At the cross tracks where the fourth and fifth branches lead off to the right, double back down to Queen Victoria Lookout on the signposted track. After the lookout the track leads back down to the head of Lodard Falls and from that point on you should retrace your outward route back to West Street. Undercliff Walk is a little overgrown but nevertheless is still easily negotiable.

MAP REF: **Wentworth Falls maps provided with this publication.** Maps 12 and 13.

WALK DISTANCE: 6 km.

GRADING: One day, easy.

One of the more interesting places in the Blue Mountains is the Grand Canyon near Blackheath. The canyon is, of course, nothing like its famous counterpart in the United States, but it is quite deep in relation to its width and has a length of about 2.0 kilometres. Greaves Creek flows through it, eroding the sandstone formations into incredible shapes, and in places one cannot see the bottom from the track because of the narrowness and darkness. Ferns, rock overhangs, a tunnel and the constant sound of rushing water all contribute to making it an excellent walk venue.

It is far better to walk downhill through the canyon so that you can really appreciate it and not think about the difficulties encountered in climbing up the other way. Also at two points the track descends from the south side on to the canyon floor and if walking uphill, one tends to miss the lower turnoff and to walk into the section of the canyon floor from which the only exit is a retrace of your route.

Take the Evans Lookout Road east off the Great Western Highway just 2.0 kilometres south of Blackheath station and proceed to a small carpark and signpost indicating a 2½ hour walk through the Grand Canyon to Evans Lookout. The spot is about 2.8 kilometres east of the Highway and is at the head of Neates Glen. If water is required, a tap exists on the north-west side of the road 200 metres back towards Blackheath. There is a tank at the walk starting point but the tap is broken.

To start the walk itself, descend the reasonable foot track south into Neates Glen which is a very ferny and pretty gully leading into, and providing access to, the deeper Grand Canyon. Steps assist in the descent but in places are slippery with constant running water. It is only about 400 metres to the Grand Canyon junction where you must cross Greaves Creek and follow its south bank downstream. At first the canyon is relatively dry and even scrubby as you contour above the stream but soon you must descend sharply from the slopes down to a cleared area on the canyon floor where there is a signpost pointing back up to Blackheath. Just downstream from this point you should pass through a 10-metre-long tunnel to put you in the canyon proper. At the tunnel the stream also flows underground. Continue downstream on the south bank through fern glades and rock overhangs. The trail is well formed and has hand rails for protection along much of the route. Eventually you will find that the stream is descending more rapidly than the trail and temporarily you come across drier vegetation on the higher slopes. Again you must suddenly descend to the canyon floor, this time via a side gully and the descent is quite steep. It is then a matter of following the bed quite closely to a signposted junction. Fork right downstream at this intersection and follow the creek as it swings round south then back north to a further intersection in just 300 metres. Take the left branch and walk along the Rodriguez Pass Track for about 200 metres so that you emerge at spectacular cliffs and get excellent views out through the valley below Beauchamp Falls. Next return the 200 metres and descend about 100 metres to Beauchamp Falls themselves which are very pretty and well worth the visit. The trail should be followed to the base of the falls for the best view. Lunch in this area would be ideal.

Return the 400 metres up the Grand Canyon then turn right up the Evans Lookout track. It ascends through extremely beautiful ferns and in places there is no other vegetation than tree and ground ferns. About a kilometre up this gully a rough horse-trail joins in from the right. It comes up from Govetts Creek valley. It is then only a short climb up to Evans Lookout shelter sheds, water tanks and picnic area. Evans Lookout is a well-known vantage point for views of the Grose and Govetts Creek valleys. The cliffs are extremely high and the valley floor is about 600 metres lower than the lookout. After a good rest and look at the view walk back along the tourist road for 1.25 kilometres to the walk starting point.

MAP REF: **Blackheath map provided with this publication.** Map 14.

WALK DISTANCE: 6 km.

GRADING: One day, easy.

17 PERRYS LOOKDOWN — BLUE GUM FOREST

The Blue Gum Forest is a name which many Sydney district walkers immediately associate with great beauty, serenity and relative isolation. It exists at the junction of Govetts Creek and the Grose River way down in the Grose Valley out from Blackheath. On a hot day the area is especially attractive due to the shady trees, park-like grassy areas, swimming holes and views up to the towering cliffs all around the valley. There is also the added attraction of an excellent camp area just 500 metres south-west at Acacia Flat.

Access to the Blue Gum Forest is difficult from any direction, but from Perrys Lookdown the walking distance is shortest at 2.25 kilometres. However, there is a difference in elevation between the two points of some 600 metres. The track is good and the upper section has properly-formed steps leading down through the cliffs so that descent time would be only about 45 minutes or even less. Ascent time, however, would be up to two hours depending on the walkers concerned and the temperature. Experienced walkers could complete the climb in one hour.

Hat Hill Road from Blackheath leads to Perrys Lookdown and at the turntable there is a small picnic ground and camping area. The track to the Blue Gum Forest veers off to the right just beside the lookout some 100 metres south-east of the car turntable. It then skirts round and across Hordern Gully to Docker Head then descends through the cliffs and down the well-defined spur known as Docker Buttress. It leads right to the confluence of the two streams at the forest.

MAP REF: **Govetts Gorge map provided with this publication.** Map 15.

WALK DISTANCE: 4.5 km.

GRADING: One day, easy.

18 BLACKHEATH — POPES GLEN — GOVETTS LEAP — BRAESIDE

Govetts Leap, just east of Blackheath is a spectacular lookout point and there is a good tourist road to it and all the amenities at the lookout. It is possible to have a very enjoyable day's walk with Govetts Leap as the main attraction, starting and finishing at Blackheath station. Two beautiful gully walks lead to and from the lookout.

Opposite the east side of the railway station Gardiners Crescent should be followed east. It leads down a small valley, becomes a gravelled road and then swings south about 600 metres from the station. Remain on the north side of the gully and walk east along Wills Street a further 300 metres to a signpost and foot track turnoff on the right hand side of the road. This is the start of Govetts Walk along Popes Glen. After 600 metres of walking along the north bank you should cross a bridge to the south bank. In this area the valley is fairly open and descends gently. Snow gums and other alpine vegetation are noticeable despite the relatively low altitude and other wildflowers are in abundance. A track joins in from the east 100 metres south of power transmission lines which cross the valley. About 1.6 kilometres from the start of Govetts Walk a rock overhang should be noted some 300 metres after crossing to the north bank where the stream turns east. Only 100 metres more to the east you should recross to the south bank and almost immediately a signposted track leads off to the left to Boyds Beach. This short detour should be taken, as it is only 30 metres to the beach beside the creek. Tea-tree and honey-flower are both especially beautiful in the area. The stream water is not suited to drinking.

Next, walk 300 metres south to the Pulpit Rock Track turnoff which leads left (east) across the stream. You should, however, go southwards and it is at this point that Popes Glen reaches a cliffline and spills over lovely Horseshoe Falls down into the Grose Valley. Two small lookouts exist on your left almost immediately you reach the cliff rim and each provide superb views. Horseshoe Falls obviously get their name from the horseshoe-shaped cliffline. The track ascends steps past a lot of ground ferns and, in 200 metres, forks. Take the left fork nearest the cliff rim for 100 metres to another lookout then fork right straight up the slopes to Govetts Leap Lookout and carpark. This is the suggested lunch place where there are all facilities. The view from the lookout would be one of the best views in New South Wales.

After lunch follow a clifftop trail from Govetts Leap Lookout southwards. In 500 metres, after having descended to Govetts Creek, you should be at the head of Govetts Leap Falls. Like Horseshoe Falls, it is one of the biggest and best falls in the Blue Mountains and would have a vertical drop of well over 100 metres. Just 100 metres east across the creek is a further lookout which should be visited for superb views before returning to the head of the falls. You should then turn south away from the cliffs along signposted Braeside Walk which follows the east bank of Govetts Leap Brook through areas renowned for hakea and wildflowers. The valley is fairly open and at the end of the trail, some 1.4 kilometres from the falls, there is a small picnic area. It is then 2.5 kilometres to Blackheath station and you must use roads for the remainder of the walk. It is suggested you should follow the gravelled road uphill south-east from the picnic area for a kilometre then join into Braeside Street which heads west. Next turn north along Boreas Street at the end of Braeside Street and then west again along Govetts Leap Road which leads back to the Great Western Highway. It is then only 200 metres north back to the station via the highway.

MAP REF: **Blackheath map provided with this publication.** Map 14.

WALK DISTANCE: 8 km.

GRADING: One day, easy.

19 FLAT TOP—THE PINNACLES—LOCKLEY PYLON

Much of the walking in the Blue Mountains is along clifflines and streams and some timbered areas. It is seldom that one finds a place where the walking trails are on elevated open tops with expansive views. This suggested walk route takes the walker across open tops with virtually no trees and with some alpine vegetation. Access to the area is, however, via Mount Hay Road from Leura and the road is quite rough in several places even in dry weather. After or during wet weather access could only be achieved by four-wheel-drive vehicles or by walking. The suggested walk starting point is 8.8 kilometres north of the Great Western Highway at the Fortress Ridge jeep track turnoff making the planned distance 9.0 kilometres return but if the Mount Hay Road is impassable the 9.0 kilometre trip could be as much as 17.0 kilometres long and the resulting 'road bash' would probably spoil the trip. The first 5.0 kilometres out of Leura however offer reasonable motoring.

The Mount Hay Road continues north-east around the western slopes of Flat Top for 1.3 kilometres but is very rough. It is therefore suggested that you initially follow the road for 500 metres, then 'scrub bash' east up onto the summit of Flat Top for an all round view. Next follow a rough jeep track north. The jeep track services a trig point on the summit and descends to the Mount Hay Road 1.1 kilometres from the walk starting point. Just 200 metres north there is a water tank supplying drinking water and a signpost at the start of a foot track which veers off to the left. The signpost indicates the way·to The Pinnacles, Lockley Pylon, Grose River and the Blue Gum Forest.

You should follow this trail north though open country initially along the western slopes of the Three Pinnacles which are small rocky knobs then north-west across two saddles and up through some trees on Mount Stead. In this area honey-flower and banksia grow in profusion. The climb over Mount Stead is quite easy and gradual and on its north-western edge the open country begins again but with expansive views. It is then only a kilometre to Lockley Pylon which is an obvious treeless knob just near the cliffline of the Grose Valley. The main trail descends around the eastern slopes of Lockley Pylon then leads down to the Blue Gum Forest. However, you should see the short minor track ascending the knob from the main trail as you approach. The view from the summit is indeed superb but, before you leave, walk 100 metres down the slopes westwards to the cliff rim for an even better view of the valley straight below. There is no water about but the area would be a good lunch spot, after which you should retrace your outward route. The short detour over Flat Top could be omitted in favour of following the Mount Hay Road.

MAP REF: ***Govetts Gorge map provided with this publication.*** Map 15.

WALK DISTANCE: 9.0 km.

GRADING: One day, easy.

20   MOUNT WILSON — WOLLANGAMBE RIVER

If you have ever dreamed of secluded white sandy beaches along a river flowing through a rugged gorge where there are plenty of swimming places, then the Wollangambe River is just the place to satisfy your dreams. On a hot day it would be very good and to take an air bed and to float about on the river would be almost heaven.

The area is only 2.8 kilometres from the main road at Mount Wilson in the Blue Mountains so that the walk's total distance is quite short. There is a small picnic ground on the east corner and a school on the west corner of a junction where the walk should start. It is 700 metres west of Mount Wilson Post Office.

Walk north-north-west 500 metres initially downhill then uphill along an earth road and then diverge slightly left at a gate and a fenceline which turns away east. Follow the road down as it leads across a grassy slope for a further 100 metres to a cross jeep track then walk 30 metres north-east along the jeep track to a small rock cairn on the left. A minor foot track leads off north-north-west beside the cairn and is the route you should follow right to the riverside. There are no branches so navigation is easy. It leaves the basalt-capped area of Mount Wilson and descends a spur to some underlying sandstone rock outcrops, sidles west around the head of a gully, crosses a saddle, contours north-west and drops to a deeper saddle, turns left and finally descends sharply to the Wollangambe River, just 200 metres downstream of its confluence with the Bell and Du Faur creeks system. The overall difference in elevation between the top of the foot track and the river is 330 metres but in the upper reaches the track is shaded by fine stands of trees and there are masses of ground ferns. On the lower stretches, the trail has a fairly gradual gradient.

MAP REF: *Mount Wilson map provided with this publication.* Map 20.

WALK DISTANCE: 5.5 km.
GRADING: One day, easy.

21   JENOLAN CAVES

Walking underground can be just as rewarding as beach or mountain walking. Jenolan Caves must surely rate as the best in Australia and are quite a good location to spend a day walking. There are surface trails in the reserve to familiarize walkers with the area and the tracks pass several interesting arches and external limestone formations such as the Grand Arch and the Devils Coachhouse, the Peephole and Carlotta Arch. Some considerable time should be spent seeing the wonderful underground caverns in the company of a guide and the usual tourist groups.

Basically, the area consists of a broad band of limestone with three streams descending to it, precipitating and running through the caves and emerging as the Jenolan River on the lower side of the Grand Arch which is so large that even the main access road passes through it. The caves are said to be of outstanding quality and there are innumerable caves which can be inspected so the choice of which ones to enter is difficult.

Initially it is suggested that you start outside Caves House, a large State-run guesthouse and walk down the main road past the Guides Office, kiosk, Post Office and bus parking bay, then pass through the Grand Arch and the entry points to a number of the caves. As soon as you emerge from under the Grand Arch, start the ascent up an excellent path into and through the Devils Coachhouse. Like the Grand Arch it is huge inside and very interesting. At the top end of the Devils Coachhouse the path leads along the banks of the Jenolan River a short distance then crosses it and ascends via many steps and hairpin bends to the Peephole. It is a small hole which enables you to view the Devils Coachhouse from above. Continue on uphill to join a main track coming from a carpark (No. 2 carpark), pass on to a ridge top and arrive at the Carlotta Arch which gives a lovely view down onto the lower Jenolan River and the small reservoir downstream from the Grand Arch. Keep going downhill via hairpin bends then sidle back down to the roadway outside Caves House to finish the circuit which is 1.0 kilometre long. The ticket box for cave inspections is across the road and the choice is yours about which caves to visit. Some of the better-known formations are in the Lucas Cave which is also the longest cave. Baal, Orient and Skeleton Caves are relatively short especially the Skeleton Cave and the River Cave is said to be quite pretty. Obviously cost must be considered as tickets are far from cheap but you should visit at least two caves. Official advice is to avoid choosing two of River, Baal and Orient if you want to see variety and to avoid seeing both Imperial and Jubilee. Lucas, Skeleton and Chifley can be grouped with any others.

MAP REF: *Jenolan Caves map provided with this publication.* Map 22.

WALK DISTANCE: Surface only, 1.0 kilometre.

	Cave walking metres	Total tour metres
Lucas Cave	527	861
Jubilee Cave	302	1574
River Cave	402	1271
Skeleton Cave	133	1016
Imperial Cave	494	1069
Chifley Cave	465	692
Temple of Baal Cave	151	363
Orient Cave	175	470

(The first six caves listed have access from the Grand Arch and the latter two from near the rear of Caves House.)

GRADING: One day, easy.

22 KANANGRA PLATEAU

About 200 kilometres from Sydney via Mount Victoria and Jenolan Caves is the Kanangra Boyd National Park. The park covers a large area and includes the Kanangra Walls and Plateau, a number of very high waterfalls and the Grand Kanangra Gorge, all of which are outstanding scenic attractions. The views are among the finest in the Blue Mountains.

Kanangra Plateau is a remarkable sandstone-capped peninsula with sheer cliffs surrounding it. Alpine type shrubs grow on the plateau and virtually no trees exist. A tourist road and lookout services the Kanangra Tops section of the park and from the carpark lookout a foot track leads east. It is sign-posted 'Kanangra Plateau: one hour' but this walk suggestion takes you well on to the plateau and much further than an hour's walk. There is no water on the plateau, so carry some for lunch.

Walk east down a rough ramp track which swings

south into a saddle known as Blacks Pass within 300 metres. There are cliffs along both the east and west sides of the saddle and rock overhangs exist along under the cliffs, especially on the east side just south of the saddle. It is well worth a detour south along the cliff base for about 150 metres just to see the overhangs before you head up a rocky ramp onto the Kanangra Plateau straight east of the saddle. As soon as you attain the plateau trees are noticeably absent and when you follow the foot track north-east close to the northern cliff rim you get superb views out north over the Kanangra Deep to Thurat Spires and Walls. The plateau is actually in three sections joined by narrow necks and it is only about 500 metres across the westernmost section to the first neck known as the Kanangra Neck. This neck is about 300 metres long. Just east of Kanangra Neck the trail divides, the left fork keeps close to the northern cliff rim and should be followed. It crosses to the second narrow neck then on to Mount Brennan which is the easternmost section of the plateau. The track then leaves the cliff tops and enters a ravine known as Smiths Pass and loses 100 metres of elevation down on to Kilpatricks Causeway. It is suggested that you do not descend the ravine but rather have a pause, some lunch and a good look at the views.

Next, retrace your route back for a kilometre to the track junction just east of Kanangra Neck. At the intersection, turn south and walk 1.5 kilometres initially past the west side of a prominent trig point on Mount Maxwell, then to the northern side of a saddle where the track turns south-east and rises on to forested Mount Murrarang. Do not bother crossing the saddle but retrace your route again. The purpose of

this part of the walk is to see the wide views southwards towards distant Mount.Colong and other peaks
in that vicinity. You also get views of the cliffs around
the Kanangra Plateau. To finish the day, walk back to
transport via the outward route but omitting Mount
Brennan.

MAP REF: *Kanangra Walls map provided with this
publication.* Map 23.

WALK DISTANCE: 7.5 km.

GRADING: One day, easy.

23   KANANGRA WALLS—MURRARANG HEAD

Kanangra Boyd National Park, south of Jenolan Caves
in the Blue Mountains, is rather interesting geolo-
gically. Basically a large plateau exists. It is capped
by granite in the north-west but at Kanangra Tops
where the main scenic attractions are to be found, it
is capped by sandstone, shale and chert belonging
to the Illawarra Coal Measures. Older Devonian
quartzites of the Lambie Group are the park's most
common rock type but are overlain in the plateau
areas. At Kanangra Walls the capping gives way
and tremendous gorges and cliffs make magnificent
scenery. Waterfalls add to the beauty. This walk
suggestion takes the walker along the clifflines to see
the best areas then includes Murrarang Head and an
undercliff section at the head where a coal seam is
protruding and the strata of the rocks is quite
interesting. Alpine vegetation on the tops is also a
feature.

Start walking from the tourist carpark lookout and
follow the signposted foot track to Kanangra Plateau.
The trail descends eastwards then south for 300
metres into Blacks Pass, the first of two necks of land

forming isolated plateau sections which you should cross. Climb east up a ramp on to the plateau, then follow the well-defined track north-east for 500 metres close to a northern cliff rim. The view is quite remarkable at the rim, and the tops are treeless in most parts. Soon you should arrive at Kanangra Neck, the second neck you must cross. It is about 300 metres long and, as soon as you reach the eastern end, the trail forks. Take the more major right fork which leads slightly uphill south-east and passes within about 50 metres west of a clearly visible trig point on Mount Maxwell. Continue south along the trail which is an old cattle pad and soon you should start to descend slightly. In the area there are a few interesting snow gums and a lot of other alpine type plants but still no big trees. Views southwards towards Mount Colong are superb and the cliffs in the locality look good too. The trail descends into a minor saddle then rises up into wooded Mount Murrarang about 2.0 kilometres from Kanangra Neck. It then forks as you descend the south-west side of the small hill and you can take either fork. The left fork is shortest but is through trees, the right fork skirts around the base of some small cliffs and gives good views. Both tracks rejoin at the cliffline on the south side of Moung Murrarang, the left fork having a short, easy descent down the cliffs. Walk east 200 metres and you should be under a fine example of rock overhang with the lower layers being coal. From appearance, man has dug away a lot of the coal (most likely for camp fires), thus causing the overhang to be more pronounced. Most likely, many cattlemen have camped there, used the coal, and thus blackened the earth underfoot. The best place for lunch would be on the clifftops above the overhang so that you get views but a short scrub bash would be required from the tracks to gain the best vantage points. No water is available. Return back via the same route after lunch to the carpark.

MAP REF: *Kanangra Walls map provided with this publication.* Map 23.

WALK DISTANCE: 6.5 km.

GRADING: One day, easy.

24   BEROWRA—COWAN CREEK—MOUNT KURING-GAI

Geologists tell us that millions of years ago the Hawkesbury sandstones began a series of uplifting movements, the creeks and rivers cutting deeper courses as the land rose. Then 6000 years ago at the end of the last ice age, the sea level rose and flooded the valleys to form such present day beauty spots as Cowan Water. The soil is poor but the sheltered valleys have thick forests and generally a large variety of plants create a magnificent display of wildflowers, from July to October especially. Additionally, Cowan Water is ideal for boating and its proximity to Sydney has meant that the inlet has become a major anchorage for boats, thus creating a picturesque setting.

This walk suggestion starts at Berowra Railway Station and finishes at Mount Kuring-gai railway station and the circuit can be completed by using the train between the two points. There is a bridge over the rail line at the north end of Berowra station with the platform ramp leading up on to it. Head up and across to the east side of the bridge, walk south 30 metres on a gravelled road, and turn east along a signposted foot track which provides fairly flat walking initially then arrives at the top of a spur where good views of Waratah Bay exist. Six zig-zags must be descended next, down to, and across, Waratah Creek, then you need to walk along the south bank through fine stands of forest amid sandstone outcrops to Waratah Bay where there are the remains of an old jetty and ferry. At this point you are about 2.0 kilometres from Berowra station.

Waratah Bay is the first of five bays you visit during this walk and all are a little different and beautiful in their own way. There are cool, tree-shaded gullies at the head of the first four bays and between each bay there are headlands providing good views along Cowan Water. Follow this good foot track known as the Berowra Track generally south along the western shore for 6.0 kilometres until you arrive at the fifth bay—Appletree Bay. The bay is well developed for boating enthusiasts, has a kiosk, boat ramps and all facilities. It would be a good place for a late lunch. The many boats in the area will certainly provide interest during the break.

After lunch you should retrace about a kilometre north-east back to the signposted good Mount Kuring-gai track which leads up steeply at first, then quite gradually on a ridge to emerge at a gate at the east end of Hardwood Street, Mount Kuring-gai. Then, you need only walk to the west end of the street which is right beside the railway station. This last section up from Cowan Creek is 3.0 kilometres long and after about 2.0 kilometres another track comes in from the left on the ridge. There are many banksias in the area too.

MAP REF: **Mt Kuring-gai map provided with this publication.** Map 2.

WALK DISTANCE: 12 km.

GRADING: One day, medium.

25 BEROWRA—BOBBIN HEAD—NORTH TURRAMURRA

Cowan Water in Kuring-gai Chase has excellent walking possibilities and is so close to Sydney that the area is well suited to use of public transport and to walking between two completely different spots. This walk route can be started from Berowra station and finished at the bus stop at the entrance to Kuring-gai Chase National Park in North Turramurra. The bus could then be taken to Turramurra station. Other walk suggestions in the area appear in this book but this walk, unlike the others, is quite long and is planned for a cooler day when time would not be spent swimming. Cowan Water is part of the drowned valley system of the Hawkesbury River which geologists tell us was caused by initial subsidence of the sandstone country then flooding at the end of the last ice age due to the higher level of the seas. The erosion of the sandstone has left the slopes quite poor in soil quality but gullies are fairly well endowed so that lush forests grow. The tops however support a wide variety of wildflowers, from July to October especially. Additionally, the proximity to Sydney has meant development of extensive pleasure boating thus adding interest to the waterways.

Once at Berowra station, walk across the bridge to the east side of the rail line, go south just 30 metres on a gravelled road, then turn east along a signposted foot track which is flat walking at first then arrives at

133

the end of a spur to give good views of Waratah Bay below. You should then descend via six zig-zags to and across Waratah Creek and follow the south bank of the creek through lovely forest and past rocky outcrops to Waratah Bay some 2.0 kilometres from Berowra station.

Waratah Bay is the first of five bays to be visited before the suggested lunch spot at Appletree Bay. Each bay is slightly different and there are lovely tree-shaded gullies at the head of the first four and between each bay headlands provide excellent views both north and south along Cowan Water. It is a 6.0-kilometre-long walk from Waratah Bay to Appletree Bay and a good trail keeps close to the water's edge all the way. One kilometre before Appletree Bay, a track leads off uphill to Mount Kuring-gai railway station, but it should be ignored. Appletree Bay is well developed for use by boating enthusiasts and has all facilities for picnics and a kiosk.

A good bitumen road leads from Appletree Bay close to the water's edge round to Bobbin Head, another major boating anchorage with all facilities and a shop selling supplies. It is suggested that you take the road for the kilometre-long walk to Bobbin Head then cross a road bridge and go to the boat repair area and supplies shop on the Cowan Arm rather than the Cockle Creek Arm. Then follow a trail which commences behind the shop. The trail leads right along the water's edge for 4.0 kilometres in a south-easterly direction then south. Mangroves and fine forest stands will be passed. The track then divides and the right branch uphill to the west should be followed. The left branch is quite minor and leads to Warrimoo Avenue, St Ives. To complete the walk you must

climb for 2.0 kilometres up to the Bobbin Head Road
entry to Kuring-gai Chase and the bus stop there. This
involves climbing 1.5 kilometres on a trail to a war-
time memorial known as The Sphinx and following a
bitumen road for the final 500 metres.

MAP REF: **Mt Kuring-gai map provided with this
     publication.** Map 2.

WALK DISTANCE: 15 km.

GRADING: One day, medium.

26   WATERFALL—ULOOLA FALLS—AUDLEY

The Royal National Park just south of Sydney is
indeed a priceless possession of the city. Its heath-
covered sandstone plateau and magnificent coastline
provide wonderful opportunities for outdoor activities
generally and especially for walkers. The sandstone
plateau supports wildflowers to such an extent that
they are a major attraction from August to November.
There are numerous species of birds and animals and
the erosion of the plateau by both sea and streams
has meant that numerous fine surf beaches. rock
pools and quiet river reaches exist. Such places as
Garie Beach and Audley are indeed well known for
their surfing and boating. Kangaroo Creek and the
Hacking River are quite mangificent streams.

Access to the park is excellent also and this walk
suggestion takes the walker from Waterfall station to
Royal National Park station. The route includes Uloola
Falls and the Gurrumboola Heights.

Start walking from Waterfall station initially up on
to the road-bridge at the south end of the station then
turn east and immediately you should see a grassy
area to the north of a Fire Brigade building. A sign
exists advising that the Uloola Track starts at the point

and extends 10.5 kilometres to Audley. Walk east on the track which is really a jeep track and which leads straight to the local football ground. At the eastern goal posts the jeep track continues east and heads into dry sclerophyll forest. The track is fairly level and easy to follow and only 500 metres from the football ground you should arrive at the signposted Couranga Track. Veer left at this junction and head north-east. After, you should emerge at the south end of Uloola Swamp just where the remains of an old training track can be seen crossing your path. Keep close to the east edge of the swamp as you continue north-east. This area has wonderful displays of Hakea in flower in December-January. At the north end of the swamp diverge left to follow the slight gully downhill rather than fork right. A kilometre north of the Uloola Swamp, Uloola Brook tumbles through the Blue Pools, which are interesting rock pools surrounded by white heath and white hakea. A further 500 metres north, cascades start and increase in size until Uloola Falls is reached shortly afterwards. The main falls drop about 20 metres in three stages. There are open sandstone areas at the top of the falls ideal for lunch beside pools. It is a bush camping place and a track to Heathcote via Karloo Pool also leads off north-west right beside the top of the falls. But the suggestion is that after lunch you climb slightly east on to the Gurrumboola Heights where the foot track swings north and follows the ridge all the way to Audley. Just as you swing north a very indistinct track leads off east to Calala and aluminium arrows exist on a tree at the point. Ignore this side track though and also another minor track to Audley leading off east 3.0 kilometres north along the ridge.

Generally the track is good and has a hard sandy or sandstone surface. It leads through a lot of grass trees, banksias and waratah. White arrows painted on the rocks help indicate your route. At the north end of the ridge two tracks lead down to Audley; take the most pronounced one with the painted arrows. It leads down directly to the west end of a bridge across the Hacking River. You will then be at Audley itself where the National Park visitors' centre, kiosk, picnic facilities, boat hire, and a host of other amenities exist. Follow the bitumen road north, re-cross the Hacking River and walk up the bitumen road to the Royal National Park railway station.

MAP REF: *Audley map provided with this publication.*
   Map 5.
WALK DISTANCE: 12 km.
GRADING: One day, medium.

27   AUDLEY—ULOOLA FALLS—KARLOO POOL—AUDLEY

Audley in the Royal National Park must surely be one of the most popular venues for outdoor leisure near Sydney except, perhaps, for some of the beaches. It is a beautiful area and has all facilities including boat hire and for those who have a yen to wander about, there are excellent walks in several directions. This walk suggestion is perhaps more ambitious than that undertaken by the average person who goes to Audley, but for any bushwalker it is of an easy standard.

Start walking across the bridge to the west bank of the Hacking River where you will see a signpost 30 metres to the right. This is the start of the Uloola Track and the sign indicates that it is 4.4 kilometres to Uloola Falls which is one of your main objectives. The track climbs up on to a spur then follows the tops of the Gurrumboola Heights southwards. There are painted white arrows as a guide and the good sandy track leads through fairly open country with bottle-brush, grass trees and waratahs in profusion. Views are fairly good too. Tracks back to Audley branch off to both east and west down from the ridge but should be ignored as should the tracks to Peach Trees trig point and to Calala. Both these latter tracks lead off eastwards and are of a minor nature only. The Uloola Track finally swings west at a saddle and the Calala turnoff, and heads down west to Uloola Falls which are about 20 metres high and descend in three stages from an area of bare sandstone. The Uloola Track continues south-west to Waterfall but it is suggested that you walk 2.2 kilometres north-west to Karloo Pool on Kangaroo Creek. This short track gradually ascends the Uloola Heights, passes between two rock stacks known as The Turrets then levels out for a while. It then descends sharply to Karloo Pool which is a beautiful rock pool ideal for swimming and sunbaking. The area is a bush camping area too and it is sug-gested that you have lunch beside the pool.

After lunch you should simply follow Kangaroo Creek back to Audley. For most of the distance you need only walk across the sandstone beds beside lovely pools and where any difficulty arises there is a streamside foot track to follow. However you need to use your judgement a bit as to which side of the stream to follow at some points and when you reach the confluence of Kangaroo Creek and Engadine Creek make sure you cross to the east bank of Kan-garoo Creek as the stream becomes a continuous deep pool thereafter as it flows east. Two tracks exist from this point. One leads up and over the ridge to Audley and the other track follows the stream bank but it is a bit overgrown and requires care. Whichever route you take will be time-consuming but you only have to cover about a kilometre. The streamside route is the more picturesque and both routes lead to the bridge over the Hacking River into the main picnic area at Audley. If you take the streamside route you must climb a little at the end to avoid some bluffs.

MAP REF: *Audley map provided with this publication.* Map 5.

WALK DISTANCE: 13.5 km.

GRADING: One day, medium.

28 FAULCONBRIDGE—SASSAFRAS CREEK— MAGDALA CREEK—SPRINGWOOD

The valleys south of Springwood in the Blue Mountains are ideally suited to leisurely walking on a hot summer day. The cool glades, waterfalls and rock pools can be appreciated to the fullest. To walk right through the main gullies is perhaps rushing a trip a little but nevertheless it is most enjoyable. The area features sassafras, ferns and rainforest set amid sandstone gorge formations. Faulconbridge is higher than Springwood so it is suggested that this trip start at the high point and descend the gully system to Perch Ponds then ascend back up some of the lost height via Magdala Creek.

From Faulconbridge Station, follow Sir Henry Parkes Drive or the Great Western Highway north-east 300 metres to a level crossing. Walk south-east 40 metres down the bitumen Wigram Road then veer off south down a foot track where there is a sign indicating the way to Springwood via Sassafras Gully.

The trail descends steeply through rocky outcrops into the headwaters of Sassafras Creek. It crosses the small stream a couple of times and about 2.5 kilometres from the station you should arrive at Clarinda Falls which have a five metre drop. From this point onwards the route becomes increasingly beautiful as rainforest is entered. Sassafras and ferns are particularly noticeable. The track remains on the western slopes of Sassafras Creek for about 2.0 kilometres below the falls but after a kilometre the confluence of Numantia Creek should be met and at the junction there is a small grassy area. There are high cliffs on the north-east side of the stream and small rock pools exist in the stream bed. Some 250 metres after crossing to the north bank a trail junction will be met. The left fork leads to Springwood but you should head south for a further 750 metres to another track junction and again the left fork should be avoided. Half way between the two junctions the track crosses to the west bank and it remains on that side for a further kilometre to the confluence of Sassafras Creek with Glenbrook Creek where there are deep pools good for swimming. The area is ideally suited to bush camping and at this point the trail crosses back to the north bank. It is the suggested lunch spot also. Glenbrook Creek, the major stream of the district is next followed for 2.0 kilometres to its confluence with Magdala Creek at Perch Ponds. There are many lovely pools along Glenbrook Creek and the rainforest is most interesting. At Perch Ponds a trail forks off to Martins Lookout but you should turn north-east up the west bank of Magdala Creek. There is a signpost at the junction indicating a distance of two miles (3.3

kilometres) to Springwood which is quite wrong as it is some 5.0 kilometres distance to the station.

Follow the west bank of Magdala Creek north-east then north 500 metres up to the 10-metre-high Martins Falls then continue on 400 metres to Magdala Falls (also 10 metres high). Both falls are particularly attractive and the gorge between the two falls is very beautiful, ferny, shady and has rock overhangs. Continue north 300 metres, cross to the east bank, walk another 300 metres and fork left (west) where a minor track leads up a side gully to the north as Magdala Creek turns west. For the next 2.5 kilometres the trail leads past rocky outcrops, and through wildflower areas, especially trigger plants, as it climbs up into the higher reaches. The trail crosses the creek some eight times then meets a signposted fork off right uphill to Lawsons Lookout but you should go north 200 metres, cross on a small bridge to the west bank yet again, the climb out of the headwaters of Magdala Creek 100 metres to the Picnic Point picnic ground which is virtually disused. Follow the road west 150 metres, turn right (north) up Homedale Street, and right (north-east) 200 metres later into Macquarie Road which skirts the south side of the Western Railway. It is then only 300 metres to Springwood railway station and the walk's end.

MAP REF: *Springwood map provided with this publication.* Map 9.

WALK DISTANCE: 13.5 km.

GRADING: One day, medium.

29 KATOOMBA CLIFFTOPS—LINDA FALLS— FEDERAL PASS—SCENIC RAILWAY.

This walk recommendation basically follows the route

of the Katoomba Falls, Echo Point and Three Sisters suggestion in this Book, but an extension is included to raise the grading and to create added interest by having some of the walk route in quieter, less frequented places.

Follow instructions as for Walk Number 12 but once at The Three Sisters do not descend the Giants Staircase but rather follow the contouring track around the cliff rim as it swings north. Within 200 metres Lady Carrington Lookout exists and as the track continues north for 1.5 kilometres other minor lookouts will be encountered. After 1.5 kilometres a track forks left up to Cliff Drive but you should continue to contour round the head of a small gully to Jamieson Lookout. From this point a steep descent down the gully's east bank starts. It is ferny, has rock overhangs and generally is very pleasant. Shortly, Lila Falls should be seen as the trail crosses to the west bank and descends through Fairy Dell. A turnoff at Lila Falls east to Leura Falls should be ignored. Further down the gully, Linda Falls should be seen and the track crosses to the east bank below the falls. Fork right (south) at this point and head down further, cross to the west bank again and soon you will be amid magnificent rain forest at an old picnic shelter and the junction of the Federal Pass and the Dardanelles Pass. Fork right up Dardanelles Pass and in a kilometre you should arrive at the base of the Giants Stairway. Keep on contouring round below The Three Sisters and head north ignoring the Federal Pass Track joining in on the left. The trail swings north-west, crosses Kedumba Creek and climbs slightly up to the lower station of the Scenic Railway. A track joins in from the right, 200 metres before the station. It is the main walking track to the clifftops and would only be needed should you miss the last car at 4.55 p.m. Carry water for lunch as the water, especially below the cliffline, is polluted. Lunch spot could be just about anywhere along the way.

MAP REF: *Katoomba Falls area and Katoomba maps provided with this publication.* Maps 10 and 11.

WALK DISTANCE: 10.5 km.

GRADING: One day, medium.

30   GOLDEN STAIRS—RUINED CASTLE—MOUNT SOLITARY

One of the main features seen from Echo Point and other vantage points at Katoomba in the Blue Mountains is Mount Solitary. It stands out alone and imposing above the Jamieson Valley so that its name seems very fitting, and walkers are attracted simply because of its isolation.

Narrow Neck Road leaves Cliff Drive west of the Katoomba Scenic Railway and other attractions. It is a rough road and only about 2.0 kilometres from its start it becomes a jeep track. Nevertheless it is well worth heading out along it to the top of the Golden Stairs and to where this walk suggestion starts. The track down the Golden Stairs starts about 100 metres before (north) of where you reach the sign warning that the road is suited to four-wheel-drive vehicles only. There is a post which apparently, in the past, supported a sign on the east side of the road at the stairs' entry.

The walk basically involves a descent from Narrow Neck to the main contouring access track, a long fairly level walk and then an ascent up Mount Solitary itself. The Golden Stairs descent is steep but relatively short and formed steps make the going easier. There are two steel ladders to negotiate and at the bottom of the descent at a 'T' junction you should turn right along the signposted contouring trail to the Ruined Castle. This trail is through rainforest and is very beautiful. It is also virtually flat walking as the route was once a busy coal miners' access route between the pits and the now tourist Katoomba Scenic Railway. Once, the railway hauled coal. After about 2.5 kilometres, a signpost indicates the track to the Ruined Castle and at this point it is well worth diverging right and climbing on to a saddle then up a ridge to the Ruined Castle. Make sure you scramble to the top of the rock stacks to get the best views. Next, continue south-east down off the Ruined Castle via a minor pad on the spur. It leads back to the main contouring trail at a low saddle called Cedar Gap.

From this point on, climbing starts and initially you need to climb up and over three knobs, keeping to the crest of the ridge and avoiding a right fork near the base of the first knob. This side pad leads to a fern gully in 300 metres where water is sometimes available.

The steep ascent of Mount Solitary involves two 'steps' each some 150 metres high and up a knife-edge formation. The track is not dangerous or even really awkward but requires use of hands as well as the feet. It is suggested that you stop at the extreme western end of the mountain's plateau and have lunch on the rocks overlooking the views to the north, west and south. There is little point in going further along the plateau unless you walk a long way. The tops are thickly covered with dry vegetation with views only if you scrub-bash. From the lunch spot (no water available) you will be astounded how insignificant the Ruined Castle appears, considering the effort in climbing it earlier. It is suggested that you retrace your outward route after lunch. You could however omit the Ruined Castle deviation by remaining on the main trail along the Castle's eastern slopes.

MAP REF: **Katoomba and Solitary maps provided with this publication.** Maps 10 and 17.

WALK DISTANCE: 14 km.

GRADING: One day, medium.

31 NARROW NECK PENINSULA—CLEAR HILL

South of Katoomba in the Blue Mountains an extraordinary peninsula-shaped, sandstone plateau exists. It is called Narrow Neck Peninsula. It is 13.5 kilometres long and only 100 metres wide in two places. It towers above the surrounding country providing excellent views for much of its length. A gravelled road leads on to the north end of the peninsula from Cliff Drive, Katoomba and conventional vehicles can drive 2.0 kilometres along it. A sign then warns motorists that the route ahead is suited only to four-wheel-drive vehicles. It is, however, good for walkers too!

Whilst the entire length of the walk suggestion is along the jeep track section and extends for 11.5 kilometres, there are extremely good views to east and west along most of the route. Thus the 'road-bash' is not so noticeable. You do need to carry water as the tops are dry with water difficult to locate.

From the walk start at the signpost warning motorists not to proceed, climb up a 400-metre-long, steep, rough hill with guard railing round the side due to the precipitous slope. Once on top the walking becomes much easier and shrubs, flowers, birds and views should draw your attention. The walk simply continues south all the way to the road end at Clear Hill, a knob on the end of the peninsula which is devoid of trees and which provides superb views, especially down over Lake Burragorang. About one third of the way along the peninsula you should cross the Narrow Neck itself and two thirds of the way south you must pass the Sydney Water Board fire observation tower on Bushwalkers Hill. The best place for lunch would be at Clear Hill before you retrace your route.

MAP REF: *Solitary map provided with this publication.*
 Map 17.
WALK DISTANCE: 23 km.
GRADING: One day, medium.

32 BLACKHEATH—POPES GLEN—GOVETTS LEAP—EVANS LOOKOUT—GRAND CANYON

This walk suggestion includes three major tourist attractions of the Blackheath district, namely Govetts Lookout, Evans Lookout and the Grand Canyon. Much of the walk route is along the cliff rim of the deep, fascinating Grose Valley. The valley is about 600 metres deep so that magnificent views should be the order of the day.

From Blackheath station head east across the Great Western Highway into Gardiners Crescent. It leads down a small valley, becomes a gravelled road and then swings south about 600 metres from the station. Remain on the north side of the gully and walk east a further 300 metres along Wills Street to a signposted foot track turnoff on the right hand side of the road.

It is the start of Govetts Walk along Popes Glen. Follow the north bank for 600 metres then cross a bridge to the south bank. The valley is fairly open and alpine vegetation is present, including snow gums. Wildflowers are in abundance. Recross to the north bank after 700 metres and in 300 metres a rock overhang should be met after the stream has turned east. In a further 100 metres you should cross back to the south bank and see a signposted track into Boyds Beach, 30 metres north and beside the stream. It is a pleasant, sandy little beach set amid tea-tree and honeyflower, which are common to the area. A further 300 metres of walking should bring you to the Pulpit Rock Track turnoff which leads east across the stream at a point where Popes Glen meets the very high cliffs of the Grose Valley and tumbles headlong over Horseshoe Falls. Two minor lookouts exist to your left just past the junction and both give wonderful views of the valley. Climb up the trail southwards and fork left in 200 metres. This leads you directly to Govetts Leap Picnic Ground and lookout where there are all facilities. The views from the lookout are among the best in New South Wales.

Next, follow the cliff rim trail southwards from the lookout. Initially it ascends a little then drops to the head of Govetts Leap Falls 500 metres south. The falls are about the best in the Blue Mountains. Turn left at the intersection at the head of the falls and walk 100 metres to another excellent lookout then climb up along the cliff rim south-east. It is 2.3 kilometres along the clifftops from Govetts Leap Falls to Evans Lookout which is the suggested lunch spot. On the way you should pass Hayward Gully Falls and have virtually continuous views as well as seeing a wonderful variety of wildflowers, including a lot of honeyflower, banksia, grevillea and heath. At Evans Lookout there are superb views yet again and all the facilities of a well-established picnic area.

Beside the picnic shelter furthest east a trail leads south, down to the Grand Canyon. Initially it descends through a cliffline into a gully and there are several tracks possible due to short-cutting. You should keep to the right in each case but continue downhill all the time. This should take you past the rough horse-trail to the Grose Valley which leads off east. The gully becomes very ferny and in some parts the only vegetation is ground and tree ferns. At the bottom of the gully you join into the Grand Canyon and a signpost points into the canyon and to Neates Glen to the right. There are good views up at the cliffs from this junction.

Walk up through the Grand Canyon next. It is indeed fascinating and in places spectacular. Rock overhangs, ferns, cascades and a tunnel all add interest. At two points the track leaves the canyon floor and climbs up the southern sandstone walls to get above waterfalls. So, be careful not to miss the turnoffs. Only the upper one is signposted 'Blackheath' and it is just after you have passed through a 10-metre-long tunnel. If you pass the turnoffs you will have to retrace your route as the canyon floor becomes too difficult to follow. At the upper end of the canyon and at a sharp bend the trail crosses the stream and ascends steeply up ferny Neates Glen to meet the Blackheath-Evans Lookout Road. The last section of the climb is through dry bushland as you get above the clifflines. To finish the walk, turn north-west and walk into Blackheath town along

148

Evans Lookout Road then north via the Great Western Highway. Regrettably, there is about 5.0 kilometres of roadside walking, which cannot be avoided, to complete the circuit.

MAP REF: **Blackheath map provided with this publication.** Map 14.

WALK DISTANCE: 16 km.

GRADING: One day, medium.

33 GOVETTS LEAP—EVANS LOOKOUT—GRAND CANYON-MOUNT GRIFFITHS TAYLOR

Govetts Leap, Evans Lookout and the Grand Canyon are undoubtedly the three major attractions of Blackheath district in the Blue Mountains. All three features are the result of tremendous erosion of sandstone and the valleys north-east of the two lookouts are some 600 metres deep. The Grand Canyon is really a hanging valley which is rapidly being eroded by Greaves Creek and it ends up plunging into the main valley at Beauchamp Falls.

To see these superb sights, travel to Govetts Leap just east of Blackheath where there are all facilities for picnics. The lookout is right at the carpark for those who feel too lazy to get out of their cars, but the person who takes the trouble to walk about will really appreciate the area so much more, and of course anyone who follows the cliffline and walks some distance will experience sights which will be remembered for life.

Start off walking south along the clifftops and within 500 metres you will not only have seen the valley views but will have arrived at the head of mighty Govetts Leap Falls and also have seen some wonderful displays of wildflowers. Ignore signposted

Braeside Walk which heads south along Govetts Creek and, instead, walk east 100 metres to a superb lookout, then climb south-east along the cliff rim. The trail continues close to the clifftop for 2.3 kilometres and passes right by Hayward Gully Falls then arrives at Evans Lookout which has a well-developed picnic area. There are shelters and tank water available so lunch is suggested whilst admiring the view.

Next, head down the Grand Canyon access track south from beside the shelter nearest to the eastern-most lookout. There are a couple of short-cut tracks and a bridle track veers off to the left so tracks are confusing. You should keep heading downhill and to the right at any forks. The track descends through a cliffline then down a gully and becomes very ferny. About a kilometre south of Evans Lookout you should come to an intersection where the side gully meets Greaves Creek. Turn right upstream into the Grand Canyon at this point. A signpost indicates the route. Look up at the towering cliffs about you. Despite their beauty there is better to come! As you walk up the canyon floor the cliffs get higher and higher and the canyon gets really narrow. In parts the daylight is all but excluded due to the depth of the canyon and the thriving ferns. The track leaves the canyon floor on two occasions to avoid waterfalls and so on, and in both cases you must climb steps up the southern sandstone walls. In the first instance there is no signpost but the track leads up a small gully. In the second case you should pass through a 10-metre-long tunnel, emerge at a streamside clearing, then climb up the signposted route towards Black-heath.

You should be really impressed by the Grand

Canyon. It is of course not as grand as its counterpart in America but its sandstone overhangs, waterfalls and underground section of river all make it a most remarkable place. At the upper end of the canyon and at a sharp bend the trail crosses the stream and ascends steeply up ferny Neates Glen to meet the Evans Lookout Road. Above the clifftops, dry bushland commences. Turn north-west and in 250 metres there is a tap with drinking water on the right hand side of the road. Continue another 250 metres then turn sharply back north-east on a gravelled road and in 150 metres fork right on a jeep track. This jeep track should be followed to its end as it crosses the plateau of Mount Griffiths Taylor. A couple of very minor jeep tracks lead off to the right to the actual summit and should be ignored. At the end of the jeep tracks you should head north, remaining on the broad spur and descend gradually through scrub until you meet the cliffline track which connects Evans Lookout an Govetts Leap. It is then only a matter of following the cliff rim trail back to Govetts Leap Falls and Lookout, retracing your outward route.

MAP REF: *Blackheath map provided with this publication.* Map 14.

WALK DISTANCE: 10.5 km.

GRADING: One day, medium.

34 GOVETTS LEAP—JUNCTION FLAT—EVANS LOOKOUT

Walking in the Grose Valley in the Blue Mountains is extremely pleasant due to the views up to the towering cliffs all around you and due to the fine forests and streams which most trails follow. However, access to the valley means an ascent of about 600 metres on the return trip which, of course, is not easy. For those wanting to see the valley floor and to climb out by the easiest route, the following walk is suggested.

Firstly, go to Govetts Leap east of Blackheath where a picnic area, lookout and all facilities exist. From the lookout you can get some idea of the walk route ahead of you. You need to take the foot track from the lookout's northern side nearest the cliff rim (not the one near the toilet blocks). Next, veer right at an intersection within 100 metres to arrive at the top of some steps.

Secondly, 1881 steps (reportedly) must be descended down the almost sheer cliff face. Avoid a left fork back to the base of Horseshoe Falls and pass right beneath the base of incredible Govetts Leap Falls which plunge about 200 metres. Follow the gully of Govetts Leap Brook eastwards downstream through ferns and forest. About one to one and a half hours after leaving Govetts Leap Lookout you should arrive at Junction Flat despite the fact that the two places are only 3.0 kilometres apart. Junction Flat is a camping area at the junction of Govetts Leap Brook and Govetts Creek. Pleasant swimming holes contribute to the attractions of the spot and there are good views up to the cliffs. Lunch is suggested.

Thirdly, walk south along the west bank of Govetts Creek. After 900 metres the track climbs up a small rise beside the stream and excellent cliff views are obtainable. Another 300 metres brings you to a junction where there is a sign which reads 'Use rough horse track when river is in flood'. The right fork here is the bridle track which leads directly up to Evans Lookout. The left fork follows Govetts Creek for a kilometre then crosses and rises gradually up alongside a tributary, Greaves Creek. It is the more scenic and easier route to take. About 1.5 kilometres from the valley floor you should enter the lip of the hanging valley of the Grand Canyon alongside Beauchamp Falls. A small track leads off to your left to the falls and a break at this point could be well worth while, both for a rest and to view the falls.

Fourthly, walk about 300 metres into the Grand Canyon and fork right (north) at a junction. At this point you get some idea of the great beauty of the canyon, as views of the cliffs, overhangs and ferns are all around you. Climb up to Evans Lookout about 1.2 kilometres away via a ferny gully and nearly at the top of the climb the bridle track from the valley joins in from the right. At Evans Lookout you are again on the clifftops and you see the superb views back down over the area through which you have walked. There are full picnic facilities including drinking water at Evans Lookout.

Lastly, follow the Griffiths Taylor Wall foot track back north-west along the cliff tops to Govetts Leap. It is a straightforward walk, fairly level, 2.8 kilometres long and only one trail leads off it. That trail, the Braeside Walk, heads off left at the top of Govetts Leap Falls, 500 metres south of Govetts Leap Lookout and the walk end.

MAP REF: *Blackheath and Govetts Gorge maps provided with this publication.* Maps 14 and 15.

WALK DISTANCE: 11.5 km.

GRADING: One day, medium.

35   BANKS WALL—EXPLORERS RANGE—MOUNT CALEY

Most of the walking areas in the Blue Mountains centre on the Great Western Highway but this walk suggestion requires access through Kurrajong Heights and Bells Line of Road. The walk offers two really magnificent panoramas and also includes the wild-flower habitats along the Explorers Range. The whole walk length is along a four-wheel-drive service trail through the Blue Mountains National Park except for several hundred metres climbing on to Mount Caley.

Initially, you need to drive along a gravelled road which leads off Bells Line of Road southwards. The gravelled road, some 4.0 kilometres on the Sydney side of the Mount Wilson turnoff provides access to a picnic ground and water supply 1.1 kilometres from the main road and then continues 2.6 kilometres around the northern slopes of Mount Banks to an intersection and two barriers. This is the walk starting point. It is 6.0 kilometres to the end of the jeep track from the left fork barrier and it is suggested that you walk the full distance then scrub bash through thick scrub across a saddle and up on to the tops of rocky bluffs on the south-west slopes of Mount Caley, some 750 metres from the road end. By walking this full distance you will see glorious views at Banks Wall at the south end of Mount Banks and from the rocks on Mount Caley. There is a water tank at Banks Wall Lookout but no other water available. The best place for lunch would be on the rocks at Mount Caley.

As you walk each way along the jeep track the wildflowers should become obvious to you. It is relatively dry vegetation with a complete lack of trees near Banks Wall Lookout. Banksia, hakea, honey-flower and acacia are the main shrubs and there are myriad ground flowers.

MAP REF: **Explorers Range map provided with this publication.** Map 18.

WALK DISTANCE: 13.5 km.

GRADING: One day, medium.

36 MOUNT TOMAH SOUTH—CARMARTHEN CANYON

Some very deep canyons exist near Mount Tomah in the Blue Mountains and the area is a popular one for people interested in exploring canyons. However, only experienced walkers should attempt this region and even they should realize their limitations. Obviously, in such wild terrain, ropes are required to get access to some parts but these notes only advise the route into the canyons and any further investigation is left up to the bushwalkers concerned. It is stressed that the route is not an easy one.

Access to the walk starting point is along Bells Line of Road to a roadside fireplace at the junction of the main road with the old Bells Line of Road some 300 metres south of Mount Tomah itself. Mount Tomah is about midway between Kurrajong Heights and Bell and the old road leads off to the south. (There is also an interesting sign near the fireplace which relates the geology of the district.) The walk starting point is some 1.4 kilometres south of the highway and, to reach it, you should head 800 metres along old Bells Line of Road then 600 metres south on Charleys Road. At the south end of Charleys Road there is a grassy paddock and a stile over a fence. A sign warning off trespassers can be ignored as it applies to the land at the side of the gazetted track which leads straight south from the stile down the spur past a trig point. Follow the track which, in 200 metres, becomes a jeep track, then, some 700 metres south of the stile, ends at a treeline. There are lovely views and tree ferns along the way.

Diverge slightly right and enter a forest on a foot pad. It swings west almost immediately down a spur through lyrebird haunts, then into drier forest and to Camels Saddle, 800 metres from the jeep track end. Cross the saddle on a rocky causeway then climb up west-south-west towards Camels Hump. About 200 metres from the saddle a rock cairn exists on the right hand side of the pad where it leads between two gum trees. The cairn marks the start of a route only north-west down a spur to Claustral Brook which is one way into the canyon area. However, a better route should be followed. Sidle round the eastern side of Camels Hump on the track then descend south-west across a gully on to a spur which leads off Camels Hump on its south side. The track should then be followed south on the spur a short distance then south-east on a subsidiary spur until it enters Rainbow Ravine via a steep descent through a ferny chasm some 800 metres from Camels Saddle. Once in Rainbow Ravine you are officially in the canyon country and it is only 400 metres to Carmarthen Brook with all its attractions. Rainbow Ravine itself is quite fascinating and where it enters Carmarthen Brook there is a six metre drop which requires a bit of agility. You could walk either direction along Carmarthen Brook, downstream being the easiest. Upstream there is a glow worm cave, falls and numerous other attractions but the terrain is very difficult in places.

How much you can see before you retrace your route back up to Mount Tomah South depends upon time.

MAP REF: **Carmarthen Canyon map provided with this publication.** Map 19.

WALK DISTANCE: 5 km, plus canyon walking.

GRADING: One day medium (or hard if you proceed well into the canyons).

37   WOLGAN VALLEY

If you fancy walking amid spectacular scenery and appreciate the solitude of the bush then the Wolgan Valley should interest you. The valley has a fairly large area of cleared land at Newnes, 47.0 kilometres north of Lithgow, and so is ideal for camping. Newnes is beside the Wolgan River and was once a town, and even had a railway station, but now all that is left are some ruins and the 90-year-old weatherboard hotel. The journey from Lithgow is largely on poor roads, used by heavy coal trucks for much of the distance, so extreme care is required in driving. During the trip you must pass over Wolgan Gap then descend sharply into the Wolgan Valley, which has cliffs about 300 metres in height. In several parts the valley is less than a kilometre wide and so the overall impression is one of great beauty. Newnes itself is dominated by impressive cliffs in all directions. There are several walk possibilities based on Newnes and perhaps the easiest one simply follows downstream along the Wolgan River. The features of the walk are obviously the river with its swimming possibilities and the towering cliffs on either side of the gorge. There are fine stands of forest along the way also. The valley is fairly broad upstream from Newnes but downstream it is quite narrow. Also the river flows north to Newnes then changes to east for 7.0 kilometres before flowing generally south-east. It is recommended that you walk to a clearing on the south bank 7.0 kilometres from Newnes where the river starts heading south-east. The clearing provides an excellent lunch spot as well as views of the magnificent cliffs in that area.

From Newnes Hotel you should walk north 300 metres, turn east on a side road across a ford where you will get wet feet, swing north again at an old railway station site, then follow the contouring road which proceeds along the route of the old railway. At a cutting shortly afterwards the road divides and rejoins. The left fork merely avoids the cutting which becomes boggy in wet weather. Soon you should be heading east along the south bank of the river, then, at a point 1.2 kilometres from the ford, there is a gateway and 50 metres east the road forks. Take the right fork uphill. It passes some old kilns which are up the slopes to your right, then bends back a bit before continuing eastwards many kilometres downstream. Follow it for only about 6.0 kilometres however, to the clearing where the river turns south-east. Then after a break and lunch, retrace the same route.

MAP REF: **Wolgan Valley map provided with this publication.** Map 21.

WALK DISTANCE: 15 km.

GRADING: One day, medium.

38   WOLGAN VALLEY—GLEN DAVIS VIEW

Newnes is a clearing on the valley floor of the Wolgan River 47.0 kilometres north of Lithgow. It was once the site of a town based on shale oil production and was serviced by rail, but now all that remains is an 90-year-old weatherboard hotel and some ruins. The clearings make the area ideal for camping and, especially, as a base from which several walks can be undertaken. The town site is surrounded by sandstone cliffs 300 metres high and the river swings eastwards and enters a relatively narrow gorge at this spot. One additional advantage that the area has for walkers is that the northern and western clifflines are the edge of a fairly narrow plateau, so that it is most enjoyable to climb out of the Wolgan Valley to the cliff rim on the other side of the plateau and see the spectacular views. The ascent and descent from the valley, however, is through dense forest and rugged gorges and, as such, it is challenging and navigation must be good. It is essential to note closely your outward route because the return journey involves trickly descents off bluffs which have access spots difficult to see from above, but easy from below. This is especially the case in the floor of side gorges which tend to be more like little canyons.

A route which provides marvellous views of Glen Davis in the valley, next north to the Wolgan Valley, should be relatively easy to follow as it has small rock cairns along much of the route. Often it is hard to find the next cairn, but if you are patient and thorough there is little chance of taking difficult routes and getting into strife. The forest and ferns in the side gully are particularly good, too.

From Newnes Hotel walk north 600 metres along the earth road, cross a small stream which flows down from the west then swing east, around through clearings ideal for camping. The road then proceeds along the north bank of the Wolgan River below a cliffline. A couple of minor tracks lead off the road and should be ignored. Some 1.4 kilometres from the stream crossing, there is a gateway and road junction. Take the left fork north-east. It soon swings north and, 900 metres from the junction, terminates on the left bank of a southwards-flowing streamlet. From this point onwards you must be very careful with navigation.

Right at the road end a very small gully enters from the west and a very obscured foot pad leads into bush from the road on the north side of that gully. Then, in only eight metres, it swings north to follow the west bank of the major gully for 150 metres. Small rock cairns exist from near where you first enter the forest but only after 150 metres of forest walking and crossing to the east bank do the cairns become easy to follow—for a while. Follow the east bank for 400 metres, then the west bank for another 400 metres. There are magnificent ferns in the area, the track is relatively easy to follow and the gradient is quite gentle. In places there are distinct traces of an old road or bridle track. Next the trail tends to follow the stream bed and to cross it many times as the gully narrows into a gorge and then almost into a canyon. Again, care needs to be taken to find the rock cairns. Eventually you should come to a small waterfall which in summer is often dry. At this point, you should climb east up to the base of some cliffs. Follow the cliff base until a fairly wide and open, bracken-filled valley is reached as a gully descends from the west into the southwards-flowing streamlet which you are following upstream. Stay as close as possible to the east side massive clifflines and overhangs but you will find that you have to descend into the awkward bracken in places and, if there are any rock cairns, then the luxuriant bracken conceals them. At the first opportunity where the clifflines become passable, climb out of the bracken-filled gully into dry forest and scrub-covered slopes. Several cairns exist on the slopes but are difficult to locate unless you left the bracken exactly where the cairns start. The correct spot is at an overhang 1.5 metres high, which requires hoisting oneself up. Once on the slopes head north-east up sandstone terraces to the summit of the plateau which is covered in dry scrub, is fairly narrow and has no view. Make sure you remember your route, especially up the terraces. Walk north several hundred metres along the plateau to the rocky outcrops and cliff tops from where there are superb views of Glen Davis and the mountains and escarpments to the north. Lunch is suggested despite the lack of water.

The return journey retraces the outward walk, but at three places you must navigate very carefully. Firstly the sandstone terraces must be descended in the right place; secondly and thirdly, at the two places where you have to follow the cliff bases along the east side of the gully to avoid falls, canyons etc., make sure you do not keep following the cliff bases too long or you will find yourself up on bluffs, with entry to the gully impossible unless you return upstream.

MAP REF: **Wolgan Valley map provided with this publication.** Map 21.
WALK DISTANCE: 10 km.
GRADING: One day, medium.

39 KANANGRA WALLS—CRAFTS WALL

Kanangra Boyd National Park south of Jenolan Caves has, as its main attraction, an exceptionally deep gorge surrounded by massive clifflines. A tourist road leads south to the focus point at Kanangra Tops and the road terminates at a carpark and lookout right beside the Kanangra Deep, within 500 metres of one of several quite high waterfalls and close to some of the best cliffs which are known as Kanangra Walls. Kanangra Tops are quite flat and open and, consequently, there are panoramic views—especially from their edges—and an unusual feature is that the tops terminate in a peninsula jutting out eastwards from the main plateau. The peninsula itself is almost divided into three sections by some narrow necks. Additionally an 'island' known as Crafts Wall is still further east but is joined to the peninsula by Kilpatricks Causeway which is somewhat lower than the other necks linking the three peninsula sections. A really magnificent walk is therefore possible. It crosses all necks out to Crafts Wall from where you get views from the isolated peak—out over all the surrounding district and back towards the Kanangra Tops themselves. Make sure you carry some water for lunch which would be best had at Crafts Wall.

Initially, walk down the signposted foot track from the carpark eastwards towards Kanangra Plateau. The rough trail swings south downhill for 300 metres Into Blacks Pass, the first neck to be crossed. A 150 metre diversion should be made to inspect fine rock overhangs on the western side of the gully just south of the saddle. Next, continue up a ramp on to the westernmost sector of the peninsula. The ramp, like much of the track, has been used by cattlemen in the past and constant treading by cattle has caused bad erosion but has left the track clearly defined. The trail keeps close to the northern rim of the plateau and, consequently, good views exist all the way as you head east-north-east. After 500 metres you should arrive at the second neck known as Kanangra Neck. It is about 300 metres long. A trail fork is immediately east of this second neck and the right fork is the more major, but you should keep walking in the same east-north-east direction along the minor route. It keeps close to the cliff rim for another kilometre crossing a lesser defined neck in the process and bringing you to the top of a ravine on the north-east corner of Mount Brennan. Small rock cairns are a guide. If you look over the cliff rim in this area you can clearly see the route of the foot track ahead, down on Kilpatricks Causeway some 100 metres lower. To reach it you should initially get on to the north side of the top of the small ravine then in about 25 metres start the descent through the ravine. Immediately you are though it, diverge left round the base of the clifflines rather than take the alternative 'rock river' or small scree straight down. There are two pads descending to Kilpatricks Causeway but the one which leads off from the cliff base is easier. The other leads off the 'rock river' well down the slopes. Once well on to the Causeway the track is less clearly defined, especially after about a kilometre where the ridge becomes rocky. The route of the track is right along the very crest of the rocky section of the causeway; then you must cross a saddle, after entering dry forest and acacia, and climb to the base of the cliffs at Crafts Wall. Wallabies may be seen in the area if you are quiet. The trail at this point divides and one branch skirts each side of Crafts Wall then they rejoin at the north-east end to continue along the range. It is suggested that you take the more minor right branch and follow the cliff base very closely southwards past some rock overhangs, then swing north-east to more overhangs. Along this side of Crafts Wall the forest is dense and little sunlight filters through, so it is a cool refreshing place on a hot day. Lunch under one of the overhangs should be most pleasant on a hot day but if it is cooler you should ascend one of the two ramps up on to the summit of Crafts Wall so that you can sit on the clifftops in the sun, admiring the view. Make sure you go to the northern rim of the tops. Later, you should wander about the tops and see Pages Pinnacle nearby—among other features. You must descend to the south-east side again as access is too difficult from other directions. If you decide to have lunch under an overhang make sure you later visit the summit; the ramps are quite obvious. Afterwards, follow the cliff base north-east then double back south-west to complete a circuit of Crafts Wall. It is then a case of retracing your route down to Kilpatricks Causeway and back up on to Kanangra Plateau, then to the carpark lookout.

MAP REF: *Kanangra Walls map provided with this publication.* Map 23.

WALK DISTANCE: 10 km.

GRADING: One day, medium.

40 BUNDEENA—MARLEY—WATTAMOLLA—GARIE—ERA—OTFORD

One of the main features of the Royal National Park just south of Sydney is the long and magnificent coastline. There are a number of fine, white sand beaches and quite spectacular clifflines along much of the distance. Additionally, several waterfalls spill over the cliffs and plunge into the sea. From August to November there are very good displays of wildflowers and in the south there is a virtual jungle, with palms being one of the main species.

It is quite feasible to walk the entire length of the coast in the park in one day starting at Bundeena and finishing at Otford, but first you should check time-tables for the Cronulla to Bundeena ferry and the train times from Otford back via Sutherland to Cronulla. Naturally, the walk length means you must not spend too much time at any one point but it is not necssary to rush the trip.

Start off with the leisurely thirty minute ferry cruise across Port Hacking. Then, from Bundeena wharf, walk south straight up Brighton Street past the shops and turn west into the second street on the right (Scarborough Street) near the top of the hill. Walk down Scarborough Street and once on the flats you should see a sign 'Marley', beside a fenceline. Follow the fenceline south, then, where the fence stops diverge slightly right across a swampy creek. Then, diverge slightly left up a jeep track into light forest. The jeep track soon becomes a foot track and climbs on to an open plateau supporting a lot of grass trees. About 1.5 kilometres from Bundeena jetty a jeep track crosses the Marley foot track and another kilometre south an area burned out in 1976 is left and good views of the south coast appear. By this stage the route has again become a jeep track. Soon you should arrive at the clifflines around the north end of Marley Beach and the jeep track splits into many confusing trails. Head for the cliff rim and follow it west down on to Marley Beach where a sign warns that in rough weather the surf can be danerous. Walk along the sand at Marley Beach then follow a foot pad through low scrub just at the edge of the rocks between Marley and Little Marley beaches. Between the two coves a track leads off west but should be ignored. Walk to the south end of Little Marley Beach and have a short break and perhaps a swim in this sheltered bay. There are lovely grassy slopes and good bush camping opportunities.

Next, follow the clifftops south towards Wattamolla about 4.0 kilometres south-west. About half way the trail turns inland through a lot of prickly hakea, west then south-west, west again, then crosses Wattamolla Creek and heads down its west bank to emerge at the head of a waterfall at the Wattamolla Picnic Ground and carpark. There are all facilities, including a kiosk, at this point. Head uphill south past the kiosk to the eastern end of the carpark from where a service road heads east. Follow it past picnic tables across grassy slopes which give wonderful views of the coast; then, when you see a toilet block well east of the carpark, head up past its west side on to a sand dune track. In 100 metres you should arrive at cliff tops. Turn right and follow the cliff rim, join a north-south jeep track, follow it south 200 metres, follow the cliffs south again and soon you should see your next goal—Curracurrong.

The trail leads down to the head of this small bay 1.2 kilometres from Wattamolla and crosses at the ruins of an old building, then leads south uphill past a sign indicating the way to Garie. There are lovely grassy slopes at this spot. The next section is about 2.5 kilometres long and leads to Curracurrong via the cliff rim. At Curracurrong there are three waterfalls dropping into the sea. A signpost between the first and second falls points the way to Stevens Drive but that route should be ignored and the pointer to Garie

(4.3 kilometres) should be followed right along the cliff rim to Garie North Head where there are spectacular views southwards from the high headland. The trail descends abruptly through rock outcrops to Garie Beach, which is perhaps the most popular beach along the park's coast. Again there are all facilities including a kiosk and there is a Surf Life Saving Club. A sign at the beach edge of the large carpark points to North Era (2.4 kilometres), Burning Palms (4.0 kilometres) and Otford (11.3 kilometres).

Wander along the cliff base south, below Little Garie Head. The trail is above the rocks along the shore and there are good views back north to North Garie Head. Cross Little Garie Beach and continue round the cliff base of Thelma Head to North Era Beach and South Era Beach, both of which are pleasant, small and isolated. About mid-way around South Era Beach, a spur heads off uphill due south and a good track leads up it on to the Burgh Ridge. It should be followed up the grassy slopes, past some small huts, then, when a main east-west spur is reached, you should climb west. Soon, a saddle should be reached just before the track leads up into forested slopes. There are excellent views from this point. Turn south down a steep gully track which leads down to Burning Palms Beach and emerges at a sign 'Garawarra'. Walk to the south end of Burning Palms Beach, climb a few steps up into grassed bush camping areas and, within 200 metres, a Rangers hut should be seen. There is tank water behind the hut and a sign points the way to Palm Jungle 1.6 kilometres and Otford 8.0 kilometres. The trail next contours through an area which has, in the past, been cleared but is now being re-vegetated. There are good coast views and views up the slopes in the Palm Jungle vicinity. Suddenly you leave the open slopes and enter the jungle. It is shady and beautiful and, as the name suggests, palms are one of the most common plant varieties. Vines are also numerous. There is no plant ground storey so the way is open and provides fast walking. Aluminium markers show the route also. You soon begin to climb up steeper and steeper then, suddenly, you emerge from the jungle into dry forest and arrive at a spectacular rock outcrop at the top of a cliffline which you have skirted around. The view is southwards over Werrong Beach in the foreground and right along the south coast. The spot is called Werrong Point. The trail then heads west through scrub for 500 metres to an intersection with a north-south jeep track called the Cliff Track. There is a signpost which points the way to Otford 4.0 kilometres south-west and to numerous other places. Follow the jeep track south-west. It soon becomes a good foot track. After crossing a saddle it climbs slightly southwards over a rocky knob, then descends steeply southwards to Otford Gap—initially by sidling down the western side of the spur then actually following the crest of the spur. At Otford Gap there are open grassy slopes, a carpark, the Lady Wakehurst Drive and an excellent south coast view. Cross the main road at the gap, walk west down Fanshawe Road which becomes an earth road then swings south, then back east. Where it turns east a foot track descends sharply by way of many steps to Otford station and the end of the walk.

MAP REF: *Marley and Otford maps provided with this publication.* Maps 3 and 4.

WALK DISTANCE: 29 km.
GRADING: One day, hard.

41 GOVETTS LEAP—JUNCTION FLAT—BLUE GUM FOREST—PERRYS LOOKDOWN

Blue Mountains walking takes two forms; walks which remain on the tops and, generally speaking, are of an easy grade, and walks which descend into the valleys and are usually of a hard standard. The Grose Valley is an extremely good walking venue and well worth the effort of having to climb back out the 600 metres difference in elevation. This walk suggestion is, therefore, for the more experienced walker who wants to see some of the valley floor attractions.

Travel to Govetts Leap Lookout just east of Blackheath which is a popular tourist lookout with all picnic facilities. Right at the lookout a track leads off from the northern side near the cliff rim. (Not a track beside the toilet blocks.) Take the track and diverge right within 100 metres, then start the long descent down the cliff face. At first sight you would think it impossible that any track could negotiate such cliffs. There are said to be 1881 steps to descend and, in the process, you must avoid the turnoff left, back to the base of Horseshoe Falls, but continue on past the base of spectacular Govetts Leap Falls, which have about a 200 metre sheer drop. The trail then follows Govetts Leap Brook eastwards down through ferns and fine stands of forest. It is only about 3.0 kilometres from Govetts Leap Lookout to Junction Flat in the valley but, because of the steepness, it takes about one to one and a half hours to descend. Junction Flat is a pleasant camping place at the junction of Govetts Leap Brook and Govetts Creek. There are good views up at the cliffs and also good swimming holes.

From Junction Flat, walking becomes most enjoyable and easy. The good foot track to Acacia Flat and the Blue Gum Forest stays on the stream's west bank and is virtually flat walking. However, about 2.5 kilometres from Junction Flat, you must suddenly climb up a bit on to a ridge just south of where Orang Utan Gully flows into Govetts Creek. The ridge gives excellent views of the cliffs around the valley and you must then descend again, on to flats. Within 750 metres you should arrive at Acacia Flat, another camping place with large grassy areas and with the appearance of a park. Keep going 500 metres and you should arrive at the suggested lunch spot and perhaps the most beautiful location in the whole valley. It is the Blue Gum Forest at the confluence of Govetts Creek and the Grose River. Swimming, lazing on the grassy flats under superb blue gums, photography, fishing or even sketching are all possibilities. Try to spend at least a couple of hours at the spot.

The next section of the trip is, regrettably, the hard climb up out of the Grose. Signposts point the way to Perrys Lookdown and state that the climb takes two hours. Most walkers, however, should be able to reach the top in a little over an hour. The climb is 2.0 kilometres long and you rise 600 metres. There are no side branches and at the top there is a carpark and lookout.

Once on the tops, follow a gravelled tourist road to Pulpit Rock 4.0 kilometres away. There is a side road to Anvil Rock to be avoided and the Pulpit Rock Road is a branch of the main road. You need to keep going left at each corner. From the carpark at Pulpit Rock, a good trail 200 metres long leads to a lookout. After seeing the lookout view, double back on a signposted cliff rim track to Govetts Leap. The track leads generally south-west for some 2.0 kilometres, joins Popes Glen Track at the head of Horseshoe Falls, then leads south for some 300 metres to Govetts Leap. Horseshoe Falls and the lookouts close to it make a fitting finish to what should have been a really rewarding circuit.

MAP REF: *Blackheath and Govetts Gorge maps provided with this publication.* Maps 14 and 15.

WALK DISTANCE: 14 km.

GRADING: One day, hard.

42 WOLGAN VALLEY—LITTLE CAPERTEE CREEK

North of Lithgow is the remote and lovely Wolgan Valley. Newnes, 47.0 kilometres north of Lithgow was once a small town serviced by rail but now only an old weatherboard hotel and some ruins are left. The town site has remained as a cleared patch ideal for camping alongside the Wolgan River, right beside the 300-metre-high sandstone cliffs characteristic of the whole valley. A number of walk venues exist and whilst other suggestions in this book describe medium grade routes, this suggestion is considerably harder. Navigation experience is essential and virtually the entire length of the walk is through forest, scrub and gorge, The reward for the scrub bash though is a wonderful view westwards from Point Nicholson some 5.0 kilometres from Newnes. The forest is very beautiful, too, and both tree and ground ferns abound. The scrub is relatively open.

From the hotel, walk north 600 metres along the

dusty road, ford Little Capertee Creek then turn left (west) and follow its north bank. Initially, bracken is thick and a little bothersome but later the going is easier. There are several side gullies flowing into the main gully so make sure you continue westwards rather than in any other direction. Some 3.5 kilometres west of the ford, Little Capertee Creek diverges south-west and you should follow a side creek from that point. The side creek flows east-south-east so you need to veer to west-north-west. At this stage you enter more rugged gorge country and a few rocky outcrops and a minor rock wall have to be negotiated. Generally speaking, it is best to remain close to the gully bed. About 1.5 kilometres west-north-west of the confluence of the gully and Little Capertee Creek you should arrive at a saddle. Directly in front of you is a tremendous drop of about 500 to 600 metres, of which 200 metres is sheer cliff. It is quite astounding to be in a gradually sloping gully one moment then, suddenly, to confront such a drop. Although the view from the saddle is excellent, it is suggested that you continue north to Point Nicholson for lunch and a 360° view. It is only an extra 600 metres although some rock scrambling is required. The return journey to Newnes is back down the same route.

MAP REF: **Wolgan Valley map provided with this publication.** Map 21.

WALK DISTANCE: 12.5 km.

GRADING: One day, hard.

43   GOVETTS LEAP — BRAESIDE — GRAND CANYON — BLUE GUM FOREST — PERRYS LOOKDOWN

For people wanting to see all the major points of

interest in the Blackheath district of the Blue Mountains, an overnight trip, camping at Acacia Flat would be most enjoyable. Whilst a 600 metre ascent out of the Grose Valley is involved, distances are relatively short so that the grading overall would be only medium.

Start walking from Govetts Leap Lookout which is one of the main tourist spots east of Blackheath. A foot track heads uphill south from the carpark along spectacular clifftops, then within 500 metres descends to the top of mighty Govetts Leap Falls and the junction of Braeside walk. A sign at the corner points the way upstream along Govetts Leap Brook. The Braeside walk is up a shallow open valley renowned for wildflowers, especially hakea. After 1.4 kilometres, you should arrive at a small picnic area and a rough road crossing. Turn east along the road and, 1.3 kilometres later, after the road has swung south and two jeep tracks have joined in from the east, you should meet the Evans Lookout tourist road. Follow it south-east for 500 metres past a water tap on the left side of the road to the signposted foot track to the south into Neates Glen and the Grand Canyon. The descent into the canyon is some 400 metres long. The glen is very ferny and formed steps make walking relatively easy. The geological layout of the area is basically a sandstone plateau with Greaves Creek eroding away a hanging valley above the Grose Valley. The Grand Canyon is thus a sandstone feature and the erosion occuring has resulted in quite narrow and deep ravines. Ferns and rock overhangs add interest for the walker. The canyon is only about 2.0 kilometres long but walking is relatively slow due to the rugged terrain and many places of interest. At one point you should pass through a 10-metre-long tunnel. Near the lower end of the gorge a track leads off north uphill to Evans Lookout but should be ignored. Instead, continue downstream 300 metres to lovely Beauchamp Falls at the lip of the hanging valley. A small pad leads to the base of the falls and should be taken. Lunch at the foot of the falls would be a good idea. Some 100 metres upstream from the falls, Rodriguez Pass Track leads off to the north and skirts the cliff base to the west of the falls. It then leaves the cliffs and descends to the valley below the falls for about 2.0 kilometres, to a spot near the confluence of Greaves Creek and Govetts Creek.

Next, you should walk north 2.2 kilometres along the west bank of Govetts Creek to Junction Flat. In the process avoid a trail turnoff left uphill which leads to Evans Lookout. There are good views up to the cliffs at several points and walking is relatively flat and easy. Junction Flat is a camp area at the confluence of Govetts Leap Brook and Govetts Creek and there are good swimming holes in the vicinity. Acacia Flat is a much better campsite than Junction Flat so you should follow an excellent trail along the north-west bank of Govetts Creek for 3.25 kilometres. Just 750 metres before the camp site the trail mounts a spur which provides good views of the cliffs then descends on to the flats which are lovely and grassy.

On the second day you should walk north-east 500 metres to the Blue Gum Forest along a flat, extremely pleasant trail and at the Blue Gum Forest you will be at probably the most beautiful spot in the whole of the Grose Valley. The sturdy blue gums tower above open grassy flats so that the overall appearance is like a park. There are good views up to the cliffs and the

Grose River is joined here by Govetts Creek, so that the stream system is very pleasant too. Camping is no longer permitted by the Blue Mountains National Park Authority as the area had become over-camped.

Next, follow the signposted trail north-west up Docker Buttress to Docker Head on the clifftops. The sign suggests that the steep climb to Perrys Lookdown would take two hours but experienced walkers would complete the trip in one hour despite the fact that there is a 600 metre difference in elevation between the two spots and the distance is 2.25 kilometres. The trail is good and the upper section has properly-formed steps leading up through the cliffs. From Docker Head the trail skirts round the head of Hordern Gully to Perrys Lookdown lookout which is a regular tourist venue. There is a picnic area and minor camping place near the lookout.

Once on the tops, follow the gravelled tourist road 4.0 kilometres to Pulpit Rock. You should avoid the branch road off to Anvil Rock on the right and, south of flat-topped Hat Hill, you need to leave the main Hat Hill Road and walk the 850 metres down a side road to Pulpit Rock. A loop road exists near Pulpit Rock so take either fork. A 200-metre-long trail then leads south from the turntable down to the actual lookout, which, like so many in the district, offers superb views of the Grose Valley. Next, follow a signposted cliff rim track from just near the lookout north. Soon it heads generally south-west for about 2.0 kilometres to Popes Glen Track junction at the head of lovely Horseshoe Falls, then leads south some 300 metres back to Govetts Leap via the cliffline and a couple of lookouts. The falls and the last 2.3 kilometres of

continuous cliff rim walking should make a fitting end
to a truly magnificent walk.

MAP REF: **Blackheath and Govetts Gorge maps
provided with this publication.** Maps 14 and 15.

WALK DISTANCE: 23 km.

GRADING: Two days, medium.

44   PATONGA BEACH — PEARL BEACH

The Hawkesbury Rier estuary is obviously one of the
most scenic features between Sydney and Newcastle.
This walk recommendation enables the walker to see
the best part of the estuary and to visit two beautiful
beaches, yet it is of quite an easy standard.

First, check the ferry timetables so that you can
catch a ferry from the Hawkesbury River station
Brooklyn to Patonga Beach. It is suggested that persons driving from the direction of Newcastle should
also catch the ferry despite the obvious extra driving
distance. Ferries do not operate very frequently so
check times carefully and allow at least five hours
ashore at Patonga Beach. The cruise will be found to
be most enjoyable and will show you lovely scenery.

Once at Patonga jetty, walk east along the beautiful crescent-shaped beach to its eastern end where
there is a line of cottages on the beachfront. A foot
track leads up the north side of the northernmost
cottage. It is steep, initially, but the climb is short and
views create interest. The track then climbs more
gradually to emerge at an east-west fire trail only
about 700 metres from the beach. Turn left and follow
the fire trail west for 50 metres to a signpost at
another fire track. Walk north 25 metres and then fork
up a foot track north-east for 200 metres to emerge at
a carpark at Warrah trig. There is a reasonable view of

the surrounds from the lookout trig. Just at the north side of the carpark a foot track leads off downhill eastwards. Follow it for 300 metres, cross a fire trail and in 100 more metres you should arrive at Warrah Lookout. The view at this lookout is superb and is especially good of Broken Bay and across to Kuring-gai Chase National Park on the other side of the Bay.

You should next return the 100 metres to the fire trail and turn right (east). Follow the trail downhill through an area that is obviously good for wildflowers especially waratahs, which should be in flower in August-September, and Christmas Bells, at Christmas time. You should pass a sandstone bluff overhang on the south side of the trail just as the trail starts to turn north and descend through a gate on to Crystal Avenue, Pearl Beach. Turn north-east along Crystal Avenue and at its end turn north across Green Point Creek, then go east on any one of the three short streets to the Pearl Beach beachfront. It is a delightful little place and you should spend as much time as possible there. Lunch and a swim are suggested. There is a store and the usual picnic facilities in the little town.

The rest of the walk is a retrace of the outward route except that you could omit Warrah trig by remaining on the fire trail rather than walking the loop deviation. The short return to Warrah Lookout would be well warranted.

Make sure you do not rush this trip. The atmosphere of the two tiny beach villages is unique in today's rush and bustle.

MAP REF: **Patonga map provided with this publication.**
  Map 24.

WALK DISTANCE: 8 km.
GRADING: One day, easy.

45 WOY WOY—KOOLEWONG HEIGHTS

Brisbane Water near Gosford has a multitude of bays, arms and peninsulas. It is surrounded by ridges up to 250 metres above sea level. These ridges often permit excellent views of Brisbane Water and one of the best places for these views seems to be at the tiny town of Koolewong just north of Woy Woy.

Catch a train to Woy Woy or drive to the south end of the bridge which connects Woy Woy to Koolewong and start the walk by crossing the bridge. Due to the expansive views up Woy Woy Bay and across Brisbane Water, it is quite a pleasant walk across the long bridge. At the north end of the bridge there is a carpark on the west side of the road for the cars of the residents of a number of bayside cottages. A foot track leads steeply up the spur which starts across the railway line from the carpark. Follow the track west, uphill. A rocky outcrop at one spot on the right of the track provides the first good view of Koolewong and there is an extremely beautiful tree framing the view. At the top of the climb the foot track becomes a jeep track and you should pass a round reservoir tank about 800 metres from where you crossed the railway.

Very soon afterwards a jeep track junction is reached and you should fork left (south) and follow it slightly uphill until you see a rock outcrop over to the right of the track. The outcrop is flat on top and gives access to a most spectacular view of Woy Woy Bay to the west. It is suggested that you have lunch at this point—however there is no water supply.

The jeep track follows power wires downhill southwards to the last pylon which transports the wires right across Woy Woy Bay's west arm. Once at the end of the track and at the top of more rock outcrops and views, you must scrub bash south-east down the main spur. There is quite a lot of prickly scrub present. Rocks also make the short descent awkward but you should arrive at a contouring foot track halfway down the slopes. Turn right and follow the contouring track despite the fact that is soon leads slightly uphill again and more scrub is encountered. Two small TV antennas on the spur knob which serve nearby houses should be met. Follow the antenna leads down a bit then swing south once again, past rocky outcrops and descend through long grass to emerge on the shore of Woy Woy Bay just west of the westernmost cottage facing the foreshore.

At this point all the hard walking is over. You need only follow the concrete pathway round the shore past the front of the line of fishermen's cottages then follow a good, gravelled foot track further north-east back to the railway and the north end of the Woy Woy-Koolewong bridge. Lastly, return across the bridge to the Woy Woy station or to your vehicle. You should have noticed the relaxed atmosphere of the fishermen and the general placidness of the lakeland wonder that is Brisbane Water near Koolewong.

MAP REF: **_Koolewong map provided with this publication._** Map 25.

WALK DISTANCE: 4.5 km.

GRADING: One day, easy.

46 PORT STEPHENS—NORTH HEAD

New South Wales is undoubtedly endowed with some spectacular coastal scenery and the image overseas residents have of Australian beaches seems to be an image of New South Wales beaches rather than of other States. Such places as Port Stephens must surely rank as world class, especially because of the fine, white sand beaches, beautiful lakeland and dominating peaks and headlands around the margin of the lake. It certainly is one of the best areas in New South Wales.

This walk suggestion commences at Hawks Nest and includes a climb to North Head for the view of a lifetime. North Head is about 250 metres high and dominates the northern side of the entrance to Port Stephens lakeland. It is connected to Hawks Nest by a 2-kilometre-long sand spit so that both Pacific Ocean and Port Stephens beaches are on the walk route.

Access to Hawks Nest is along the Pacific Highway past Karuah then to Tea Gardens and over the recently built birdge over the Myall River, then east along Kingfisher Street, south along Mungo Bush Road and east along Booner Street to the ocean foreshore camping ground. Start the walk at a carpark in the sand dunes a kilometre south of the camping ground along Beach Street. At the carpark the spit is only about 300 metres wide.

Walk on to the ocean beach then turn south and walk about 200 metres on to some bare sand. dunes for a good general view. Keep going south over the dunes and then diverge westwards across the spit to Wanderrebah Beach on the inlet. There are good views to the west across Port Stephens and to Nelsons Bay. Walk south-south-east for 1.4 kilometres along Wanderrebah Beach. The relatively calm waters will probably be dotted with yachts and fishing crafts.

As you arrive at the foot of North Head, cross the spit to the ocean beach. You will see a jeep track leading uphill off the ocean beach just at its southern end where some rocks start to appear along the foreshore. Follow the jeep track up through beautiful open forest which contains particularly good banksia trees, and, after about 600 metres, you will arrive at a turntable from which a short-cut foot track heads straight up towards the summit of North Head. The jeep track however continues for another couple of hundred metres east to a second turntable and lookout with a fine view of Hawks Nest. From the second turntable a sidling foot track leads up to join the very steep short-cut track. Then the track bends back north-east (initially), climbs further, then swings up steeply, southwards to the crest of the ridge of North Head where a second excellent view of Hawks Nest can be seen. By walking 10 metres west there is also a reasonable view towards South Head and Nelsons Bay. A small foot pad leads east for 100 metres to a trig point on the actual summit and from it there are very good views to South Head and Nelsons Bay and also out to the several rocky islands in the ocean. There is no water supply on the top but lunch could be eaten whilst you have a good break after the steep climb and before you retrace your outward route back down to the ocean beach. Once on the ocean beach, a swim might be very welcome and then you should merely follow the ocean beach north-north-west back to the carpark.

MAP REF: *Port Stephens map provided with this publication.* Map 27.

WALK DISTANCE: 6 km.
GRADING: One day, easy.

47   ALUM MOUNTAIN

Bulahdelah on the Pacific Highway is dominated by some rocky peaks east of the town. The view must inspire walkers—at least to some extent. However, if the range is viewed from the east side—for example from Sams Forest Road—walkers would most likely feel compelled to investigate this range known as Alum Mountain. As the name suggests, alum is present in the mountain and, in the past, quarries were operated on a small scale to obtain the alum. There are two large caverns and steep cliffs, too. The starting point for this suggested walk is opposite a road house on the Pacific Highway as you head uphill out of the town to the north. There is a round concrete tower on the lower slopes of Alum Mountain, to the east of the road house, and a grassy track leads uphill directly from the highway to the tank. Of necessity. the walk distance is quite short due to the rugged terrain and a fair amount of exploration time is needed.

Start walking up the short track to the concrete tank which is only 400 metres from the road house. A small foot pad exists just to the north side of the tank and it should be followed; however it soon becomes indistinct. Head straight uphill to a power pylon, less than 300 metres from the tank. A jeep track services the pylon and should be followed north up on to the range top saddle, only about 200 metres away. The jeep track forks on the saddle and you should follow the right fork southwards uphill. The track is a bit hard to see due to the presence of many loose rocks and some grass. The track continues up the ridge for several hundred metres then stops at a rocky outcrop.

There are two main peaks on the range and the northernmost one is the objective. To reach it, descend down the east slopes a little. As you follow the rocky cliff base generally southwards, you should see a natural ramp leading steeply up, southwards. Follow it up and at its top the summit is only 15 metres north. There are excellent views of Bulahdelah and the Pacific Highway northwards. No easy way exists off the summit except to return the way you came up, so head down the ramp and turn south again and continue to follow the eastern cliff base until you see a large cavern high above you. There are excellent natural steps and handholds to enable you to climb straight up the rocks and into the impressive cavern which is about 20 metres wide and 10 metres deep.

Return down to the eastern cliff base and double back north 200 metres to another natural ramp leading up southwards. This ramp is far bigger than the first one climbed and in one place you must pull yourself up a very small rock face but the spot is not unduly difficult. The ramp leads directly to a saddle immediately south of the peak that you climbed earlier.

From the saddle, the walking is easier and you should follow the crest of the range southwards until a small quarry is noted, almost on the actual crest. At this point it is suggested that you descend due west to below the rocky slopes then sidle north-west gradually descending until you reach the power wires which run north-south along the western lower slopes. A small foot track follows the power wires and you should walk north on the foot track until another track intersects the one that you are on. Turn left and, within about 400 metres of walking downhill very slightly, you should arrive back at the road house area via a paddock.

MAP REF: *Alum Mountain map provided with this publication.* Map 28.

WALK DISTANCE: 4 km, approximately.

GRADING: One day, easy (but with a lot of rock scrambling).

48   MYALL LAKES—VIOLET HILL

The Myall Lakes area is one of the more picturesque coastal lakelands on the north coast. It is particuarly pleasant because of the numerous hills surrounding the lakes. The vegetation in much of the area furthest from the ocean is virtually jungle but a number of hilltops have been cleared and so provide spectacular views. One such hilltop is Violet Hill which stands on the end of a long peninsula between Boolambayte Lake and Myall Lake. There are numerous coves, islands and other hills in full view from the summit.

To reach the area, travel to Bulahdelah then on a short distance to the Lakes Highway. Follow the Lakes Highway for just a few kilometres until you cross Boolambayte Creek on the newly-aligned section of the road not shown on the Military series map. A kilometre past the bridge, Violet Hill Road leads off to the right. It is signposted, is gravel and immediately crosses Branch Creek at a ford. Follow Violet Hill Road (which has some annoying potholes) for 4.4 kilometres south-east to the base of Toms Hill and a turnoff minor road to the east. You should then proceed on Violet Hill Road a further 3 kilometres to where you cross a saddle, then another 500 metres down to a very minor track on the west side of the road. The track leads 50 metres in to the shore of Boolambayte Lake and to a very pleasant camp site if required. It is here that it is suggested you start walking, too. The spot is actually just at the north-west end of Violet Hill but from this point it is impractical to climb the hill, due to dense vegetation.

Initially, walk out on to Violet Hill Road and follow it south-east then east for 500 metres to a minor crossroad. Uphill to the right leads directly to Violet Hill Lookout and a sign exists at the point. Climb up the 500-metre-long track to the lookout which is open and rounded but with limited views. However, if you walk north-west 100 metres you will get very good views of central and northern Boolambayte Lake. Next, walk south-east over the top and out along a high open ridge which provides really first class views of southern Boolambayte Lake, Myall Lake and their connecting channel plus a panorama right along the Pacific coast. The ridge is quite open and you should get excellent views all the way as you descend the 700 metres distance right down south-east to the isthmus between the two major lakes. It is grassy and pleasant there despite the intrusion of two houses on the slopes. Lunch at the point is suggested.

A gravel road leads north up the valley from the point and should be followed after lunch. At the top of the climb there is a road junction about 900 metres from the lunch spot. Turn right and follow the road east down across a grassy saddle then steeply up north-east to another junction on a ridge top. Fork left down a grassy jeep track then follow it as it sidles up

185

on to a knob. This knob is also open and provides wonderful views of Myall Lake.

The return walk to the camp area is only 2 kilometres long. Follow the outwards route back for the first kilometre to the second junction and then turn right (north-west). After 500 metres you will arrive back at the turnoff to Violet Hill Lookout and, thereafter, you should retrace your outward route again for the final 500 metres.

MAP REF: *Violet Hill map provided with this publication.* Map 29.

WALK DISTANCE: 6 km.

GRADING: One day, easy.

49   GLOUCESTER BUCKETTS (SOUTHERN END)

Gloucester township is dominated by the rocky Bucketts range just to the west. The range is only 7 kilometres long and a stream cuts through the middle of it forming two separate sections but both are aligned north-south. This walk suggestion is in the southern sector which, although much lower than the lofty northern sector, is nevertheless just as rocky.

Just out of Gloucester along the Barrington Road and just after the Gloucester River is crossed, Bucketts Road leads off west to the left. Follow it west then south for 6.5 kilometres until after you pass through a road cutting as the road curves gently round south-west. Just past the cutting are two paddock access gates opposite each other. This is the suggested walk starting and finishing point. The whole route of the walk is in full view from the gates.

Walk through the north side gate and turn west. Follow the contour. Soon you will arrive at a point where two gullies converge. Cross the gullies and swing right up the west bank of the westernmost gully. The whole area is a grassy paddock and the climb is easy. Head directly up to the saddle between the two southernmost knobs on the Bucketts Range. There is only a grassy covering most of the way but some gum trees are on the higher slopes. The saddle is not quite a kilometre from the walk start.

Next climb the southern knob which is relatively easy and only a couple of hundred metres. The view from its top is largely obstructed by vegetation but the southern rim gives excellent views to the south and west. Return to the saddle then diverge slightly left as you climb the north side knob which is dome-shaped. Once to the left and on the rock face swing right up on to the crest of the ridge then again diverge left where you should see a narrow sloping slit with two grass trees at its top. This slit makes for very easy climbing up what otherwise could be awkward sloping rock. From the grass trees it is only a few metres to the summit where there is an uninterrupted 360° view and from where the dome shape can be really appreciated. The top is the suggested lunch spot, although there is no water supply. Then you should walk north down across a smaller dome to a saddle which is extremely narrow. the east side of the saddle has a rocky gully leading straight down it which, in wet weather, probably acts as a small cascade. The width of the gully permits relatively easy descent though and is the return route of this walk suggestion.

However, whilst sitting on the dome having lunch, you should have been inspired by the great rocky knob just to the north and you should not miss climbing it despite its awkward appearance. In fact the climb is relatively easy. From the saddle, which, incidentally, has very high western cliffs and many ferns on the slopes below, climb straight up the first steep pinch. Next, there is an almost level walk to the last main climb. The summit view is marvellous.

Return to the saddle, turn left down the awkward gully and then descend the tree-covered slopes to the south-east until you meet a fence. Stay on the north side of the fence and follow it east right down until you are level with the walk starting point. It is then only 200 metres across the paddock past two small dams to the gateway and walk end.

MAP REF: *Gloucester Bucketts map provided with this publication.* Map 30.

WALK DISTANCE: 2.5 km.

GRADING: One day, easy.

50   PATONGA BEACH—WONDABYNE

Patonga Beach and its hinterland are fascinating at any time of the year due mostly to the tremendous variety of scenery and flora. This walk suggestion enables the walker to see much of the area but excludes the awkward mangrove regions.

Follow the instructions for Walk Number 54 as far as where Dillons Valley Road crosses a saddle before descending southwards into the headwaters of Patonga Creek. Turn north on a jeep track at the saddle, ignore a turnoff west in 100 metres but, after a further 400 metres, turn west and follow a jeep track up to a turntable on the ridge just immediately south of the summit of Mount Wondabyne. From the turntable, there is a foot track heading north for 100 metres to the actual rocky summit with its expansive views. Retrace the 100 metres next, and descend the foot track which leads off north-west down around the western slopes of Mount Wondabyne and through an area renowned for wildflowers (especially waratah) in August-September and Christmas bells in December. Honeyflower is very widespread, too. The foot track soon joins a jeep track once below the rocky areas and then you should arrive at a 'T' junction at the highest point on the east-west fire trail which, roughly, runs above where the railway tunnels through, under the ridge. Turn left (west) and follow the fire trail downhill, more or less on the south side of the railway line after it emerges west of its tunnel. In just over a kilometre, the track starts to turn south as Mullet Creek (a long inlet of the Hawkesbury Estuary) comes into view. Here also a jeep track doubles back north-east down to end at the railway line. It should be ignored. Some power poles are in the area and you should look for a small foot pad on the north side of pole number 86, then follow it down a spur until rocky clifftops are reached and you can see the railway crossing Mullet Creek. Veer well left and descend the rocky outcrops to the water's edge, then turn right and walk to the start of the rail causeway but not walk on the tracks as the line is the main northern electrified line and is very busy. It is also probably illegal to walk on the lines. Rather, walk along the water's edge (despite the difficulty of the rocks) and continue in this fashion for the short distance to Wondabyne railway station. To complete the circuit you could then travel by train to Hawkesbury River station then cross to Patonga Beach by ferry or, alternatively, use the train to Woy Woy then catch a bus to Patonga.

Naturally, all timetables should be checked before starting this walk and Sydney residents no doubt would do best to leave transport at Hawkesbury River station and cross to Patonga Beach by ferry.

MAP REF: *Patonga map provided with this publication.*
Map 24.

MAP DISTANCE: 12 km.

GRADING: One day, medium.

51   DHURAG NATIONAL PARK CIRCUIT

The Hawkesbury River country around Wisemans Ferry consists of Hawkesbury sandstone deposits eroded by the river to form a huge valley. The Hawkesbury's erosive power has been such that it has left steep slopes on both sides of the valley and this in turn has caused side streams to descend very rapidly from the heights, causing the countryside to be quite rugged.

Dhurag National Park covers part of this rugged tract on the north side of the river and it is because of the ruggedness that there is such a wide variety of birds and animals to be seen, including lyrebirds. The creek valleys have fairly dense forest which includes vines, ephiphytes, sassafras and coachwood, whilst the high sandstone outcrops and peaks support many eucalypts and angophoras. South-east of Wisemans Ferry, along the Gosford Road and about a kilometre past Hazel Dell Picnic Area, is a road which leads into a camp area and a further picnic area in the Mill Creek watershed. Some 2.3 kilometres up this side road a good circuit walk route has been established to show visitors features of the park. The circuit is only 9.0 kilometres long but is through quite difficult country. Signposts indicate the commencement and the two ends of the track which·are both near one another at the rear of the grassed picnic area. Take the right hand (northerly) track first across a log bridge so that the most difficult sections are walked first; then you should have a relatively easier walk back down Biamea Creek valley to finish the circuit. On a hot day, especially, the creek valley is quite pleasant due to its thick forests, rock pools and sandstone bluff over-hangs. About 600 metres before the carpark, as you return down Biamea Creek, an alternative track called the Grass Tree Track should be avoided unless you particularly want to see grass trees. The first two thirds of the circuit is over high sandstone ridges which are quite dry and, therefore, it is essential that you carry some water. Good views exist on the high points, too.

MAP REF: *Dhurag National Park map provided with this publication.* Map 26.

WALK DISTANCE: 9 km.

GRADING: One day, medium.

52 GLOUCESTER BUCKETTS (NORTHERN END)

Just beside the town of Gloucester and dominating the town's western skyline is the Gloucester Buck-etts, a rugged line of peaks with really rocky tops and cliffs. The range is only about 7 kilometres long and runs north-south but is bisected by a stream. The northern sector is the highest and the closest to the town. It is the suggested venue for this walk.

North-west of the town along the Barrington Road, and after having crossed the Gloucester River, Buck-etts Road branches off west. Follow it and it soon turns south. Then proceed south 2.5 kilometres, until you see two parallel fencelines forming an easement running west opposite a milking shed. There is an electricity pole (number 787) at the spot and there is a farm house south of the easement. The area is devoted to dairying and grassy slopes extend well up to the base of the Bucketts Range.

Start the walk by following the easement west through two gates (one at each end of the easement), then continue in the same direction through a third gate. Next, diverge right up the slopes on to a spur with a fence running up it. Follow the spur up to the point where the grass extends furthest west then diverge slightly left through bracken so that you enter the lower part of a very steep gully. There are some rocky outcrops on the north bank which are best avoided but, generally, you must climb up to the saddle on the range by way of following the north bank of the gully. The climb is steep, rocky and spiders are an annoyance. Also many plants are very shallow-rooted and cannot be relied upon as handholds. Although the distance to the saddle from the walk start is only 1.5 kilometres, it will take at least an hour for the climb. The vegetation is luxuriant in the gully itself, so you need to try and keep to the more grassy parts.

Once at the saddle, which is just south of the highest point on the range, turn left (south) and wander along the tops, then down the extremely narrow ridge for really spectacular views. The going is slow but tremendous cliffs and views both west and east make the walk most enjoyable. The town of Gloucester is, of course, in full view. Nearly a kilometre south of the saddle, the ridge suddenly 'dives' and southern cliff faces prevent further descent. It is suggested that you have lunch on the rocks at this point, whilst you admire the views—especially of the rugged southern section of the Bucketts. There is no water supply though. You may also see rock wallabies in the area. After lunch, retrace your route back to the walk starting point.

MAP REF: *Gloucester Bucketts map provided with this publication.* Map 30.

WALK DISTANCE: 5 km.

GRADING: One day, medium (but with awkward climbing).

53   MYALL LAKES

The Myall Lakes area is of particular interest to walkers because of its beautiful views and because of the variety of vegetation, ranging from virtual jungle in inland gullies to heathlands and moor near the ocean.

To reach this recommended walk area, follow the Pacific Highway north-east past Bulahdelah, turn right along the Lakes Highway and, just one kilometre past the bridge over Boolambayte Creek, turn right again into signposted Violet Hill Road. The road immediately crosses a ford, is gravelled and is inclined to have bad potholes. Follow it for 4.4 kilometres then fork right rather than go on to the minor left branch road. But note the minor road as the walk route includes this junction later. The junction is at the base of Tower Hill. Travel 3.5 kilometres further, crossing a saddle in the process. You should then find a very minor road to the right into a camp site only 100 metres away and beside Lake Boolambayte. The spot could be useful if you wish to camp and is also the start of this walk suggestion. It is actually just at the north-west end of Violet Hill.

Initially, walk back on to Violet Hill Road, turn right and in 500 metres of walking generally eastwards you should meet a minor cross road. Turn right (south), up signposted Violet Hill Lookout jeep track, which leads for 500 metres directly to the rounded hill top. Walk 100 metres north-west for an excellent view of central and northern Boolambayte Lake, then south-south-east for 200 metres for wonderful views of southern Boolambayte Lake, Myall Lake, their connecting channel, numerous surrounding peaks and the Pacific coastline. Return back down to the crossroads, then walk north-east generally for about a kilometre, fork right, cross a stream, start to climb a little and then fork left. (The right fork is quite minor.) Climb steadily up northwards, gaining over 100 metres elevation, then continue north-west up a second incline of about a further 50 metres rise — to a hilltop. This top is about 1.3 kilometres from the start of the initial climb. The main jeep track continues down to a saddle, west-wards through a gate, but you should double back on the hilltop and follow a minor fire trail, at first east then downhill northwards on a spur. After a kilometre of descending you should meet a larger jeep track which forms a 'T' junction. Turn left and walk 3.0 kilometres through jungle vegetation northwest up to a saddle then west down a gully to Violet Hill Road. Turn left and follow Violet Hill Road 3.5 kilometres to the camp area and walk end.

MAP REF: **Violet Hill Map provided with this publication.** Map 29.

WALK DISTANCE: 12.5 km.

GRADING: One day, medium.

54 PATONGA BEACH AND HINTERLAND

For a walk with tremendous scenic variety including heath country, mangrove swamps, white sand beaches, sandstone country and a very wide variety of flowers go to Patonga Beach and start this walk suggestion at the jetty. Perhaps the ferry from Hawkesbury River station to Patonga Beach could be used for transport and thus add the interest of a cruise on the Hawkesbury.

First, walk to the east end of the beautiful beach where you will see a number of cottages lining the shore. To the north of the northernmost cottage a small foot track leaves the beach beside the building and steadily rises up on to a ridge. Soon you should come on to a sandstone bluff which provides good views south over Broken Bay. The track then rises further but less steeply up the spur until a fire trail is met. Turn right (east) and walk 300 metres then fork right along a 100-metre-long foot track to Warrah Lookout which provides very good views of Broken Bay, Return the 100 metres, cross the fire trail and climb up a signposted foot track to Warrah trig, only 300 metres away. The trig point provides only minor views. A National Park access road services the trig area. Follow the road north-west along the ridge top for 1.2 kilometres until the main Umina-Patonga Road is met. Turn right and, in 200 metres, turn left through a gate, west down a National Park fire trail. The ridge top vegetation will have been uninspiring for the last kilometre but from this point on is noticeably more interesting. Broad views also will become apparent. In 200 metres you should fork north and continue 300 metres until a more important fire trail is met as it heads east-west. Turn downhill and follow the fire trail west for 200 metres then generally northwards, along the western slopes of the Ettymalong Heights, which are of broken sandstone. Wildflowers are a feature of this section of the walk. Flowers include heaths, grevillea, hakea, banksia, flannel flowers, fringed lilies and Christmas bells in large numbers and also many others. After 3.0 kilometres, you should arrive at the suggested lunch spot at a gully with a sandstone bridge crossing and a dam just to the east. Also there is a camp cave just south-east of the crossing.

From this point you temporarily leave Brisbane Waters National Park, which you have been crossing so far, and, regrettably, the next kilometre is not so pleasant. You must climb north several hundred metres to a saddle where you will be confronted with a quarry and the Woy Woy garbage disposal tip. A gravelled road skirts the western edge of the tip and should be followed. It soon swings west away from the tip up the southern side of the valley of South Woy Woy Creek. There is a gateway where you re-enter the park and the road is known as Dillons Valley Road but is not signposted. Walk west uphill to a saddle in 1.5 kilometres; ignore a track off north, then turn south to the headwaters of fascinating Patonga Creek. The road descends to an isolated pocket of farmland surrounded by the park and, from this point south, the walk grading becomes considerably harder, due mostly to navigation requirements. As the road emerges at Dillons Farm a grassy foot track leads off south-east at a point where the road doubles back to cross Patonga Creek and enter the farm. Follow the foot track down and, within 200 metres, you will be amid sub-tropical forest with palms, vines and lush green grass. You will be on the east bank of Patonga Creek at this point. A small pad heads north and another crosses the creek, but you should remain on the quite minor pad along the east bank for 50 metres then cross to the west bank, where a reasonably defined, almost contouring track exists. Follow the track south through luxuriant growth and through some truly magnificent palms and ferns until the pad becomes indistinct, about 600 metres along the west bank section. Once the track has been lost, keep up out of the creek valley and you should shortly arrive on a spur which descends to the point where Patonga Creek swings west temporarily. Descend the spur at this point by heading virtually due south. The creek gully becomes more open and grassy. Cross Patonga Creek at this point without concerning yourself about wet shoes and feet as you will certainly get your feet both wet and muddy later. Swing south again shortly as you continue to follow the east bank for 3.5 kilometres — initially along grassy river bank then along the margin of mangroves, where it should be a bit muddy. A foot pad exists up out of the mangroves for some of the distance but it is not continuous. The mangrove section is quite time-consuming, especially where you need to avert oyster beds as Patonga Creek broadens into an estuary. Eventually, you will find that the foot track joins a large area of dry flats which are extenisvely used by trail bikes and appear like roads. Head south along the bike tracks until you have passed the base of a steep spur on your left. At this point an excellent foot track leads east for 300 metres, crosses a creek where you can wash your muddy legs, then follows a gravelled road east which joins into Jacaranda Street, Patonga. Proceed east along Jacaranda Street then into Patonga Street and, within a couple of hundred metres, arrive back on the Patonga beachfront. It is then only

200 metres east back to the jetty and walk finishing point.

MAP REF: **Patonga map provided with this publication.** Map 24.

WALK DISTANCE: 16 km.

GRADING: One day, hard.

55 BARRINGTON TOPS

Barrington Tops is rather unique in northern New South Wales in that it receives winter snow falls and has snow grass plains, snow gums and icy tarns. Its fairly extensive plateau is generally about 1500 metres or more above sea level. It is a wild, remote part of the state where dingoes can be heard most evenings. As the plateau rises from rugged mountains north-west of Newcastle there is plenty of sub-tropical rain forest on the slopes. Obviously abundant too on the tops are wombats, wallabies and rosella parrots and, on the slopes, lyrebirds and beautiful beech trees. The ordinary motorist can reach 700 metres altitude in his car by travelling through Maitland, Paterson, Eccleston, the Allyn River valley and up to Lagoon Pinch where there is a turntable and tank water. The road continues but is only a jeep track, due to its steepness. In 4.0 kilometres it climbs to 1400 metres, just north of a peak called The Corker where the Barrington Tops National Park is entered. Beyond this point, vehicles are not permitted without authority. Make sure you carry some water, then head off up the 4-kilometre-long ascent northwards. It is anything but easy. North of The Corker there is still 3.0 kilometres more climbing but it is only of a very gradual nature. The views, beech forests, lyrebirds and snow gums should create interest too. You should arrive at a junction and sign-

198

post 7.0 kilometres from the Lagoon Pinch turntable. The sign indicates the way to Careys Peak, 2.0 kilometres to the left, and Wombat Creek, 300 metres to the right. If it is a hot day or if water is needed, first go to Wombat Creek for water. To reach it you should follow the 20-kilometre-long Gloucester Tops track for 200 metres, then fork left for 100 metres to the water supply.

Next, continue uphill north-west towards Careys Peak for a further kilometre to another junction and sign showing the way to the Big Hole. Fork right (north-north-east) and walk generally downhill past a swamp to the Big Hole which is a magnificent, large, deep pool on the Barrington River and which is in an alpine setting. It is ideal for swimming, camping and your lunch break which will be well overdue. Big Hole should take some three to four and a half hours to reach from Lagoon Pinch.

After lunch and perhaps a swim, retrace 3.0 kilometres to the junction and turn right for a kilometre walk westwards to Careys Peak for a first class view. After 700 metres walking you should turn left downhill for 100 metres to Careys Hut, an old tin hut with an earth floor and no bunks or water supply. It is in a saddle immediately north-east of Careys Peak. Walk from the hut up a 200-metre-long foot track for the very fine view southwards along the access ridge that you earlier climbed. If you go 10 metres west on to some rocks you should be able to see the alpine plains to the north, too. From the peak you will really get to see how the Barrington Tops are indeed a real high plateau and how the Allyn River and other streams have eroded the southern slopes so deeply. It is also interesting to see the well-defined line where

sub-tropical forests meet snow gums on the ridge
south towards The Corker.

The return journey is a retrace of the outward route
but excludes the Big Hole. On the way down you will
perhaps feel less weary than on the way up and so
appreciate more the fine forests and views.

MAP REF: *Barrington Tops map provided with this
publication.* Map 31.

WALK DISTANCE: 17 km.

GRADING: One day, hard.

56   BARRINGTON TOPS

Undoubtedly one of the best places for bushwalking
reasonably close to Newcastle is Barrington Tops; a
high plateau rising to about 1600 metres above sea
level. It is remote and has wonderful views and
peculiar flora for northern New South Wales in that it
is alpine and receives winter snows. It is a National
Park and much of the surrounding slopes are declared
State Forest.

Best access is from Maitland via Paterson, Eccleston, the Allyn River valley and up to Lagoon Pinch on
a main southern spur some 7.0 kilometres from the
edge of the true plateau and, therefore, the best
walking areas. At Lagoon Pinch there is a water tank,
carpark and minimal picnic facilities. The road continues as a jeep track up the spur for 4.0 kilometres to
enter the National Park and vehicles of any descrip-
tion are not permitted into the park without authority.
The 4.0 kilometre stretch is the main climb to the
plateau and the park is entered just at the northern
side of a knob known as The Corker. Should you wish
to camp out before starting the walk, for instance on
a Friday night, it would be advisable to camp beside

the Allyn River rather than at inappropriate Lagoon Pinch.

Start off walking up the 7.0 kilometre climb following the Careys Peak Track and make sure you carry some water. After the initial steep pinch to the park entry 700 metres higher than Lagoon Pinch, you ascend gradually and beech forests, ferns, snow gums, views, wallabies, wombats and rosella parrots will all be present to make the climb most enjoyable. At the 7.0 kilometre mark there is a junction which indicates a walking track to Gloucester Tops, 20.0 kilometres, Wombat Creek, 300 metres and Careys Peak, 2.0 kilometres. It is suggested that you detour to Wombat Creek for lunch by the stream. You need to walk 200 metres along the Gloucester Tops Track then fork north 100 metres.

After lunch retrace the 300 metres, turn north-west and walk a kilometre to another junction where Big Hole Track branches off north. Fork left and walk west 700 metres then fork south 100 metres into a saddle where Careys Hut exists. It is an old tin hut which has an earth floor, no bunks and no water supply. Only 200 metres south-west up a foot track is Careys Peak summit with its wonderful views to the south and the ridge that you climbed that morning. On some rocks, just 10 metres to the west, you can look out to the north over alpine plains.

Retrace 300 metres back to the main track and head off west, initially downhill through a gateway. Then, keep going roughly westwards for 3.0 kilometres, until you reach a wonderful lookout to the south where the jeep track runs alongside the top of the cliffs on the southern edge of the plateau. The view is down the Paterson River valley mainly. From the lookout set a compass course due north and scrub bash 300 metres downhill to emerge on some delightful alpine plains along Edwards Creek. Follow the creek downstream as closely as possible along its southern bank without getting into marshy tracts and avoiding obvious patches of scrub. After 2.5 kilometres you should arrive at the confluence of the Barrington River as it winds across broad alpine plains. Only 400 metres downstream is Jacksons Hole, a pleasant rock pool. It is the suggested camp site. To reach it, it is best to stay on the southern bank of the Barrington River but you will have to cross Saxby Creek and most likely get wet feet. The camp site at Jacksons Hole is very picturesque and grassy with excellent snow gum wood to ensure a good campfire. The spot is on the north bank of the Barrington. During the night you will probably hear dingoes howling but they are no danger.

Next morning, walk downstream following the river's north bank. Animal pads exist for much of the distance but are a little hard to follow at times. Nearly 2.0 kilometres downstream, and after having crossed a stream flowing into the river from the north, the river flows south-east and a natural series of stepping stones exist so that it is usually easy to cross to the south bank at this point. You should then walk east-south-east, generally following the south bank despite a little scrub and, within a kilometre, you should arrive at a river gauge and a jeep track crossing. Turn right (south) uphill away from the river and follow the jeep track over a saddle and down to the east. Within only 500 metres you should arrive at Big Hole which is a large tarn, excellent for a cold swim and for a morning tea break. It is set in idyllic surroundings of snow gums and snow grass plains. The pool is deep, large and clear. Wild duck and other waterbirds appear to be in the area, too.

Next, climb south then south-south-west uphill for 3.0 kilometres past a swamp and back to the Careys Peak jeep track. Turn left and walk a kilometre then fork left twice within 300 metres to see yourself back at Wombat Creek for lunch again.

Finally, after lunch retrace the outwards route back down the 7.3 kilometres past The Corker to Lagoon Pinch turntable.

MAP REF: **Barrington Tops map provided with this publication.** Map 31.

WALK DISTANCE: 30 km.

GRADING: Two days, medium.

57   FITZROY FALLS EAST RIM TRACK

Fitzroy Falls are one of the better falls in the Morton National Park and are on the edge of the Southern Tablelands near Nowra. Despite the fact that a reservoir is immediatley upstream of the 80-metre-high falls they are well worth visiting. The National Park headquarters and facilities for tourists are also at the head of the falls, whilst walking tracks exist along both west and east rims of the gorge of Yarrunga Creek. Neither rim walk is very long, but for anyone interested in walking rather than just driving to the falls, the trails provide a pleasant opportunity to spend several hours wandering about.

The east rim return trip is 5.0 kilometres long, taking about two hours — if only two or three minutes are spent at each lookout along the way. It is therefore suggested that you use facilities at Fitzroy Falls themselves for lunch, either before or after the walk, and thus help make a pleasant day's activities. The trail starts at the foot-bridge over Yarrunga Creek just above the falls and follows the clifftops southwards. A track to the camping area veers off left almost immediately and should be avoided. The East Rim Track then leads directly to May Lookout only 200 metres south and, at the lookout, you get reasonable views of Grotto and Twin Falls which cascade over the western rim of the gorge virtually opposite May Lookout. Next, the track leaves the cliff rim, turns east and gently descends to Ferntree Gully, a pretty little gully which is cool and refreshing on a hot day. As the name suggests, it is a good place to see ferns and there are two branches of the gully, so that the length of track among the ferns is longer than would normally be expected. You then wind uphill to a high point on the south side of Ferntree Gully and should arrive at signposted Warragong Lookout which is a kilometre from the walk start. From it you get views towards Fitzroy Falls, although it is a side-on view and not as good as that from West Rim lookouts. Virtually straight below is Lady Hordern Falls and across the gorge are Twin Falls and Grotto Falls. The trail then turns in from the cliffs for a little while and leads through dry forest with banksia and honeyflower being quite prolific, among other flowers. Within 400 metres of sidling then descending, you should arrive at signposted Lamond Lookout which provides views westwards and downstream along Yarrunga Creek Valley. Again you should climb up, away from the escarpment, then sidle southwards cross a relatively dry side gully and head up to an un-named lookout 500 metres from Lamond Lookout. The view is a general one. South

200 metres again a further unnamed lookout exists, giving similar views but with a better northward aspect. Still further south 300 metres, is signposted Valley View lookout where there are excellent views southwards towards the plateau of Mount Carrialoo and the lower Yarrunga Valley. The trail continues for another 200 metres to join a road terminus. This road joins in from the Kangaroo Valley Road, 350 metres east, but there is little point in walking the final 200 metres to the terminus. There are no views and the vegetation is relatively uninteresting, so it is suggested that you retrace your outward route.

MAP REF: *Fitzroy Falls map provided with this publication.* Map 32.

WALK DISTANCE: 5.0 km.

GRADING: One day, easy.

58 FITZROY FALLS WEST RIM TRACK

The Southern Tablelands of New South Wales have been deeply eroded along their eastern margins especially, and such rivers as the Shoalhaven and Kangaroo have created quite deep gorges. Yarrunga Creek has also eroded the tablelands and, where the harder, overlaying rocks have given way, the beautiful 80 metre drop of Fitzroy Falls exists. The scope for water reticulation in conjunction with electricity production in such an area has been recognized and a reservoir has been built immediately above the head of the falls. The aim is to supply additional water to Sydney and the South Coast and to obtain peak load electricity. However, the dam does not appear to have spoiled the falls and they remain one of the main features of Morton National Park.

A 2.5-kilometre-long track exists on the east rim of

the gorge below the falls but it does not give views directly at the falls. On the west rim, however, a 3-kilometre-long return walk includes excellent views of the falls and, from Renown Lookout at the furthest point, there is an excellent view of both Fitzroy and Lady Hordern Falls as well as the cascade on Yarrunga Creek between the two sets of falls. Therefore it could be classed as the better walk of the two choices. Full tourist facilities and National Park Headquarters are at the head of Fitzroy Falls so it is suggested that you have lunch there and complete the walk either before or after lunch. It would of course be quite feasible to walk the east and west rim routes in the one day as the total distance would be only 8.0 kilometres.

Start the West Rim walk at the footbridge over Yarrunga Creek at the head of Fitzroy Falls. Walk west along the top of the escarpment for 400 metres to Jersey Lookout, which gives a close up view of Fitzroy Falls and a view to Mount Carrialoo, a plateau to the south. On the way there are a number of steps to be negotiated. A branch track which used to lead down to the bottom of the falls should be passed. The trail is now closed. From Jersey Lookout, walk south-west uphill to Richardsons Lookout which gives good views especially to the south then turn away from the cliff rim to join a fire trail in only 8 metres. The fire trail is the continuation of Gwen Road and it is not open to general vehicular traffic beyond this point westwards, but continues for some distance along the west side of the gorge.

Walk along the fire trail for only 20 metres west, then veer off left on the signposted Western Trail for 150 metres to the next lookout which is Twin Falls lookout. Twin Falls and Grotto Falls can be seen from this vantage point and both falls are on minor side gullies flowing over the western escarpment into Yarrunga Creek. Next, you should head north-west 150 metres to cross a creek alongside the fire trail which crosses the same creek on a concrete ford. The foot track then skirts round into the pretty fern gully called The Grotto. This spot is very cool and refreshing. Head 400 metres south along the cliff tops to Starkeys Lookout which again gives reasonable views both up and down the Yarrunga Valley. The lookout is actually 30 metres off the main track and just a few metres south of the junction a branch of the fire trail ends at the foot track to form a 'T' shape. You should keep walking south for a further 200 metres to signposted Renown Lookout which provides the best views from any of the lookouts around the gorge. For the return journey it is suggested that you retrace the last 200 metres, then turn left (west) along the fire trail branch, then in another 200 metres turn north along the main fire trail. You should then follow the road back to the concrete ford 800 metres away then rejoin the foot track and retrace the remainder of the route back to Fitzroy Falls. The walk along the fire trail takes you through pleasant open forest which has many wild-flowers—especially in springtime.

MAP REF: *Fitzroy Falls map provided with this publication.* Map 32.

WALK DISTANCE: 3.0 km.

GRADING: One day, easy.

59   BERRIMA

Berrima, a small town on the Hume Highway, is probably the best example of a small Australian town of the 1830s still existing, and today there remain over forty buildings aged between 100 and 135 years, most of which are in use and are in an excellent state of repair. A number of the buildings are classified by the National Trust and many are registered with the Trust.

The town consequently provides a very pleasant venue for a day's ramble to see the various points of interest. The town's history started in 1829 with the selection of the site as county town for Camden County by Major Mitchell, then Surveyor General. The nearby settlement of Bong Bong was established earlier in 1821 on the original Sydney to Goulburn Road. However, the road ran over the Mittagong Range and was unsatisfactory for horse- and bullock-drawn traffic, so Major Mitchell decided that the road should be re-aligned via Berrima. From that time on, Berrima saw a continual stream of bullock teams pulling drays laden with wool, hides and other produce to Sydney and returning with stores for Goulburn, especially. There were soon four inns in Berrima and fourteen hotels and the population grew to 600.

In 1867 the southern railway opened, bypassing Berrima, and the town went into suspended growth to await the arrival of the motor car. By 1914 the population had dropped to eighty but since then the Hume Highway has brought · passing traffic and the town, whilst still small, has grown again. The buildings remaining in the town were often constructed elaborately yet many remained in use for only a short time. The most beautiful building in the town is an excellent example; it is a sandstone court house finished in 1838 at tremendous cost, yet only twelve years later, court hearings were transferred to Goulburn and by 1857 the building was falling into disrepair until 1936, when it was rejuvenated as a school of arts. The gaol in the town, completed in 1839, remained in use until the 1860s but after that was left unused for long periods. The First World War saw it used for internment of Germans living in Australia and the survivors of the crew of the Emden. It was re-opened in 1949.

As you walk around the town, you will notice that the majority of the old houses are sited near the Wingecarribee River. This is because all water had to be drawn and carried from Lambies Well or the river. The town is laid out so that major buildings are all either around or close to the small town square or near the main road. Also it can be seen that the town was without churches for some twenty years as the Church of England was not opened till 1849 and the Catholic Church in 1851. Both builings were constructed in sandstone in Gothic Revival style. The Presbyterian Church building was originally built in the 1860s as a Masonic Temple and School of Arts and was later donated to the church. Like the churches, the public school was a latecomer to the town. It dates from 1869, even after the southern railway had opened. There was, however, a tiny, earlier school which still stands in Jellore Street. To really appreciate any walk around the town, one needs to linger, and to ponder about what life must have been like in those early days. Take notice of the mangificent old trees, including the oak in the town square, and enter buildings wherever possible.

Start a town tour at the bridge over Wingecarribee River and walk north to the west end of the small town square park, known as Market Place. A small museum is located there with a few interesting relics. Turn left into Jellore Street to see the oldest house in the town

Berrima House which was sold in 1837 for £18 and resold in 1841 for £24. Just west of it is the original school building which is in poor repair. Return to Market Place and walk east along its northern side to see three inns, including the Coach and Horses Inn and the Victoria Inn. The first bank building is also there. In the park across the street is an old oak tree. Continue north up the Hume Highway's west side to see Australia's oldest continuously licensed hotel. It dates from 1835 but has been modified since. All other inns and hotels in the town closed with the decline of the town and only some re-opened. Just north is the old police station in front of the gaol. The gaol looks quite elaborate with a magnificent gateway. Turn left into Wiltshire Street to see the courthouse on the right and the old police barracks further along the street also on the right. The famous Bullshead Fountain, providing water for horses, is on the north wall of the gaol too, and at the end of the short street there is a track down to the riverside and Lambies Well. The little deviation to the river is most pleasant.

Next, return to the east end of Wiltshire Street and turn north up Argyle Street to see two old houses on the left and rear of Breens Hotel on the right. Just north again is the Presbyterian Church where you should turn west along Oxley Street. There are four old houses at the eastern end of Oxley Street, one on the south side next to the church and three on the north side. The westernmost north-side house is Bellevue, a lovely house named because of its view of the town area. Walk back east again, cross Argyle Street and turn north into Wilkinson Street at its junction with the Hume Highway. Just 200 metres north on the right hand side is Harpers Mansion built in 1829. It is the biggest house in the town, is set on a hillside and is double storeyed. Again, return to the Hume Highway and turn east up Oxley Street to see the Public School then return to the highway and follow it back to Market Place. The old post office is passed at the corner of Oxley Street and the highway; there are then old houses on either side of the highway followed by Taylors Hotel on the left and Breens Hotel on the right. Breens was the last to close after the railway bypassed the town, leaving only the Surveyor General. Breens has since been restored to its original condition. South again, on the corner of Wingecarribee Street is the old bakery, now a motel and tea rooms, but you can go into the tea rooms and inspect the old bakery section and a small gallery with an interesting display. You should then arrive back at Market Place but walk along its east end to see Holy Trinity Church of England, then along the park's south side to see the Magistrate's House (1870s) and Holsberrys Inn. This brings you back to the bridge and walk starting point. To finish off the day, walk across the bridge to see the Catholic Church then walk 2.0 kilometres east along Oldbury Street (from alongside the church) to the Berrima Cemetery. A browse around the cemetery reveals some interesting stories of life in the so-called 'good old days'. Lastly, return to the bridge in town.

MAP REF: *Berrima map provided with this publication.*
  Map 33.
WALK DISTANCE: 6.0 km.
GRADING: One day, easy.

There are not very many places in New South Wales where you can see glow worms and certainly there is none that can rival New Zealand's Waitomo Caves. However, Bundanoon on the Southern Tablelands has a Glow Worm Glen where you can be assured of seeing glow worms after dark. The display is quite good. This walk suggestion leads to various lookouts along the cliffs of Bundanoon Creek then finishes with a visit to see the glow worms. Of course timing of the walk would be important as you would not appreciate the glow worms in daylight. You should carry a torch for each person in your group, and it is suggested that you take your evening meal rather than lunch with you. The walk circuit is only 7.5 kilometres long so there is no point in starting the trip too early. Allow yourselves about an hour for the evening meal which could make use of a fireplace at Riverview Lookout Picnic Ground and another hour of daylight walking after the meal break. It should take around an hour to reach riverview Lookout so that really you need to start the walk at Bundanoon shops three hours before dusk.

From the shops, walk south down Constitution Hill on Church Street for a kilometre then turn east along a gravelled road through pleasant farming land for 1.3 kilometres. The road is lined with fine stands of trees. It then forks and the right fork should be taken into the Morton National Park. Then only 400 metres south-east is Amphitheatre Lookout. It gives good views down over the steep-sided valley of Bundanoon Creek. The name Amphitheatre is derived from the arc of cliffs at the spot. Right beside the lookout, a

700-metres-long trail leads north into Ferntree Gully then swings east up to Mark Morton Lookout and Riverview Lookout, both of which provide further views of Bundanoon Creek, one to the north-east and the other to the south-west. Picnic facilities should then be used for your evening meal.

Next, follow the minor road that services the picnic area, north-west 800 metres through relatively wet forest compared to the drier forests previously encountered. You should arrive at a track off east (right) which is signposted Dimmocks Creek, then follow it east, down past a track turnoff to the left within 150 metres then north to another intersection after 250 metres. Veer right then turn down the west bank of the creek for about 200 metres to see the lush ferns and rock overhangs beside the creek. It descends steeply so do not go more than about 200 metres, as dusk should be approaching. Retrace your route 200 metres back uphill then veer left at the junction so that you are climbing uphill following the slopes on the west side of Dimmocks Creek. After 200 metres you should come to a 'T' junction. Turn right and follow this grassy jeep track 200 metres to another 'T' junction which has farmland just west of it. Turn right again and head along a good trail on a fenceline north 600 metres to cross a gully, then meet a main trail which runs from William Street Bundanoon east to the Glow Worm Glen. It is then only 150 metres east of the gully crossing via the excellent trail down some steps to the glow worm display.

To finish the walk, after seeing the glow worms, simply walk west initially on the good track up through a farming area then along William Street until you meet the main road. Turn left, 1.3 kilometres from

Glow Worm Glen and arrive back at the Bundanoon shops after another 400 metres of walking.

MAP REF: **Bundanoon map provided with this publication.** Map 34.

WALK DISTANCE: 7.5 km.

GRADING: One day, easy (evening walk).

61 BUNDANOON — FAIRY BOWER — BONNIEVIEW LOOKOUT

Bundanoon Creek, a tributary of the Shoalhaven River, has some interesting cliffs along both its flanks and there are numerous lookouts on the cliff rim. The creek valley is about 300 metres deep and much of it contains dense rainforest. Regrettably, the views are serviced only by road in nearly every case and there is no provision of tracks for walkers between lookouts, with the exception of the short trail between Echo Point and Bonnieview Lookouts. However the roads are quiet and walking along them is relatively pleasant as there is a wide variety of trees, shrubs and wildflowers as well as an abundance of rosella parrots.

Start a walk at the Morton National Park's main entrance at the south end of Church Street, Bundanoon, where there is an unmanned Rangers Station, a picnic ground and a camp area. Take the left fork at the entrance for 650 metres then leave the gravelled road and follow a foot track for 850 metres down to Fairy Bower, a pleasant little waterfall area, with Spooner Lookout providing valley views. Retrace 100 metres then turn south-west uphill. In 400 metres you should rejoin the tourist road. Next, follow the road south to Sunrise Point Lookout 500 metres away, then to Grand Canyon Lookout and a further 200 metres walk to the Fern Glen. The glen is south of the lookout just upstream along the gully which meets the cliffline in the area. As the name suggests, it is ferny and has rock overhangs. Head along the road north-west 700 metres then turn left on another road, following it 500 metres to another intersection. Then go left 200 metres again and finally 550 metres to Beauchamps Cliffs Lookout and Bonnieview Lookout, which are only 100 metres apart. These two lookouts give good valley views especially to the south-west. Just 15 metres from the car park, a sign indicates a trail to Echo Point. Follow it for 750 metres to emerge on the Echo Point access road then turn left and in 300 metres you should be at Echo Point for another south-westerly view. To finish the walk simply follow the Echo Point access road back north-east then north 2.0 kilometres to the park entry. To really appreciate this walk, try and avoid choosing a busy public holiday in summer when the dusty gravelled roads can mar an otherwise pleasant day.

MAP REF: **Bundanoon map provided with this publication.** Map 34.

WALK DISTANCE: 7.5 km.

GRADING: One day, easy.

62 BUNDANOON — GLOW WORM GLEN — BUCHANANS LOOKOUT

Bundanoon, on the Southern Tablelands, has a number of interesting walk venues, all of which are short but good. The main focus is the cliff line of Bundanoon Creek. Buchanans Lookout is one rarely visited, and is not even mentioned in Morton National Park literature yet it is as good as any of the other vantage points. Additionally, one must pass Glow Worm Glen about midway between the town and the lookout.

Start walking at Bundanoon Railway Station and head north-east along the main Mossvale Road for 400 metres then veer east along William Street and continue to its end. A good trail leads east from the end of William Street, passing along an easement between farmland then entering Morton National Park at the bottom of the hill. It then is only 150 metres distance east to Glow Worm Glen which is a cool ferny gorge with rock overhangs. The glow worm display is very good but of course is only visible at night. Retrace about 50 metres to the uppermost pipe handrail at some steps and, about four metres down from the handrail, there is a red metal marker. It is at the start of the track to Buchanans Lookout but, because of boulders and the magnitude of the main track, it is difficult to see. Soon it leads down to Dimmocks Creek, just upstream of the Glow Worm Glen, and crosses the creek on a badly deteriorated bridge made from two logs. It then leads up steps eastwards into dry forested areas and swings south-east to follow the contour. In 400 metres a paddock should be noted on the left. It is a good navigation guide as the track is hard to follow due to many cattle pads crossing it but, for nearly a kilometres, the paddock remains about 25 to 50 metres from the track. It is then only 400 metres slightly downhill east-south-east to the lookout. The last 1.4 kilometres of the track is through dry forest and there are no markers so navigation needs care. The lookout view is mainly down on top of the lovely stretches of Bundanoon Creek, some 300 metres below. The forests in the valley are obviously quite lush and their beauty can be appreciated from above by all the varied colours of green present.

It is suggested that you make the lookout your lunch spot or dinner spot depending upon whether you want to return to the Glow Worm Glen late enough to see the glow worm display. Carry a torch for each member of the party if you intend remaining in the area after dark. To finish the walk simply retrace your route back up William Street and to town.

MAP REF: *Bundanoon map provided with this publication.* Map 34.

WALK DISTANCE: 7 km.

GRADING: One day, easy.

63 OALLEN—SHOALHAVEN RIVER—WELCOME

Many stretches of the Shoalhaven River have excellent scenery and are very pleasant places to visit but generally are fairly inaccessible. Such is not the case at Oallen, which is readily accessible and has the added interest of being an old goldfield; hence the name Welcome. In the future the area should become well-known as the second stage of the Metropolitan Water Sewerage and Drainage Board Shoalhaven Water Supply Scheme is planned for completion in the 1980's. It will involve the construction of a large dam some 10.0 kilometres upstream of this suggested walk location, and the purpose of the dam is to regularies the river flow into dams downstream, so perhaps this walk area will not be spoiled. Oallen is south-east of Goulburn on the Goulburn-Nerriga Road and the recommended walk starting point·is at Oallen Ford where the road crosses the wide Shoalhaven bed. The spot has good swimming, long beaches and is ideal for camping—on the south bank. Debris lying high up the river banks gives some indication of the fury of the river when in flood. The walk route involves no necessity for navigation experience as you need only follow the south bank of the river south-east then east until you reach the mouth of Ningee Nimble Creek which flows in from the south at Welcome Homestead ruin. The whole of the distance is easy walking and it caters very well for those wanting to swim and laze on a hot day. When you reach Ningee Nimble Creek 4.75 kilometres from the walk start follow it south a few hundred metres to the gravelled Goulburn-Nerriga Road then turn west and follow the road back to the walk starting point. There are pine plantations between the road and the Shoalhaven for about half the distance back and you should also pass Oallen Homestead on the left.

MAP REF: *Oallen map provided with this publication.* Map 37.

WALK DISTANCE: 10.0 km.

GRADING: One day, easy.

64 MITCHELLS LOOKOUT—MORTON NATIONAL PARK

The Morton National Park is quite a large park and has within its boundaries some of the best walking country in New South Wales. The park is however, largely isolated and access to walk areas is extremely difficult especially because former trafficable roads have been allowed to deteriorate, or are now cut off by surrounding private property. Places such as The Castle and Mount Owen are, of course, well-known to experienced bush walkers but are only visited on extended trips whereas, in the mid-1960s, it was feasible to take a day walk to Mount Owen. One access route which remains allows a day visitor to see the rugged country from a high vantage point and thus gain some appreciation of the great beauty of the district. The access road, however, is for dry weather only and even then must be travelled very cautiously as there are rock ribs across the road. The road commences at Sassafras on the Nerriga to Nowra Road and leads south 10.9 kilometres to the base of a hill, near Newhaven Gap. There is an unlocked gate across the road end at Sassafras and the spot looks more like a farm entrance. A very old house is on the south-west corner, a newer shed on the south-east corner and an old shed opposite. A sign on a tree opposite the turnoff displays a reference: 6/329.322. As a guide during your approach, it should be remembered that the turnoff is just 100 metres west of the highest point on the road through Sassafras and eight kilometres west of Tianjara Falls.

The road south from Sassafras gets far too rough for conventional vehicles and so walking must begin at about the 10.5 to 11.0 kilometre stage.

A further 500 metres along the road as it leads south-west a minor foot track leads off uphill to the left (south) and there is a sign on a tree indicating the way to Folly Point. There is also a bulldozed side bay just ten metres past the turnoff. The area was burned out in 1976 but does not spoil the walk because the burnt section is regrowing vigorously.

Follow the pad up over the western end of a hill and then across a broad, flattish valley sloping west. Wooden stakes and square metal markers indicate the route south across the regenerated grasslands, and there are expansive views. Soon the pad leads up to a small saddle. Banksia and many wildflowers flourish and Christmas bells make a particularly good show at the appropriate time of the year. The pad continues its general southward route among low hillocks on a plateau then, 3.0 kilometres from the road, arrives at the top of a hill with steep southern slopes down to a saddle. This is Mitchells Lookout. The view is especially good to the south and east. There are a host of peaks to the south, The Castle, Mount Cole and Castle Rock being the most obvious. To the south-east is Pigeon House Mountain with its 'pimple' on top, and to the east is the Clyde River Gorge, way below. The scenery will no doubt make you want to continue on the foot pad but from this point on, walking is considerably harder, due to many ascents and descents and because the track becomes poorly defined in places and so requires good navigation. It is therefore suggested that you have lunch then retrace your route.

MAP REF: *Budawangs map provided with this publication.* Map 38A.

WALK DISTANCE: 7 km.

GRADING: One day, easy.

65   BADGERYS LOOKOUT—SHOALHAVEN RIVER

The Shoalhaven River near Marulan assumes grand proportions and has eroded a gorge about 500 metres deep. The valley is quite steep-sided and winding but the river bed is relatively broad with lovely, sandy beaches and delightful camping spots. It provides endless possibilities for swimming, fishing, sunbaking, climbing, photography and even floating about on airbeds; the catch is that to return from the river you must ascend 500 metres. Most people are deterred by the climb so you could have a paradise virtually to yourselves.

Some 7.0 kilometres south of Tallong Railway Sta-

220

tion, a small town on the main southern railway, is Badgerys Lookout. It is a little-visited lookout on the gorge rim. There are several other places one could descend to the river by foot track but this route is the shortest and hence the steepest. It is only 2.5 kilometres from the lookout to the riverside.

The lookout carpark has picnic facilities but no water. Next to a picnic table and seats at the western end of the carpark the trail starts by leading north down into a gully, then turns west to follow that gully and swings south right around the western end of the knob on which the lookout is situated. It then sidles on to Badgerys Spur and descends generally southwards to the river. Despite the short distance involved, you should allow well over an hour for the steep, slow climb out later.

MAP REF: *Shoalhaven Gorge map provided with this publication.* Map 35.
WALK DISTANCE: 5.0 km.
GRADING: One day, medium.

66   LONG POINT—SHOALHAVEN RIVER

If you enjoy a lazy time by a magnificent river with white sandy beaches, plenty of swimming, lovely grassy flats and virtually no-one else about, you will enjoy a visit to the Shoalhaven Gorge near Marulan. Several access trails to the river exist, but all involve an ascent of 500 metres back out of the gorge again and this climb deters most people. The trail from Long Point Lookout is extremely well graded. It is, therefore, the longest, but, it makes the ascent back out relatively easy and few tracks anywhere, in terrain as rugged as the Shoalhaven, could compare for grade.

Long Point Lookout is 5.7 kilometres south of Tallong Railway Station, a small town on the main southern railway. There are tank water and picnic facilities at the lookout.

The track from the lookout to the river is 4.0 kilometres long and has a number of zig-zags. It starts at the lookout carpark and leads south-west on a prominent ridge. At first you actually climb a little and two alternative tracks can be taken for the first 300 metres. One stays on the tops and spur crest and the other minor pad sidles around the southern slopes of a knob. The forks then join on a sharply defined spur, turn south, lead into a saddle and then descend gradually down the western and southern slopes of Kingpin Mountain which is really just part of the Long Point Spur. The trail meets the river just at the confluence of Barbers Creek, from where there are lovely grassy flats to the east and sandy beaches to the west. The choice is yours as to how you spend the day before returning back up the spur. The climb should take about one hour fifteen minutes, depending on the walkers.

MAP REF: *Shoalhaven Gorge map provided with this publication.* Map 35.

WALK DISTANCE: 8 km.

GRADING: One day, medium.

67 FOLLY POINT—MORTON NATIONAL PARK

Walk number 64 to Mitchells Lookout provides track notes for the first half of this walk suggestion and, as mentioned in those notes, the aim is to view the wonderful country in the vicinity of The Castle in the Budawangs. However, south of Mitchells Lookout, the foot track would be hard for inexperienced walkers to follow. The route continues to be blazed with square metal markers, has a number of pink arrows painted on rocks and has many small rock cairns. However, marking is far from clear in parts and it is extremely easy to lose the track, but for those who persevere, Folly Point is some 4.0 kilometres further towards The Castle and the views become really superb.

Follow track notes according to the Mitchells Lookout walk then descend the south-eastern slopes from the viewpoint towards a saddle. A wide, open, grassy gully slants westwards from the saddle and the track swings down through some of the grass. Some wooden stakes show the way as the track swings south then south-east up a grassy side gully to arrive at a knob right alongside the Clyde River Gorge edge. The route then follows the top of the knob, descends into a small saddle and ascends a second knob, remains on the rocky top, then descends south-east down the crest of a spur to a deeper saddle. Excellent views of Pigeon House Mountain can be seen from the spur top. At the saddle the pad swings west and rises only slightly then, strangely, heads north-west down the northern edge of a rocky gully and suddenly 'dives' into, and up, the other side of the gully and continues westwards. It next turns south, basically sidling round just below the treeline on a well-wooded high hill. In parts there are soaks draining down the western slopes and the track can easily be missed in boggy conditions or among the vigorously growing grasses and ferns. The main form of guide in the area is the square metal marker on trees but there are a few stakes too. Soon the pad heads south-east into more rocky country and on to a long narrow saddle. The trees cease and scrub and grass make the pad quite hard to follow. Rock cairns, and occasional pink painted arrows, show the way south, until you arrive at a reasonably large, flat, rock clearing with a rock cairn on it and a metal sign implanted in the rock. The sign, however, is only about 30 cm high and is impossible to see from any approach. The sign points west to Folly Point but actually the lookout point is on a bearing of 210° magnetic and there is no track to it. You must cross bare rock and shrubs for 200 metres and it is suggested that you make the viewpoint your lunch spot before retracing your route.

MAP REF: *Budawangs map provided with this publication.* Map 38A and Map 38B.

WALK DISTANCE: 15 km.

GRADING: One day, medium.

68   BUNGONIA LOOKDOWN — BUNGONIA GORGE

Bungonia Lookdown is a lookout 11.0 kilometres from the small town of Bungonia, east of Goulburn. The lookout is within a reserve which has some interesting caves in it, but the major attraction is the superb view down into the gorges of Bungonia Creek and the Shoalhaven River. In this area, the Shoalhaven has eroded a gorge some 500 metres deep and Bungonia Creek similarly has eroded very deeply. Bungonia Creek, however, has formed a canyon and it is the canyon area, primarily, that this walk suggestion covers. There are three routes down to the gorge but one from nearby Adams Lookout north is extremely steep and awkward and is not recommended. Adams lookout, however, has the best view of Bungonia Canyon. The other two lead off jointly southeast from

224

Bungonia Lookdown itself. Red markers on trees show the way. The trail remains fairly level near clifflines for 400 metres then sidles up a little, round a knob where there is a track fork. The left fork, which continues to have red markers, should be followed in preference to the right fork with white marks. The right fork leads over the southern slopes of Mount Ayre then descends. The descent via the left fork is initially into the head-waters of a gully eastwards, then the trail swings north and sidles down the slopes of Mount Ayre on to a spur. Bungonia Creek is then reached in a little over a kilometre. You should then turn west and follow the creek right through the canyon where it is suggested you have lunch. Huge boulders slow progress in the Troy Walls area. The canyon is very narrow and has pools which may occasionally require a swim if you are to go right through. After a good look around, and perhaps a swim if it is hot, head downstream, along sandy beaches to the mouth of Bungonia Creek and the Shoalhaven River, where there is a lovely small grassy flat, fine beaches and excellent swimming. A quarry nearby blasts periodically so obey signs and sirens. It should take up to one and a half hours to ascend back up to Bungonia Lookdown. The climb is steep at first, too, so if it is a hot day wet a towel in the river just before you leave. It will be useful to wipe your face, as you climb. The track leaves right from the confluence of the two streams and, at first, fol-lows the crest of a very sharp little ridge. As you walk the ridge you have the streams on either side of you, then, about 300 metres south, you should cross a narrow saddle and ascend straight up the steep spur south then south-westwards. Once at a knob about 600 metres from the saddle, the trail swings just south of west and is relatively flat for a little while until it approaches Mount Ayre where it again becomes steep. It finally passes just south of the summit of Mount Ayre, descends a little then rejoins the outward route. Some 400 metres north-west sees you back at Bungonia Lookdown where, if you again peer over the edge, you will be amazed at the country you have just traversed.

MAP REF: *Bungonia Gorge map provided with this publication.* Map 36.

WALK DISTANCE: 7 km.

GRADING: One day, hard.

69   LONG POINT—SHOALHAVEN RIVER— BUNGONIA GORGE

The Shoalhaven River has eroded a gorge 500 metres deep near Marulan. At a number of places sidestreams, such as Ettrema and Bungonia Creeks, have carved impressive ravines on their way to the mighty Shoalhaven. This walk suggestion, like other overnight recommendations in this book, must surely be one of New South Wales' best walks. The Shoalhaven has lovely, white, sandy beaches and camping places and Bungonia Gorge would probably rank as one of the most rugged anywhere in Australia. Take your bathers, a lightweight airbed for floating about on the river and a bath towel (rather than a huge beach towel).

Long Point Lookout, 5.7 kilometres south of the small town of Tallong on the main southern railway, is perhaps the easiest place from which to descend to the Shoalhaven as the track is well graded. The track leads off south-west from the lookout carpark which has picnic facilities and tank water on a prominent ridge. Within the first 100 metres of walking, the track divides. The left minor fork sidles down the southern slopes of a knob whilst the right main fork follows the crest. Both tracks re-unite within 300 metres on a sharply defined spur and then lead down south into a saddle. Kingpin Mountain, which is really just part of the Long Point Spur, is then skirted via its western and southern slopes. There are a couple of minor uphill grades to cross gullies and there are a number of zig-zags before the trail emerges at the confluence of Barbers Creek and the Shoalhaven River, some 4.0 kilometres from the carpark.

Whilst the area near the bottom of the trail is very pleasant, it is suggested that you follow the river's north bank upstream for 2.0 kilometres to the mouth of Bungonia Creek. Along the way there are magnificent sandy beaches and perfect swimming places so it is suggested that you linger and enjoy it. At the mouth of Bungonia Creek there is not only sand and swimming places but also a lovely grassy camping place. It is suggested that you establish camp there and, after lunch, set off without packs and, perferably, in just bathers and sandshoes (providing it is warm enough) up Bungonia Creek. Initially, it is easy walking simply following the stream bed and beaches but, in 2.0 kilometres, you should reach the start of the Canyon area at Troy Walls. From this point upstream the scenery is breathtaking and the walking becomes far more difficult. Huge boulders slow progress but aim to get right through the canyon. Go as far upstream as time permits but ensure you at least reach a point 3.0 kilometres from the Shoalhaven so that you get a good idea of this incredible place. Return to camp in idyllic gorge surroundings.

Next morning you should return to the base of Long
Point Spur by about mid-afternoon. Lunch should be
somewhere by the river, and plenty of time should be
spent swimming and floating about on that airbed.
Fishing may interest you, too. If the weather is cooler,
you could take a stroll upstream along the Shoalhaven
beyond Bungonia Creek or wander along the lovely
grassy flats downstream from the base of the Long
Spur. When you must leave this paradise, allow at
least one hour fifteen minutes for the climb back out
to Long Spur Lookout.

MAP REF: *Shoalhaven Gorge an Bungonia Gorge
maps provided with this publication.* Maps 35 and
36.

WALK DISTANCE: 18 km.

GRADING: Two days, medium.

70   NEWHAVEN GAP—MONOLITH VALLEY

Some of the best walking country in New South Wales
lies within the bounds of Morton National Park. Such
places as The Castle and Mount Owen are quite well
known to experienced bushwalkers. However, the
district is remote and reaching the main points of
interest requires at least an overnight walk. One of the
best approaches is from the Newhaven Gap area,
south of Sassafras on the Nowra to Nerriga Road.
This route, however, requires use of a very rough
access road and the start of the road is difficult to
locate. The rough road starts at Sassafras and looks
like a farm entrance as an unlocked gate exists at the
spot. It is eight kilometres west of Tianjara Falls and
there is a building on each side of the gate as well as
one opposite. You then need to travel 10.9 kilometres
south along this dry-weather-only road. Here the road

becomes too rough to continue in conventional vehicles and walking must begin.

Initially, follow the road, basically south-west, through open country. Within about a kilometre pass the Folly Point foot track turnoff left, and keep walking roughly south-west to cross Camping Rock Creek some 3.5 kilometres from the walk start. A camp spot exists as the jeep track veers west and heads on from the creek. A little further on and to the left is conspicuous Camp Rock with its rock overhang facing the jeep track. One kilometre onwards ignore a left fork which rejoins the main jeep track within a couple of hundred metres. The deviation provides access by a short pad to a beautiful clearing. Head on north-west up through rain forest for 300 metres to fork left onto another jeep track at a hillcrest. Climb west amid eucalypts to a hilltop where the jeep track becomes a foot pad. The pad has no track markers and descends south-west into more rain forest, then basically contours around the headwaters of Kilpatrick Creek then rises onto a ridge some two kilometres from the jeep track junction. At this point the pad broadens to become the Styles Creek jeep track and it should be followed for 1.5 kilometres down to Styles Creek. The forest is left just before the creek ford an expansive views of cliff lines occur. Camp areas exist on both sides of the ford, and the spot would be excellent for a lunch break.

Next follow the jeep track south, then south-west, for 500 metres up to a small crest in the midst of open country. Some 1.3 kilometres due south is a wooded ridge rising westwards to Mount Houghton's eastern cliff lines base. Walk across country to this ridge crossing upper Styles Creek in the process. There is no defined pad. Once on the wooded ridge a foot track starts right on the crest and should be followed for 500 metres up to the cliff base westwards. There is a waterless camp cave at the cliff base.

Follow the unmarked pad south-west around the eastern cliff base of Mount Houghton past tiny streams, through damp forest and to the south west end of the mountain. It is about 1.3 kilometres distance but quite slow walking and near the cliff base all the way. Near the end of this sector is an interesting rock amphi-theatre. Next turn south-east and descend the track across a saddle and climb up to cliffs on the north end of Mount Tairn 700 metres away. Follow the cliff base a little to the right then ascend through them onto the open plateau of Mount Tairn. Walk south across the plateau for 700 metres, then swing south west through a gap between two rocky ridges. These ridges are aligned north-south. From the gap a huge anvil shaped rock can be seen westwards on Mount Tairn's summit. Walk west 250 metres towards this rock, crossing a gully in a heathy area. Next turn south for 100 metres following small rock marker cairns, then again turn west for another 100 metres to cross another gully. Head down this gully 100 metres and descend the southern cliffs of the plateau via a small waterfall which is often dry. The going is a little awkward, but ropes are not needed. Turn west along the cliff base for 400 metres to the top of a spur at the south-west end of Mount Tairn. Swing south-south-east down the eucalypt covered spur pad and onto an open ridge. Join the foot track from Wog Wog which enters from the west some 1.5 kilometres from Mount Tairn's cliffs.

Walk south-east through eucalypts then down across a gully, and on down across a deep saddle and up to the base of the cliffs of Mount Cole (Mount

Roswaine). It is 1.3 kilometres from the track junction to the cliff base. Two routes exist from this point to Monolith Valley which lies on the other side of Mount Cole. The northern route is the easiest but both routes are of about two kilometres length. The northern track simply leads to the left round the cliff base north-east, swings east up through a gap then swings south between Mount Cole and The Seven Gods to reach the Monolith Valley Campsite. The southern route leads right 400 metres round the cliff base south-west to the second of two ravines. Climb up through this ravine. Halfway up, sloping sandstone rock must be scaled to get above sheer sectors. The sloping rock could prove dangerous when wet. At the crest of the ravine turn south up a smaller side ravine to gain access to the plateau of Mount Owen (Mount Renwick). Rock marker cairns should then be followed south-east then east for 800 metres then down a steeply disected ravine northwards to rejoin the main ravine which separates Mount Cole and Mount Owen.

Turn east next and walk into the Monolith Valley campsite making sure that you do not turn south down a right fork pad in the main canyon after 200 metres, but rather climb up and over a little rise. A second right fork pad just short of the camp should also be ignored. It leads uphill onto adjacent rocky vantage points.

Monolith Valley is an area of incredible sandstone formations and as much time as possible should be spent exploring among them. The longer one lingers in this valley, the more one marvels at its grandeur so spend as long as you can discovering its wonders, even though you are tired after the long day's walk.

On the second day retrace day one's route, except that the alternative route around Mount Cole could be used. The wise course of action would be to avoid the southern route if it is wet. It cannot be over-emphasised that this walk suggestion as a whole is only suited to experienced bushwalkers skilled at navigation.

MAP REF: *Budawangs map provided with this publication.* Maps 38A and Map 38B.

WALK DISTANCE: 39 km.

GRADING: Two days, hard.

71 THE BREADKNIFE

Near Coonabarabran is the Warrumbungle National Park. It is an area of volcanic spires, domes and mesas, all of which are the remains of composite volcanic activity about 13,000,000 years ago. Formations such as the Breadknife are dykes developed along cracks in a volcanic cone. The lava was a viscous, trachyte type containing a lot of silica which caused rapid hardening. In many cases, hardening blocked the throat of volcanic vents and, with the passing of time, the surrounding area was eroded leaving the lava plugs. Such features as Belougery Spire and Crater Bluff are excellent examples.

The park is noted for a wide variety of flora and fauna and grey kangaroos, echidnas, wedge-tailed eagles and galahs abound. Cypress pines, grass trees and ironbark are common. Generally speaking, the park is quite dry and water is often a problem. Any walking on hot summer days is, therefore, not the best.

Canyon Camp on Wambelong Creek is the park centre and just east of it is Camp Blackman, the main camping area. There is also accommodation available in cabins at Canyon Camp. The cabins are actually old Sydney trams. Other less developed camps exist. The park has an excellent system of good tracks, especially radiating from Camp Pincham 3.1 kilometres south-east of the Canyon Camp entrance. This walk to the Breadknife starts at Camp Pincham and, although it scales the heights above the Breadknife, it is not very hard. Make sure you carry some water when you leave Camp Pincham, heading south along the Spirey Creek valley. There is a tap right at the start of the track, just before the track crosses to the east bank of the usually-dry stream.

After 400 metres of walking, fork left upwards; then, in 300 metres, fork right, avoiding the signposted Macha Tor track. Continue south and pass the Bress Peak track after 800 metres and pass the Macha Tor return track after 200 more metres. Some 700 metres further south, avoid the signposted Spirey View Lookout track heading off east uphill, and after another 900 metres you should arrive at the foot of the climb at the turnoff to Hurleys Camp where there is a bush camp often used by rock climbers. So far the track will have been of excellent standard through wooded country and wildflowers.

It is a further kilometre to a track junction at the lower end of the Breadknife but there is a steep climb involved. Excellent views of Belougery Spire and western cliffs plus a seat at Wilsons Rest all help to make this climb more pleasant. Cypress pines also provide some shade. Fork left uphill and, in 400 metres, you will arrive at Lughs Hut, which is just a roof and drinking water supply. It is at the top of the main blade of the Breadknife. However, you need to climb a little further for spectacular views. Follow the track east around the base of another blade parallel to, and south-east of, the Breadknife and, as you reach its top end, walk 10 metres west up on to the blade for a view. Next continue up some rocky slopes following paint marks showing the track route and, within a few metres, you will arrive at the Grand High Tops. A wonderful view is obtained from the knob at this point. It is about the best view in the park and is particularly good towards the Breadknife. Belougery Spire, of course, is in full view as it has been for much of the ascent. It is suggested that you have lunch (no water supply) at this point, then head 628 metres west, initially along the tops, then down to Dagda Gap. There is a sign at the gap; '5.4 km to Camp Pincham' (via the Dagda short-cut track). Follow it down as it sidles to the lower end of the Breadknife. There is a hut (Balor Hut) at this point, a kilometre from Dagda Gap. The hut can be used as an overnight stop if required and if previously arranged with the Park Ranger. Drinking water is also available there. Just around the lower end of the Breadknife, you rejoin your outward route which should be followed for the 4.3 kilometres back to Camp Pincham.

MAP REF: *Warrumbungle map provided with this publication.* Map 39.

WALK DISTANCE: 11 km.

GRADING: One day, easy.

72   MOUNT KAPUTAR — BUNDABULLA LOOKOUT

Rising out of the north-west plains, east of Narrabri, is the Mount Kaputar National Park. It is a volcanic park centred on Dawsons Spring 53 kilometres from Narrabri. The whole area is a heavily-eroded one which has left trachyte plugs and massive lava flows. Dawsons Spring is the site of the Ranger's office and camping facilities. It is also the starting point for this walk suggesiton, featuring alpine vegetation and extensive views, combined with volcanic interest. The highest peak in the park is reached on this walk and at such a height (1524 metres) snow gums are very common. Wildflowers also proliferate including the vivid purple false sarsaparilla.

At the Dawsons Spring camp ground you will notice a shed to the north-west, across the creek which flows through the area (and over a small waterfall). Cross to the shed, then walk up a jeep track which heads uphill to the north-west to the main Narrabri road—within 400 metres and at a sign: '4670 feet'. Cross the main road and continue on a jeep track while it initially runs parallel to the main road. Then it swings to the right and scales a spur. Within 400 metres you will meet the tourist road to Mount Kaputar itself. It is a one-way road at this point, used by uphill traffic only. Follow it up for a very short distance to arrive at the summit carpark. Next, walk up the 20-metre-long track to the peak top for a 360° view at the summit cairn. The view to the west, along the clifflines, is perhaps the best but, to the south, can be seen the TV tower and the general area of the rest of this walk which, from now on, becomes considerably easier. Just 25 metres north of the cairn is another knob which you should definitely inspect. It provides superb views to the north-east of the clifflines and valleys. Snow gums and everlastings are also present.

Return to the summit carpark and turn left down the exit one-way road. In 250 metres, the road becomes a two-way road and you should continue downhill for 400 metres to the Narrabri Road. Walk south for 500 metres to the turnoff into Dawsons Spring Camp but turn left (east) at this point. The short road east leads into a carpark and the start of the foot track to Mount Lindsay.

Follow the foot track through an area abounding in trigger plants and, in 200 metres, turn right on the signposted track, to Bundabulla Lookout 1.5 kilometres. This fairly good track is extremely pleasant. It leads through areas of rocky outcrops and hosts of wildflowers as it gradually descends southwards. Soon, the track mounts some rocks and views to the southeast become superb. Bundabulla Lookout is down the slopes a little from the roughly contouring track but a loop track exists to the lookout. It is far better to take the loop than to short-cut and miss the views. The ascent after the lookout is quite gradual and easy. There are a number of white posts in the area to indicate the route as the track is often on open grass slopes and rocks. Bundabulla Lookout is 300 metres from the main track and, from the lookout, views over the 150-metre-high cliffs are excellent. There are many rocky ridges in view. To return to the main track, follow painted marks on the rocks which lead you, roughly, straight towards the TV towers which are in view. Once on the main track again, turn left (west) and follow white posts across delightful grassy areas full of wildflowers such as bluebells, fringed lilies and pincushions. After 350 metres of virtually flat walking, you will arrive at Eckfords Lookout which is at the top of a cliff about 300 metres high and which again gives excellent views. There is a sign at the lookout indicating the way to Dawsons Spring and the track should be taken uphill towards the TV tower. Shortly before reaching the tower there is a track junction and the left fork should be taken. It sidles round the west side of the tower to another track junction and an Aboriginal bora ground—a ceremonial place. It is interesting that the ancient bora ground should be right at the base of one of modern man's TV pylon stays.

To end the walk, head west past the Bora Ground, following painted markers at the edge of some cliffs, then descend steeply through a forest for about 300 metres to emerge in the camp ground west of the Ranger's Office.

MAP REF: *Mt Kaputar map provided with this publication.* Map 40.

WALK DISTANCE: 6.5 km.

GRADING: One day, easy.

73   CORRUNBRAL BORAWAH (THE GOVERNOR)

East of Narrabri is the southern section of the Mount Kaputar National Park. The Park is a vastly eroded remnant of an old volcano and features trachyte intrusions and lava flows. Mount Kaputar itself reaches 1524 metres above sea level and so can be subject to snow in winter. Snow gums grow profusely on the high points. The Park centre is at Dawsons Spring where there are camping facilities and the Ranger's office. Aboriginals once inhabited the area and named it the Nundawar which is today corrupted to Nandewar Ranges. An Aboriginal bora ground still exists near the television tower on one of the highest rocky peaks.

To really appreciate this park one definitely needs to walk to several vantage points and to walk amongst the volcanic wonders which are, of course, in areas too rough for cars to reach.

Corrunbral Borawah (also called the Governor) is a spectacular peak resulting from lava flows. It is, perhaps, the most interesting point one can walk to without having to really exert oneself. It also provides spectacular views.

From Dawsons Spring Campground, go 3.7 kilometres back down the Narrabri Road to a road turnoff to the north where a sign indicates the way to the Governor. Then drive 100 metres north to a carpark to start this walk which is only 3 kilometres long. However it is over rocky terrain and consequently takes about two hours to complete if taken slowly.

To appreciate the area fully, it is suggested that, initially, you walk 300 metres north-north-east up the road to a spectacular lookout beside some repeater station towers and power pylons. The view is over the northern cliffs and towards Corrunbral Borawah to the west. Next return to the carpark and a sign which says: '1 km to the Governor'.

Follow a good, wide track west-south-west for about 400 metres to a sign advising that rock climbing with ropes etc., on the Governor is prohibited. It will be obvious to all visitors to the park that it lends itself well to rock climbing. The foot track narrows near the sign and descends south-west through some rocky parts where yellow everlastings abound in early summer. A short ladder is next encountered and you should descend it, cross a small saddle at the base of a cliffline then climb another ladder up out of the saddle. There is a good view towards Euglah Rock to the south from this area. White paint marks indicate the route up the rocky slopes on to Corrunbral Borawah's summit. There are two knobs on the summit and both should be visited to ensure that the best views are obtained. A lunch break on the top (without a water supply) could be most enjoyable before retracing the outward route back to the carpark. While you have your lunch you may be lucky enough to see one of the birds of prey which are fairly common in the park and, as you wander through the gums towards the carpark, you will probably see some of the parrots which are very common.

MAP REF: *Mt Kaputar map provided with this publication.* Map 40.

WALK DISTANCE: 3 km.

GRADING: One day, easy.

74   CORYAH GAP—MOUNT CORYAH CIRCUIT

Mount Kaputar National Park, east of Narrabri, is renowned as a volcanic park. There are many trachyte intrusions which have left spectacular plugs jutting skywards.

As the road climbs up the mountains towards the Park centre at Dawsons Springs, it crosses Coryah Gap 6 kilometres short of the centre. At the gap there is an entrance arch to the park, a sign indicating that the point is 3850 feet above sea level and a carpark.

This walk suggestion enables the walker to see large sections of the park form the tops and the incredible Yulludunida Crater depths, to the west of Mount Coryah. A sign at the carpark states that it is 3.2 kilometres to Mount Coryah but it appears that the sign exaggerates the distance. A more accurate distance may be 2.5 kilometres. It is a steep climb and at least two hours should be allowed for walking time. Lunch on the tops could be worthwhile but there is no water supply.

Initially, walk westwards uphill on the narrow foot track from the carpark. The track leads through a forested area with many wildflowers. After about a kilometre the track becomes much steeper and steps have been cut to make the walk easier. It rises up through rocks to the base of the summit cliffs of Mount Coryah. A track junction is met at this point. Turn left and walk downhill along the base of the cliffs. Soon you must scale more steps up past the cliffs and on to the summit ridge which is broad and forested. Continue over the ridge and down the foot track to arrive soon at a lookout down the western slopes. The view is of Yulludunida Crater. It is quite spectacular and this could be a pleasant spot for lunch.

Next, walk back uphill, still following the track. Soon it starts to sidle along the base of the cliffline on the northern side of Mount Coryah. Views to the north become very good and grasstrees, some of which must be hundreds of years old, abound along the cliff base. There are several rock overhangs, too. Just before the track swings back south-east, there is a very good view of the Narrabri Road about 400 metres— virtually straight below. The track then rejoins the outward route and you should then simply retrace your outward route back to the Coryah Gap carpark. You will have noted that the circuit track does not reach the actual summit of Mount Coryah. In fact the peak is surrounded on three sides by cliffs and the only access is through trees and scrub from the south west. Unless you are a 'peak bagger' there is probably little point in including the summit in the walk itinerary.

MAP REF: *Mt. Kaputar map provided with this publication.* Map 40.
WALK DISTANCE: 5 km.
GRADING: One day, easy.

75 MOUNT WARNING

A glance at the Tweed Heads National Mapping 1:250,000 map sheet reveals the immensity of a vast ancient (early tertiary) volcano which we are told last erupted about twenty three million years ago. It is on the border of northern New South Wales and southern Queensland. The Tweed River and other streams have eroded the central explosion crater making it larger, but leaving an 'island' of the more acid lava rock dome, now called Mount Warning. The old mountain once attained about 2000 metres or nearly twice the present 1156 metres height. The flanks of the old mountain's basaltic dome remain along the State border in the form of the McPherson Range and Tweed Range, but erosion has created great low angle spurs (or Planeze) with deep gorges between. Such dramatic features as the Pinnacle mark the rim of the eroded crater where the harder surface rocks have given way. The erosion caldera is about 30 kilometres in diameter.

A most informative and enjoyable day walk to Mount Warning can be taken from the Breakfast Creek car park serving the National Park which encompasses the peak. Access is via Murwillumbah and the south arm of the Tweed River valley, then up the valley of Karrumbyn Creek. Many Gold Coast visitors find the walk to be an excellent day's outing during their stay.

An excellent foot track leads from the car park to the summit and is 4.4 kilometres long. It is well graded except for the last short steep ascent above 1000 metres elevation which has a chain handhold to assist with scaling sloping rocks. Seats along the way and kilometre markers also help make the walk enjoyable. Rain forest is abundant and is confined to the igneous rock areas of the main peak and associated peaks where soil depth and moisture is adequate. The upper rock faces feature shrubby and grassy plants such as tussock grass, grass tree, blunt leaf mountain wattles, tea trees and broad leaved cassinias. Views occur only on the upper reaches and at the summit where there are spectacular views to the explosion crater walls which on average, are 15 kilometres distant. The North Coast of New South Wales and the Queensland, Gold Coast are within view as is the Tweed River and the town of Murwillumbah. The summit of Mount Warning, by reason of elevation and easterly aspect, is the first part of the Australian mainland to receive sun rays at dawn. The summit would be the ideal place for lunch, water needs to carried. There is no branch track and walkers need simply climb and descend via the same route. At least four hours should be set aside for the return walk.

MAP REF: ***Mount Warning map provided with this publication.*** Map 41.

WALK DISTANCE: 8.8 km.

GRADING: One day, easy.

76   TIA FALLS

The New England plateau has been deeply eroded by numerous streams flowing to the Pacific coast. The erosion has been great and such rivers as the Tia have cut tremendous gorges which provide spectacular walking places.

The Tia River is crossed by the Oxley Highway south-east of Walcha and, 1.3 kilometres further south-east along the highway a signpost indicates the way to Tia Falls. The side road is actually the old Oxley Highway for the first 300 metres, then you should turn right (north-east) and follow the falls road for 4.0 kilometres to a gate at Old Wombi Homestead. Go through the gate (leaving it how you found it), then go a further kilometre north-west to an undeveloped picnic area close to Tia falls. The falls themselves cannot be seen from this point and in fact, even with a short walk, cannot be seen properly.

This walk suggestion enables you to obtain superb views of the entire falls and the incredible valley downstream. First, it is recommended that you follow the tourist track north 200 metres to see the head of the falls and a very limited section of the gorge; then return and start to walk east around the contour following as closely as possible the gorge rim. There are some animal pads which make walking easier and there are some kangaroos in the area. The Tia River curves northwards around in a big bend, and so a 'peninsula' exists, east of the main falls. Smaller falls occur near the northern tip of the peninsula and, on the east side of the peninsula, the gorge is about 500 metres deep. It is, therefore, suggested that you continue to walk as closely as is safe around the rim of the gorge. By the time you reach the northern end of the peninsula, views of the main falls are spectacular and their whole drop is visible. Further around the rim the lower falls come into view, then the main downstream gorge appears. By this time you should be walking south-east. Keep going around the cliff rim as it turns generally north-east about 1.5 kilometres from the walk start, then follow it north-east for another 1.8 kilometres to another peninsula where the cliffs head south-east once more. Here, the downstream view is superb and time should be spent at the spot. It would be a good place for lunch but there is no water supply.

243

After lunch, retrace the outward route which should be most enjoyable as the gorge walls change colour as the day progresses. The effect of sunlight is perhaps one of the features of this walk.

MAP REF: *Tia Falls map provided with this publication.*
Map 43.
WALK DISTANCE: 7 km.
GRADING: One day, easy.

77   APSLEY FALLS

South-east of Walcha, just off the Oxley Highway, is Apsley Falls which are about 300 metres high. An archway exists over the entrance to the Falls Reserve and a one-kilometre-long road leads to a picnic area. Halfway along this drive there is an extremely good lookout over the gorge, downstream from the falls. A plaque at the picnic area indicates that John Oxley discovered the falls on 14 September 1818 and crossed the river at this point, before going on to Port Macquarie.

Like most other falls in the district, Apsley Falls are at the eastern edge of the New England Plateau and are caused by massive erosion by the river flowing to the Pacific coast.

There is a lookout at the falls which gives a first class view but there are some 113 steps down to it. The effort is well worth while, before you cross the head of the falls (assuming the river is not in flood and therefore dangerous). Once across the river, climb slightly to a fenceline, turn right and follow the fence; then, once the gorge rim is reached, stay as close as you safely can. Skirt around from east to south, then east again and, finally, north—thereby walking three sides of a square shape. No doubt you will be surprised at the depth of the gorge, which must be at least 500 metres deep and with sheer sides. Kangaroos, rosella parrots and other fauna abound in the forest along the rim. False sarsaparilla flowers provide a pretty sight, too, at certain times of the year.

At the point where the gorge heads east again, some 3.0 kilometres out from the walk start, have some lunch whilst the gorge is still in view (there is no water supply), then head west uphill to the top of a high knob. The slopes are tree-covered, but the summit is reasonably open and provides a good view of the surrounding country and, to a lesser extent, the gorge. It is then an easy walk downhill to the southwest, back to the falls.

MAP REF: *Apsley Falls map provided with this publication.* Map 42.

WALK DISTANCE: 5 km.

GRADING: One day, easy.

78 WAMBELONG MOUNTAIN (MOUNT EXMOUTH)

One of the better walks in the Warrumbungle National Park, west of Coonabarabran, is to Wambelong Mountain, the highest point in the park. For general information about the park, it is suggested that you read the introductory remarks in the walk suggestion to the Breadknife (Walk 71). This walk also starts at Camp Pincham and is through dry country, so water should be carried. The feature of this walk is the views of the entire volcanic park and surrounding plains.

Initially, proceed 400 metres south along the track beside Spirey Creek; then turn right, down and across the creek. There is a sign; 'Ogma Hut 3 Km' at the junction. Follow the Ogma hut track south-west along West Spirey Creek's valley, through forested areas and past a small cave on your left; then, after about 2 kilometres, ascend steeply up to the hut. There is a drinking water tank and four bunks at the hut.

Turn right (west) and gradually ascend the track up past signposted Churchill Rock and the Grassy Glades Ramp and, in 1.2 kilometres, meet a track junction. Fork right uphill over a saddle then descend the Danu Scree ramp for 400 metres to Danu Hut and another junction. Again, there is drinking water at the hut.

A signpost indicates Wambelong Mountain 2.6 kilometres uphill and this track should be followed. The climb is quite steep but well worth while as the view from the top is superb. Lunch is suggested on the top whilst you admire the view but there is no water supply. At this point you are 7.6 kilometres from Camp Pincham and the return trip is simply a retrace of the outward route. The walking however will be mostly downhill.

MAP REF: **Warrumbungle map provided with this publication.** Map 39.

WALK DISTANCE: 15 km.

GRADING: One day, medium.

79 BREADKNIFE—BLUFF MOUNTAIN

This walk in the Warrumbungle National Park features the pick of the volcanic spires, plugs and lava flows. For an introduction concerning the park generally it is suggested that you read the notes for the suggested easy one-day walk to the Breadknife (Walk 71). This walk also starts at Camp Pincham and, because it is through dry country, water should be carried.

At first, follow instructions as for the walk to the Breadknife and see the spectacular view from Grand High Tops. Once at Dagda Gap, proceed west 1.4 kilometres to Nuada Gap, via a pleasant, forested area and, then, through many cypress pines. At Nuada Gap, turn left up the 1.3 kilometre track to the summit of Bluff Mountain. The track heads, first, steeply up to the south end of the great dome which is Bluff Mountain; then, it turns back north and ascends the rock spine of the southern slopes. At the summit there is a cairn but the best views are about 150 metres before you reach the summit. If you walk north-west from the cairn you will also obtain good views over the awesome cliffs.

Next, descend back to Nuada Gap and turn left. In 100 metres you will reach Dows Hut where there is a drinking water tank. Lunch is suggested here. After lunch, head north past Nuada Peak and the Mid Spirey View to Point Wilderness with its views to the north, then descend sharply past Ogma Rock to Ogma Hut which is in a saddle. There are four bunks and tank water at the hut. The distance from Dows Hut is 1.6 kilometres. A signpost shows the way to Camp Pincham and you should descend this track which drops steeply at first, then levels out as you wander down the pleasant wooded valley of West Spirey Creek. At one point there is a small cave on the right side of the track. There are many wildflowers and parrots seem to be common. After 3 kilometres the track rejoins the main Spirey Creek valley track to the Breadknife and at this point you need only retrace your outward route northwards back to Camp Pincham, a distance of only 400 metres.

MAP REF: **Warrumbungle map provided with this publication.** Map 39.

WALK DISTANCE: 14.5 km.

GRADING: One day, hard.

West of Coonabarabran is the wild Warrumbungle National Park. It is a park featuring volcanic trachyte plugs and lava flows. The whole area is heavily eroded yet it is a dry region and few streams flow for any length of time. Undoubtedly this is one of the State's better parks and it is certainly well developed as far as tracks are concerned. There are good camping facilities at Camp Blackman and other camp areas at various points. This walk suggestion is to camp out at Ogma Hut on the tops and to see the beautiful colourings of sunrise and sunset on the peaks. The hut has four bunks and a drinking water tank behind it. However, it is suggested that you also carry come water. The park centre is at Canyon Camp and 3.1 kilometres from the entrance to Canyon Camp is another camp area named Camp Pincham. It is at this point that you should start walking. There is a tap for water just to the right of the start of the trail.

A signpost indicates Febar Tor 2.1 km to the south and the Tor is your first objective. Cross to the east bank of Spirey Creek, which is usually dry, then walk 400 metres and fork left uphill. Next, walk 300 metres and fork left again uphill, this time eastwards on the Goulds Circuit track. After 1.4 kilometres of steady climbing through forest, you should fork left again and descend the southern slopes of Fabar Tor. There is a view southwards to Belougery Spire, then a small saddle and a steep climb up to another track junction, just below the summit of Macha Tor and 800 metres from the last junction. Fork right very steeply uphill to the top of Macha Tor, only 100 metres distant. The top provides wonderful views and has a few cypress pines for shade. The view is especially good to the south and the route this walk suggestion leads through.

Next, return down the 100 metres to the Goulds Circuit track and continue to the right downhill, south then west through open forest and back to the main Spirey Creek valley track. Just 182 metres short of the main track, there is a viewpoint towards the Breadknife, some 20 metres to the left. Once on the main track, this suggested route is identical to the one day easy walk to the Breadknife; you should follow track notes in that suggestion, until you reach Dagda Gap. In the process you will see spectacular views from the Grand High Tops—especially down over the Breadknife. The Grand High Tops would be a good place for lunch but there is no water supply there.

From Dagda Gap, head west 1.4 kilometres up through forest and some cypress pines to Nuada Gap. Turn left here and take the steep track up to Bluff Mountain, a distance of 1.3 kilometres. The track initially climbs south-west then reaches some cliffs, steps and grass trees, then ascends the rocky, southern slopes of Bluff Mountain. There is a rock cairn on the peak but the best views are just south of the summit, as you climb the track. The views are very good eastwards to the Breadknife and Crater Bluff. Next return to Nuada Gap, fork left and pass Dows Hut almost immediately. There is tank water at the hut. Continue north past Nuada Peak and the Mid Spirey View to Point Wilderness for more views to the north. There are excellent views of the cliffs of Bluff Mountain to the left, too. Finally, to end the day's walk, head down the track past Ogma Rocks to Ogma Hut which is in a saddle. It has tank water and four bunks but is only rudimentary has an earth floor. Ogma Hut is 1.6 kilometres from Nuada Gap.

Next day entails a climb westwards to Wambelong Mountain which is an 8.4 kilometre return trip from Ogma Hut. Packs could be left at the hut and only lunch and a first aid kit taken to the summit. Initially, the route is up past signposted Churchill Rock and the Grassy Glades ramp for 1.2 kilometres—to the Cathedral Arch turnoff. Fork right on to a saddle then descend across the Danu Scree ramp for 400 metres to Danu Saddle. Danu Hut is in the saddle and tank water is at the rear of the hut. The Burbie Spring track leads off downhill to the right (north) but you should head westwards generally, up the slopes and to the top of Wambelong Mountain which is also known as Mount Exmouth. The distance from Danu Hut to the top is 2.6 kilometres but the steep climb involved is well worth while as the views are superb. It is the highest peak in the park and has snow gums growing on it. On the way up you may see wild goats and there are many ancient grass trees.

Return back down to Danu Hut and Ogma Hut, collect your pack if necessary, then walk north-east down the signposted Camp Pincham track. It drops steeply at first but soon flattens out and follows the West Spirey Creek valley through woodlands and numerous wildflowers. At one point there is a small cave to the right of the track. After 3 kilometres, you should rejoin your outward route and then you have only 400 metres to walk back to Camp Pincham.

MAP REF: **Warrumbungle map provided with this publication.** Map 39.

WALK DISTANCE: 24 km.

GRADING: Two days, medium.

81   MOUNT FRANKLIN AND MOUNT AGGIE

The Brindabella Range along the western boundary of the A.C.T. has easy access and is relatively close to Canberra. It also rises to an elevation of 1857 metres and so has beautiful alpine scenery. In winter the range is snowclad but, once the snow melts, the plants grow rapidly and blossom in summer making à carpet of colour in places. It is therefore best to attempt this walk in summer.

Two peaks close to the range top road provide both wonderful views and displays of flowers. They are Mount Franklin (1644 m) and Mount Aggie (1480 m). Access to them is via the Cotter Road and Brindabella Road to the A.C.T.— New South Wales border, then south along Mount Franklin Road on the range crest for 14.3 kilometres to a saddle with a yellow survey peg indicating a jeep track with a reference 'R685' on the peg. Actually, the saddle is north of Mount Aggie. It is suggested that the walk should take a figure eight shape and that lunch should be eaten on top of Mount Franklin but water would need to be carried.

Set off south along the minor jeep track to Mount Aggie. The track initially runs almost parallel to the main road but it climbs gradually through open snow gum forest then rises above the treeline just near the summit of Mount Aggie. The summit, 2.0 kilometres from the walk start, is quite rocky on the western side; consequently, views to the west are exceptionally good. There is a great variety of wildflowers near the top, too, and both trigger plants and everlastings appear in masses. Next, walk 1.1 kilometres south down the jeep track back to the main road at Aggie Gap where a signpost points back to Mount Aggie and also advises that you are 1303 metres above sea level. The jeep track crosses the main road and continues on, generally south, up to Mount Franklin. It gets steep in parts but the way is well defined and open through snow gums so that, as you gain elevation, the view improves and glorious flower-covered, grassy slopes welcome you to the summit area. Views include Canberra, Coree Mountain and various peaks southwards. The climb to the summit is 1.5 kilometres long and you rise 250 metres in the process. There is a trig point just 125 metres north-east of the 'T' junction formed by two jeep tracks. The best views towards Canberra are from near the trig point although trees block some of the view.

After lunch, follow the jeep track south-west down the main spur for 1.5 kilometres. The route makes wonderful walking as a wide swathe of trees were cleared for the jeep track and now it is flanked by flowers and grassy slopes. The view south-westwards has been greatly improved too by the clearing and Mount Ginini is in full view. You should pass the Franklin Chalet and then join the main road again. The roads actually form a triangle at the junction, so take the right fork. Then, at the main road, turn right (north) and simply follow the main road back 5.5 kilometres to the walk starting point. The road is a very quiet one and the bush along the way should make a most enjoyable finish to your walk.

MAP REF: *Mount Franklin map provided with this publication.* Map 47.

WALK DISTANCE: 12 km.

GRADING: One day, easy.

The Brindabella Range west of Canberra has indeed got some lovely places to walk. The range rises to 1857 metres above sea level at Mount Gingera and, as such, is quite alpine in its vegetation and receives regular snow falls in winter. The Mount Franklin Road provides easy access except, of course, when blocked by snow. From Canberra you need to travel via the Cotter Road and Brindabella Road to the range top, then south past Bulls Run, a skiing venue, to Mount Ginini, 21.5 kilometres south of Piccadilly Circus. There is a radio link station on the summit of Mount Ginini. Some 600 metres before the installation a lesser road forks off left and after 300 metres is barred by a locked gate. Walkers are authorized to pass the barrier which gate marks the suggested walk start and finish. It is best to contact the area Ranger by phone (Canberra 478153), or at Bendouva Dam, to advise him of your walk plans.

The first 2.9 kilometres of the walk route are along the eastern slopes of 1763-metre-high Mount Ginini to Stockyard Gap. There are old, gnarled snow gums and a few wildflowers beside the road to hold your interest. Stockyard Gap has a small clearing on the west side of the road with a small dam in the clearing. You should next walk a further 1.4 kilometres up around the north-eastern slopes of Little Ginini to a lovely grassy alpine saddle on the east side of the road. The saddle has a marvellous alpine flower display in summer and should be noted, as it is the point where you later rejoin the road on the way back to Mount Gingera. Continue for another 500 metres on the road to a saddle at the northern end of Mount Gingera. There is a small hut and an alpine garden on the west side of the road, together with a sign advising the mountain's name and height.

Leave the road and climb south-west, straight up through lovely grassy and flowering slopes to the north-western end of the elongated summit of the peak. The climb is over a distance of only about 600 metres and the altitude difference is some 200 metres. Once on the top, though, there is easy walking for the rest of the day among alpine vegetation and the views are certainly unrivalled anywhere else near Canberra. Large areas are virtually open and wild horses are sometimes seen grazing on the lush grasses. From the tops you can look down on large areas of alpine plain immediately to the north of the peak and to the distant Cooleman Plains away to the south-west. Numerous far-off peaks can be seen, including much of the northern Kosciusko National Park. It is suggested you wander south-east along the summit and pick a spot for lunch. There is no water supply. The tops extend for about 1.2 kilometres and culminate at a trig point at the south-east end where there are more views.

From the trig point, descend north-east 100 metres to where you should locate a minor jeep track which services the trig area. The track should be then followed down, roughly east-north-east then north through a barrier and on to the Mount Franklin Road. The descent is most pleasant and through fine snow-gum slopes. Turn right at the Mount Franklin Road and walk north-east for 400 metres until you are approaching a saddle through which the road passes. Just before the saddle, leave the road, then cross alpine grass, low shrubs and flowers to follow the eastern side of Snowy Flats, an alpine plain. Keep up, away from the creek which drains the flat. Also keep below the line of trees on your right and this should provide good easy walking on grass rather than through scrub or bogs. Downsteam 1.3 kilometres, Snowy Flat Creek turns east to leave the plain and it should then be crossed. If you walk eastwards a little before crossing, you should not get wet feet or scratched legs from shrubs. The aim is to turn north-west after crossing the stream and follow the alpine plains for 500 metres, back to the saddle and Mount Franklin Road, just east of Little Ginini. From that point onwards the route is simply a retrace of the outward route.

To really enjoy this walk it is essential to linger, to take particular notice of the alpine flowers and shrubs, the old gnarled snow gums, twisted by severe winters, and to admire the views. It is essentially a summer walk which needs fine weather. If mist or fog persist the trip would not be very enjoyable.

MAP REF: *Mount Gingera map provided with this publication.* Map 48.

WALK DISTANCE: 13 km.

GRADING: One day, easy.

83 BILLY BILLY ROCKS

The Corin Dam Road passes through some delightful country, especially near Smokers Gap where, at about 1250 metres above sea level, there is alpine vegetation. North of Smokers Gap is Billy Billy Rocks, a cluster of large granite boulders near Billy Billy Creek, a tributary of Paddys River. The distance between the road at Smokers Gap and the rocks is only 3.0 kilometres but there is no track and fallen timber in scrub makes progress slow and difficult. A map and compass certainly must be used and, in winter, snow often covers the district. Therefore, inexperienced walkers should not attempt this walk unless in the company of some-one experienced.

To reach the area, travel to Tharwa and then north along Paddys River Road and Corin Road, or bypass Tharwa by taking the Point Hut Crossing road between the Monaro Highway and Paddys River Road, if you wish. Point Hut Crossing is a wide ford at the Murrum-bidgee River but can become too deep to cross at times. Another access route is through the Cotter Picnic Area then south, along Paddys River Road. Smokers Gap is 45.0 kilometres from central Canberra via Point Hut Crossing, the shortest route. The road at the gap is a bit too narrow for parking but, some 200 metres east of a Smokers Gap sign, there is a reason-able parking place on grass. The walk route is difficult to follow unless a compass is used, especially on the return journey, as trees prevent navigation by sighting distant objects in most parts. Consequently it is best to use two hills as navigation aids.

Walk in a north-westerly direction across a snow grass plain and up to a hilltop about 400 metres from the parking area. At the top of the hill there is no view and nothing of particular interest but, from it, you should take a bearing of 325° magnetic and descend to a small creek which is densely lined with tea-tree and somewhat difficult to penetrate. Continue on the same bearing and ascend steeply for a kilometre to a hill-top with granite boulders on its summit. The ascent is quite awkward due to fallen logs. Burrs in summer can be most annoying. Skirt round the northern side of the summit rocks and scale one or two for a bit of a view towards your destination, Billy Billy Rocks, which are about a kilometre further on and at a bearing of 335° magnetic. To reach Billy Billy Rocks, however, it is best to walk north-west until you cross Billy Billy Creek then swing sharply north-east rather than walk in a direct line. The deviation removes the need to descend so far to the creek and the valley area is more open and pleasant. Once at the rocks, you should go to their eastern end from where they can be easily climbed. However, the best views are from the higher rocks nearer the north-western end and these should be approached from the eastern end—not directly from the southern side where the boulders are too steep. It is time-consuming to find access to the highest boulder but an easy route exists. The highest rock is about 20 metres high and provides spectacular views of the Tidbinbilla Range and Valley. Canberra can also be seen. Lunch is suggested but there is no water. The return journey is a retrace of the outward route but a word of warning—use your compass!

MAP REF: **Billy Billy Rocks map provided with this publication.** Map 46.

WALK DISTANCE: 6 km.

GRADING: One day, medium.

84   URIARRA CROSSING—GINNINDERRA FALLS

The Murrumbidgee River near Canberra is excellent for walking and swimming. Many sandy beaches exist and Uriarra Crossing is one of the more accessible points from the city. Leave transport at the crossing to start this walk, but do not attempt it if the river is very swollen. Follow the south bank (Canberra side) track downstream past a YMCA camp. The somewhat polluted Molonglo River then joins in from the south and it is necessary to walk south from the YMCA area for about 500 metres to a derelict concrete bridge across the

Molonglo. It may be necessary to wade the river a little using the foot bridge as a aid against current.

Next return to the Murrumbidgee's south bank and continue downstream for many kilometres. Near vertical slopes line the river at one point and a little scrambling over river debris may be needed if the river water is high. Normally it is best to stay close to the waters edge. Eventually, about seven kilometres from the walk start, a minor road should be met as it descends to the river bank. Have lunch is the area before leaving the water, then walk up the road north-east. After 700 metres, Cusacks Crossing road is joined. Keep on uphill until the road swings south-east after passing under high voltage power wires 1.6 kilometres from the river. Next turn left into the Ginninderra Falls Reserve. A 400 metre long pad leads to the 25 metre high falls and gorge.

The falls reserve is now accessible from Canberra via Southern Cross Drive, Belconnen, so walkers may wish to operate a transport shuttle instead of retracing the walk back to Uriarra Crossing. The retrace however would be most enjoyable and especially good during the long hot summer days.

MAP REF: *Uriarra Crossing map provided with this publication.* Map 45.

WALK DISTANCE: 18 km.

GRADING: One day, medium.

85   COREE MOUNTAIN

West of Canberra on the New South Wales-A.C.T. border is an imposing peak with a forestry firewatch tower on it. From the summit, Canberra and all its suburbs can be clearly seen and a feature of this peak, named Coree Mountain, is the rocky cliffs on its south-western and western slopes. It is quite a high peak, with alpine vegetation well down the slopes. A rough jeep track leads to the fire tower and thus provides walkers with an easy access route.

The jeep track leaves the Brindabella Road (west of Cotter Dam) at the crest of the dividing range at the State border. It leads northwards for 11.0 kilometres to the summit and is known as Two Sticks Road. It is suggested that the walk start 3.5 kilometres north of the Brindabella Road—at a saddle where there is a clearing on the left (west) side. The jeep track worsens, north of that point but conventional vehicles should easily reach the saddle except in very wet weather. You should simply walk the jeep track generally northwards for 4.0 kilometres to a junction on the north-west side of Coree Mountain. As you walk along the road especially at the 2.0 kilometre mark, you no doubt will look up at the great bulk of Coree Mountain and wonder how any road could possibly reach the top. However, the turnoff jeep track to your right (east) scales the crest with little trouble. At first you must descend slightly to a dam and the only water supply in the area. Grassy slopes and pleasant snow gum surroundings make it a good lunch spot. The jeep track then climbs south-east and, in 500 metres, divides. You should fork right then negotiate about ten hair-pin bends to put you virtually 'on top of the world', with a spectacular 360° view. The fire tower is not high but by climbing on to the low platform the view is even better. You will probably be amazed how many pine trees grow near Canberra. After a good look around and rest, retrace your outward route. Do not try and short cut down the mountain's south-west slopes. It is extremely steep, rocky and scrubby.

MAP REF: *Coree Mountain map provided with this publication.* Map 44.
WALK DISTANCE: 15 km.
GRADING: One day, medium.

86   SAWPIT CREEK NATURE TRAIL—
WATERFALL TRACK

In the vicinity of the Sawpit Creek accommodation area and park headquarters of the Kosciusko National Park, two circuit trails have been constructed. A walking combination of the two trails is both informative and attractive. The area's altitude is only 1200 metres so trees are substantial and the routes are quite different to routes at higher elevations in a lot of the park. For each trail a leaflet is available from the park head-quarters but, at the time of writing, only the Sawpit Creek trail leaflet described numbered points along the track. Pegs existed along the Waterfall Track, too.

There is a day visitors' carpark outside the park accommodation area and it is the obvious place from which to start walking. The Sawpit Creek Nature Trail leads off from the carpark and has twelve numbered points of interest along its route. To follow it, take the signposted trail and cross Sawpit Creek; then im-mediately fork right (east) and follow the north bank of the creek downstream. Several varieties of eucalypt are present and are named in the leaflet. Tea tree grows along the creek itself. Between points two and three the trail returns to the south bank and slowly descends until point eight where a junction is reached. To the left is the Piallabo Track to the Crackenback River picnic ground and park entrance. It is signposted. Turn to the right and follow the nature trail up west-wards, on to a ridge. The area is drier and such flowers as trigger plants are common. Soon the track swings north, back into the park accommodation area, near some cabins. It is then a case of walking a couple of hundred metres out the front entrance of the camp back to the day visitors' carpark at the Kosciusko Road. The circuit totals only 1.6 kilometres.

On the other side of the road, right beside Sawpit Creek, the signposted Waterfall Track begins. It has 25 numbered points along its 7.0 kilometre length and at least two hours should be allowed for actual walking time. Additionally, lunch is suggested by a waterfall at point No. 11. The track forms a loop and returns back to the exact spot where it starts but there is a 500-metre-long side trip from the loop which leads up to North Sawpit trig point, 1393 metres elevation. The spot has a view of Lake Jindabyne from the top of some boulders. The leaflet does not indicate what the numbered points represent and it is impossible to decipher what is the attraction in most instances. It is understood that a new leaflet is under preparation.

The trail follows the south bank of Sawpit Creek north-west for 3.0 kilometres then crosses the creek at a waterfall. At point number six, trigger plants are in abundance and between points ten and eleven an old gauging station track, once used by the Snowy Mountains Authority, is crossed. Generally the 3.0 kilometres are through pleasant tree-covered bushland with a few wildflowers and birds. Occasionally small streamside, grassy flats are passed. From the waterfall, which is only small, the track climbs up about a kilometre on to a ridge, then turns east. Between points fourteen and fifteen a sign indicates the return route still 2.0 kilometres long. It is at a point where a very old jeep track takes over as your route rather than the more recently made foot track. Shortly afterwards you should fork left up to North Sawpit trig for the Jindabyne view then return to continue along the main trail. The deviation adds only a kilometre but also a little climbing. The remainder of the walking is generally flat or downhill, mostly on an old jeep track. A number of large granite boulders should be seen along the way, many with a lot of lichen growing on them. At point number twenty five the jeep track is left and you should follow a foot pad back across Sawpit Creek to finish the walk.

MAP REF: *Sawpit Creek map provided with this publication.* Map 55.

WALK DISTANCE: 8.5 km.

GRADING: One day, easy.

87 RAWSONS PASS—LAKE ALBINA—BLUE LAKE—CHARLOTTES PASS

Apart from Tasmania, Australia has very few mountain tarns—one of the more beautiful features caused by ancient glaciers. Lake Cootapatamba, Lake Albina, Club Lake, Blue Lake and Hedley Tarn are, in fact,, about the only sizeable tarns on the Australian mainland. This recommended walk route takes the walker to two tarns and to see two of the other three and at the same time, remains alongside the highest peaks in Australia. If possible, the walk should be undertaken in December or January, when the additional interest of wildflowers makes for an extremely pleasant trip.

The Kosciusko summit access road is no longer open to the public beyond Charlottes Pass except on foot. At the time of writing, a mid-summer time bus operates between Perisher Ski Village and Rawsons Pass and it is possible to board the returning buses at Charlottes Pass. The bus service may not be a permanent feature and it may therefore be necessary to walk up the road for eight kilometres to Rawsons Pass to start this walk. Obviously some checking is best first, and an early bus should be used to maximize walking time available. The whole area is treeless, extremely exposed and subject to sudden changes in weather. Commonsense dictates that you keep warm. There is no point in attempting the walk in fog as distant views and views down on to tarns are the feature of this walk.

From Rawsons Pass you should, initially, make the traditional climb to Australia's highest summit: Mount Kosciusko, 2228 metres above sea level. No true walker would miss out on this goal, especially when all you need to do is walk up a road for a kilometre. There is no doubt that the 360° view is superb, particularly to the west and across into Victoria. Lake Cootapatamba is just below the peak to the south. About midway between Rawsons Pass and the summit, via the road, a good foot track leads off north, downhill along the main northern spur of Mount Kosciusko. Follow the track down to a saddle where Hannels Spur Track joins in from the west. (Incidentally, it is the longest climb in Australia.) Continue on and up the eastern slopes of Muellers Peak to another saddle between it and Mount Northcote. At this point you are some 2.0 kilometres from the summit of Mount Kosciusko and Lake Albina Lodge and Lake Albina itself can be seen in the valley northwards. The main track actually leads up the western slopes of Mount Northcote bypassing Lake Albina, but another track leads down past the lodge to the lake and should be followed. It is a really lovely valley and you should not rush. Gentians and other flowers are normally thick in summer. It is best to follow the lake's eastern shore around to the outlet at the northern end and to have lunch by the lake. Make sure you climb a little west of the outlet, up the slopes, to gain views of Watsons Crags and Lady Northcote's Canyon.

After lunch, climb east from Lake Albina to regain the main trail. The climb is steep and you must climb right to the ridge top as the trail is on the tops at that stage. Once on the ridge, walking is far easier and you can see Club Lake down the slopes to the east. Its colour often looks magnificent from above. The trail should be followed up over lofty Carruthers Peak then down to the north-east fork about 500 metres where the main divide is left at a jeep track and you should fork right to descend gradually eastwards past a locked hut and after 600 metres for left onto a foot pad to beautiful Blue Lake, the biggest of the tarns. It is surely one of the best features of the National Park. Its northern side is cliffs and its south-west side is grassy and ideal for a rest to admire the surroundings. It is also excellent for camping.

You should retrace the last 600 metres of your route and veer left (south); then follow the well-defined jeep-trad south-east for 2.5 kilometres down to the Snowy River ford and for a further 400 metres up and back to Charlottes Pass.

MAP REF: *Kosciusko map provided with this publication.* Map 54.

WALK DISTANCE: 11 km. (19 km if no bus available)

GRADING: One day, easy.

88 CHARLOTTES PASS—BLUE LAKE—HEDLEY TARN

Blue Lake must rate as one of the best features of the

Kosciusko National Park. It is a wonderful place for seeing flowers, for lazing, camping, photography and admiring the alpine scenery. It was formed by a glacier gouging out the southern slopes of Mount Twynam, one of Australia's highest mountains. As a result, the northern side of the tarn is lined with cliffs. The southwest side is grassy and relatively flat although a certain amount of glacial moraine is present.

Travel up the main Mount Kosciusko summit road to Charlottes Pass where there is a barrier and a carpark. A good jeeptrack leads off on the north side of the road from the pass and should be followed. It leads west 400 metres down to the youthful Snowy River, then fords it and climbs gradually north-west for 2.5 kilometres to a sharp left bend in the jeeptrack. Turn right (east) at this bend and then it is only 500 metres down to Blue Lake via a foot pad. Most of the route is through treeless alpine slopes which can be extremely exposed at times but in fine weather are really pleasant. Being in a hollow, Blue Lake is relatively sheltered. Try and time your trip for December or January, when the weather and the flowers are at their best. A cold swim and lunch by the tarn is suggested.

Next, go to the tarn's outlet at its south-east side. Moraine left by a glacier makes the area rugged but if you follow Blue Lake Creek downstream you should arrive at Hedley Tarn within 500 metres. It is also glacial in origin and whilst not as big as Blue Lake it is still very beautiful. From the tarn, walk west-south-west across broken and scrubby terrain with no trees, for about 600 metres to rejoin the jeep track, then turn left and retrace the outward route back to the Snowy River then up to Charlottes Pass.

MAP REF: *Kosciusko map provided with this publica-*
tion. Map 54.
WALK DISTANCE: 7 km.
GRADING: One day, easy.

89   PERISHER VALLEY—THE PORCUPINE

From Perisher Ski Village in the Snowy Mountains, an
interesting alpine walk is highly recommended. It is
also one of the routes recommended by the Kosciusko
National Park authorities and a leaflet is available from
park headquarters. It describes interesting points
along the route. The trail starts near The Man from
Snowy River Motel and climbs to a group of boulders
on the Ramshead Range known as The Porcupine.
During the ascent open snow gums proliferate, inter-
spersed with alpine herbland. Wildflowers are especially
good about January and distant views are superb.
However, if fog is about do not undertake the trip as
the attractions would automatically be hidden. The
main views are of the Cracken back Valley.

Turn south at The Man from Snowy River Motel then
right soon after, at the next fork. Follow this road until
you reach the Sundowner Lodge on your left; then
veer right along a wide track which leads to, and
crosses, Rock Creek. The foot pad then leads off up
hill south-south-west, following a snow pole line. It
continues basically in the same direction right to The
Porcupine, some 2.5 kilometres away. You rise 200
metres in elevation but only gradually and the extremely
pleasant surroundings should make you want to linger
along the way. The peak has superb views, a rocky top,
and is 1960 metres above sea level. It is south west of
Mount Duncan nearby which has a trig point on its top.

266

The pole line continues past the peaks, so do not go too far. Return via the same route.

MAP REF: **Guthega map provided with this publication.**
 Map 53.
WALK DISTANCE: 5 km.
GRADING: One day, easy.

90   THE BACK PERISHER—THE BLUE COW

Perisher Valley, in the Kosciusko National Park, is a well-known ski resort and, amongst the many amenities, there is a chairlift from the village to the summit of the peak just to the west which is known as Back Perisher. The chairlift operates In summer as well as the snow season and, as such, is ideal for use by walkers wanting to enjoy the alpine tops without having to first climb steeply. The lift actually saves about 250 metres of climbing and terminates at an altitude of 2017 metres, thereby placing you on top of one of Australia's higher peaks. From the peak, walks to nearby mountains called The Perisher and The Paralyser would be feasible but extremely exposed. A better alternative walk is one northwards to a peak with the strange name of The Blue Cow. It is only 3.0 kilometres away and, between the two peaks there is lovely alpine country with just enough snow gums to make the scenery really beautiful without hindering the views. Rocks and myriad flowers are present and the general level of the country remains high so that you do not have to descend too much between the two peaks.

Unless fog is present, the whole route of the walk can be seen from just about any point along the way and navigation would not normally be a problem. However, if fog is about, extreme care is needed and, in some circumstances, it would be better to abandon the walk. Lunch would be best in the sheltered spots among snow gums rather than on the top of The Blue Cow. The ascent to the summit of The Blue Cow and to the summit of The Back Perisher on the return trip is steep in each case, but both are short climbs. During the walk, views include the Snowy River and of course the main Kosciusko Range and also Perisher Village.

MAP REF: **Guthega map provided with this publication.** Map 53.

WALK DISTANCE: 6 km.

GRADING: One day, easy.

91   THREDBO—RAMSHEAD—NORTH RAMSHEAD

Thredbo Ski Village, like other ski resorts in the Snowy Mountains, has chairlifts and like the Perisher Lift, the one at Thredbo operates during summer. The Thredbo lift rises from 1370 metres above sea level to 1965 metres, so saving a lot of arduous climbing for those wanting to see the tops. It is suggested that you make use of the lift and spend a day seeing two of Australia's highest peaks; Ramshead (2190 metres) and North Ramshead (2177 metres). Once at the top of the chairlift, the country becomes quite open and almost treeless in parts. The open places, of course, are good for views and alpine flowers. The peaks are rocky yet climbing them is relatively easy, despite the lack of any track for most of the day's walk. The only track leads from the lift north-west across to Rawsons Pass and Charlottes Pass. No specific route is suggested other than that you should follow the trail from the lift for about a kilometre then cross grasslands to climb the two peaks. You should generally spend the day exploring, then return to the lift. Do not attempt the walk in bad weather; it could prove most uncomfortable and even dangerous. A feature of the walk is the views so there is little point in heading off on the walk in fog. Once back at the lift, save a return fare. There is a good nature trail, called Merritts Path, down to the valley terminal. It is 5.0 kilometres long. A brochure about the walk is available in Thredbo Village and could be obtained before the walk. It describes points of interest along the way although most points are obvious and do not need the leaflet explanation. The feature of the trail is the strata of vegetation as you descend, ranging from open tops to tea tree-filled gullies on the lower slopes.

MAP REF: **Kosciusko map provided with this publication.** Map 54.

WALK DISTANCE: 12 km, approximately.

GRADING: One day, easy.

92   WOLSELEYS GAP—SNAKEY PLAIN

To most people, Snowy Mountains walking seems to involve a trip to the Kosciusko summit area; it is quite obvious that very few people walk to many of the other beautiful places further north in the National Park such as the area right next to the Kiandra-Khancoban main road. No doubt many people travel through Cabramurra and see some of the alpine plains, flowers and snow gums but do not make the effort to walk. If only they knew how lovely such places as Far Bald Mountain, Round Mountain and Snakey Plain were!

Snakey Plain does not appear to have snakes, but maybe the name keeps people away. It is right alongside the Big Dargal Mountain. It gives a really good view of massive Mount Jagungal to the south-east and has a crystal-clear stream flowing through it, with grassy banks providing a perfect lunch spot.

To reach the area, travel the Tooma Road to a point 2.5 kilometres west of Tooma Dam. A sign on the south side of the road reads: 'Snakey Plain Fire Trail'. At this point you are about 1300 metres above sea level and Snakey Plain is at 1500 metres, so a little climbing is involved. The trail should be followed south initially, through open forest without views. About 1.5 kilometres from the Tooma Road, after mostly fairly level walking, you should descend slightly to Wolseleys Gap, where there is a sign and a very old east-west road. At the junction, go 50 metres west to cross tiny Shingle Creek then continue south up grassy Snakey Plain Fire Trail. Once away from the lushness of the small gully, the trail becomes more pronounced and climbs steadily on to open grassy slopes above the treeline, on the northern side of the Jagumba Range. Views to the north-west become quite good and alpine flowers proliferate. Tooma Reservoir also comes into view as you ascend. The trail reaches some tops just 100 metres west of a trig point, on a small summit, which is worth visiting as a minor side trip. The trig is 3.0 kilometres from the Tooma Road.

It is a further 1.5 kilometres from the range top to Snakey Plain and the trail traverses some truly delightful alpine 'garden' settings. About December-January especially, the area must rank as one of the best displays of flora in the Snowy Mountains. The trail is well defined and gradually descends to Snakey Plain. Some of the snow gums are particularly beautiful and photographers will probably be well satisfied. On arrival at Snakey Plain you could not help but be impressed; it is very green and dominated by the Big

Dargal Mountain. The stream, flowers, views and snow gums all contribute to make It a paradise for walkers. There is a sign in the middle of the plain indicating the route of overgrown Wheelers Hut Fire Trail which leads south-east down off the plain. Spend a lot of time and perhaps laze in the sun for a while until you have spent your time, then retrace your route back to Tooma Road.

MAP REF: ***Dargals map provided with this publication.***
  Map 52.
WALK DISTANCE: 9 km.
GRADING: One day, easy.

93   ROUND MOUNTAIN

The Tooma Road, in the Snowy Mountains between Kiandra and Khancoban, skirts the northern slopes of Round Mountain and the summit is actually only about 600 metres from the road in a direct line. The crest, however, is about 200 metres higher than the road and, as such, any climb directly up is rather steep and also rather scrubby. The view from the top is superb as it is the highest point around and the effort of climbing is well worth while. An old jeep track scales the peak from the western side and is by far the best access route, despite the extra distance, and it is recommended that you follow the jeep track to start a really good, but short, walk.

It is best to leave transport right opposite the junction of the old track and Tooma Road as there is a wide area suited to parking. The spot is 200 metres west of the old mile peg (Cabramurra 13 miles) and 500 metres west of the kilometre peg (Cabramurra 20 kilometres). A sign facing west-bound traffic warns of an approaching steep descent just as you reach the site. The jeep track leads off uphill south-west and is quite over-

271

grown in parts. After 400 metres a hut should be reached on the right; at that point, the old electric supply poles end and you can no longer use them as an additional guide. The track swings south-east then east and ascends through lovely snow gums. It stays right near the crest of the broad spur and is traceable virtually right to the summit of Round Mountain. Rocky outcrops occur over the last 100 metres and need to be scaled. You should then be 1.2 kilometres from the walk start.

From the peak you should see the long expanses of Ogilvies Plain, the Tumut River Valley and across to Farm Ridge. Also partly visible should be the Round Mountain Track, heading south towards Mount Jagungal and the Thiess Village Track, which runs east-west across Cool Plain and past the south side of Round Mountain. Thiess Village Track is not far away but there is dense scrub between it and the summit and, as you must next proceed down steeply to it, you should take the shortest possible distance between the two points which means walking due south 600 metres. The descent will be quite awkward at times but, once on the Thiess Village Track, the rest of the day's walk is easy—amid rather pleasant alpine plains, snow gums and flowers.

Turn east and follow the track about 500 metres down slightly to the signposted junction with Round Mountain Track, then turn left (north) so that, within a further 500 metres, a small tributary of the Tumut River is reached. Water is reliable at this point and it is also a lovely grassy spot so lunch is suggested. There are actually two streams joining at Round Mountain Track crossing and, after lunch, you should follow the west bank of the right fork stream which is the broader of the two. About 500 metres upstream you should fork left and follow the south bank upstream so that you continue to walk up a long, grassy alpine valley. A kilometre from the lunch spot you should arrive at a saddle on the plain. Cross the saddle and descend 200 metres back onto the Tooma main road. You may need to skirt around a small boggy place in order to reach the road though. To finish the walk you should then head generally westwards for 500 metres along Tooma Road to complete a circuit.

MAP REF: *Jagungal map provided with this publication.*
Map 51A.

WALK DISTANCE: 4.5 km.

GRADING: One day, easy.

94   THREDBO—MOUNT KOSCIUSKO

Some walkers are content to wander about, simply appreciating their surroundings, while others have that extra yen for 'peak bagging' and, of course, no peak bagger could ever let an opportunity pass to climb Australia's highest mountain, even if the climb does involve a lot of physical effort. There is, however, one way for all walkers to reach Mount Kosciusko and be satisfied and that is to take the Crackenback Chairlift from Thredbo Ski Village to an altitude of 1965 metres. It is then a pleasant ramble to Mount Kosciusko at 2228 metres. The route is across often treeless, but pleasant, grassy and flower-decked tops. Flowers are at their best in summer, especially January. Lake Cootapatamba, a tarn near the mountain, is one of the better places to see flowers and is also the suggested lunch spot. The tops can become quite dangerous in foggy conditions and it is comforting to know that a snow pole line extends from the top station to Rawsons

Pass. There is a foot pad that basically follows the pole line but, about a kilometre from the top station, the pole line divides. You should take the left fork. About 4.0 kilometres from the pole line junction you should cross grass and walk west down slopes to Lake Cootapatamba. It is only 500 metres from the pole line, and the area is ideal for lunch.

From the tarn, it is only about 700 metres up the valley to Rawsons Pass and, from the pass, an old road leads right to the summit of Kosciusko, a kilometre away via the road. The 360° summit view is superb and all of Australia's highest peaks can be seen. Some snowdrifts always seem to remain throughout summer.

The return journey is basically the same as the outward trip, but, for variety, it is suggested you bypass Lake Cootapatamba by remaining near the direct snow pole line and then deviating further south to climb North Ramshead, 300 metres west of the line and 2177 metres high. The deviation should satisfy peak baggers as North Ramshead is one of the ten highest Australian peaks. It has a rocky top and extensive views, too. When you arrive back at the top station of the chairlift, try descending the slopes on foot. The slopes have largely been cleared for ski runs and, in summer, flowers are in abundance. There are also good views of Thredbo Village. The descent is from 1965 metres down to 1370 metres so is quite substantial. It is some 1.5 kilometres long.

MAP REF: *Kosciusko map provided with this publication.* Map 54.

WALK DISTANCE: 14.4 km.

GRADING: One day, medium.

95   GUTHEGA—THE PARALYSER—THE PERISHER—THE BLUE COW

Tiny Guthega Ski Village in the Snowy Mountains is surrounded by excellent walking country. The area has just enough snow gums to make the landscape really pretty without blocking views. Most slopes are alpine meadow and herb-covered; numerous small streams descend to the youthful Snowy River and there is always the magnificent backdrop of the Main Range. A first class circuit walk could be taken south and east of the village, including just enough climbing to satisfy those who want more than just an easy ramble.

Go to Guthega Village and leave transport at the western end of the village. The spot is up the slopes south of the Guthega Pondage which is part of the Snowy Mountains Hydro-electric Scheme. Cross Farm Creek first. It flows northwards into the pondage·and you need to reach the main spur leading south up to The Paralyser. The creek crossing is awkward due to herbage but, once on the spur, walking becomes easier. The Paralyser is one of the bigger peaks in the Snowy Mountains but you can rest assured it is not so big as to paralyse you in the effort to climb it. In fact the climb is extremely pleasant. The only thing is that the spur has several knobs on it so that you think you are approaching the top then suddenly find you have further to go. The summit has a trig point, is boulder strewn and is open alpine meadow. It is 2.8 kilometres from the walk start.

Next, you should aim for The Perisher, an even bigger peak to the east. However, there is a small ridge between the two points and, due to boggy and mossy conditions, it is best to keep to the highest ground as you progress, rather than walking a straight line. Go south-south-east as you leave the trig to avoid granite outcrops then gradually swing east. As you approach The Perisher it looks most formidable but is deceptive and not very difficult. At its peak, some 2.2 kilometres from The Paralyser, there is a top station for a chairlift and a ski tow rising from near the Perisher Ski Village which can be clearly seen to the south-east. The top is quite rocky, like other peaks in the district, and can be very exposed to cold.

A minor jeep track ascends the slopes from Perisher Ski Village and divides in the saddle north-east of The Perisher and south of your next goal—The Back Perisher. Cross the saddle, using both forks of the jeep track so as to avoid awkward herbage. It is only a kilometre between the two tops and The Back Perisher is also serviced by a chairlift from the village. It operates in summer as well as the ski season. From The Back Perisher, views are also quite superb and, again, there are granite boulders on the crest.

The most enjoyable and interesting section of the walk must be crossed next. It involves descending the northern slopes of The Back Perisher then rambling through delightful snow gums, herbage and alpine flowers up on to The Blue Cow, the final big peak in the circuit. The whole route can easily be seen and the general direction is north-east over some 3.0 kilometres. Views are superb and the area could best be described as a walkers' paradise. The climb to The Blue Cow is steep but relatively short.

Finally, you should descend westwards 2.5 kilometres down the range back to Guthega Village. Several small knobs exist along the range before the descent to the top of a ski lift; then you should follow the lift for the remainder of the walk.

MAP REF: *Guthega map provided with this publication.* Map 53.

WALK DISTANCE: 11.5 km.

GRADING: One day, medium.

96   BRINDABELLA ROAD—CAVE CREEK

Cave Creek is located in the northern Kosciusko National Park and it has carved quite bold limestone formations, both above and below the ground surface. The area is remote and access roads are too rough for conventional vehicles. A jeep track access from the Brindabella Road is, however, a more interesting walk route than via an alternative jeep track from the south. It is 8.0 kilometres from the Brindabella Road to Cooleman Caves on Cave Creek but little extra walking is needed to see points of interest in the Cave Creek area. The distance between Murray Cave and the Cave Creek Falls is 3.0 kilometres and these two places are at the extremities of the area of interest. Make sure you take a good torch for each person, a ball of string, a hard hat if possible and an old outer garment to protect you from muddy caves. The string should be used for underground guidance by laying it as you progress through the cave. Tie it to some object at the entrance.

The jeep track turnoff from the Brindabella Road is 37.0 kilometres south of Brindabella, at a point where the road is sited nearly a kilometre east of electricity transmission lines which, until that point, remain near the road along the northern approach. There is a gateway at the turnoff and the track leads into snow gums almost immediately, at the eastern edge of Long Plain.

Navigation from Brindabella Road is quite easy as you only need to follow the jeep track known as the Blue Waterholes Track for the 8.0 kilometres. At first, it climbs slightly for 2.0 kilometres then descends sharply, to emerge from snow gums and cross Cooleman Plains. A wooded ridge must then be crossed in the abandoned Cooleman Homestead area, before a final short rise and a kilometre of descent—through more open country to the Caves area. Have lunch beside Cave Creek, then wander east 1.5 kilometres downstream to see the limestone gorge and the waterfalls beyond the gorge. A foot pad leads all the way to the falls and the stream must be forded a couple of times in the gorge or bluffs must be scaled. The best view of the falls is from the south bank, downstream of them.

Return back to Blue Waterholes Track then head upstream to inspect the underground wonders at Cooleman Cave; if time permits, also Murray Cave, a kilometre beyond Cooleman Cave. The jeep track in the Cave Creek picnic area forms a loop, basically, and, from the south side, a track leads off via a usually dry ford. Within a few hundred metres, Cave Creek enters the grassy valley from the west and bold bluffs can be seen upstream. Cooleman Caves are at these bluffs on the northern bank. Murray Cave is further upstream. Allow about two and a half hours to retrace your route back to Brindabella Road but spend as much time as possible at the caves. Camping is excellent in the caves area.

MAP REF: *Cooleman Caves maps provided with this publication.* Maps 49 and 50.

WALK DISTANCE: 22.0 km.

GRADING: One day, medium.

97   COOLEMAN CAVES

New South Wales has a number of limestone areas with caves and, of course, places such as Jenolan Caves are well-known and highly developed. In a remote part of the northern Kosciusko National Park there is an almost unknown cave area which is not developed, yet it has some good limestone formations, both underground and on the surface. It is, therefore, well worth while taking a walking trip through this area known as Cooleman Caves and doing a little caving as an extra interest. Provided sensible preparations are made, a little fossicking would be quite safe and rewarding. Take a long piece of string, a good torch and, If possible, a hard hat. Wear old clothes, too, as it could be muddy underground but comply with normal bushwalking routine by keeping your pack light so as not to spoil the surface walking. Use the string by tying it to some object outside the cave entry then lay it as a guide while you walk underground. Also, take great care not to break any of the limestone formations and thus spoil the cave for others later.

Access to the district is from either of two directions, both of which involve long journeys on rough gravelled roads. Perhaps the best access is from the south, along the Tantangara Road from the Snowy Mountains Highway, to a point 37.3 kilometres from the highway and 19.7 kilometres north of the Tantangara Dam wall. The spot is at the start of the Murray Gap track and south-east of the Goodradigbee aircraft landing ground. It is on the eastern edge of Currango Plain. If the road is quite dry, you may even be able to go a further 2.5 kilometres along the airstrip and to the western edge of the plain but beyond is for four-wheel-drive vehicles. Try and negotiate the plains crossing if

279

possible as it is not a very good start and finish to a walk.

Across the airstrip, at the Currango Plain's western edge, the jeep track forks. Take the left fork which swings west and rises up to a saddle within a kilometre. At the saddle, leave the jeep track and follow the crest of the broad ridge north-west through open forest and through a fence, soon after leaving the track. A small hill is a kilometre away and should be climbed as it is an excellent guide for navigation. From its summit veer just west of north and descend the western side of a gully which is a tributary of the Goodradigbee River. By doing this you avoid high Black Mountain, on your left. The gully, however, swings east after about a kilometre and should then be left, so that you remain on the same bearing to cross several gullies and finally arrive high above the southern bank of Cave Creek which, at this stage, is in a gorge downstream of a waterfall. The route to Cave Creek will have been through pleasant, quite open forest, offering easy walking.

Turn west next, and follow Cave Creek upstream. Keep up high until upstream of the waterfalls as, otherwise, limestone outcrops will make walking awkward; then descend to grassy flats and a reasonable foot pad along the south bank. Follow the pad upstream into a gorge of sheer limestone which is quite interesting, especially if you look back east as you head to the western end of the gorge. The sheer sides mean Cave Creek must be forded several times too or alternatively bluffs could be scaled for bypassing.

About 2.0 kilometres upstream from the waterfalls, a small picnic area and jeep tracks should be meet in an area known as the Blue Waterholes. Have lunch by the stream and, perhaps, a paddle, then follow left fork jeep tracks twice so that you remain by streams; then cross a ford which is usually dry. You should then turn south up the track, through an open, grassy valley. Within 300 metres, Cave Creek enters from the west but the jeep track continues up southwards. At this point, you should follow Cave Creek upstream into another interesting gorge to where Cooleman Caves are located on the north bank, 300 metres approximately from the jeep track and to Murray Cave a further kilometre upstream. Spend as much time as possible exploring caverns, then return to the jeep track at least two hours before dusk, if the day is getting late. To finish the walk it is then only a case of following the jeep track uphill, south past Spencers Hut ruin on the right, then across extensive Cooleman Plains back to the saddle where you left the jeep track on the outward route. The last section is on a south-east bearing. You should then retrace the outward route back to your transport.

MAP REF: **Cooleman Caves map provided with this publication.** Map 50.

WALK DISTANCE: 22.0 km (ex eastern side of landing strip).

GRADING: One day, hard.

98   OLDFIELD HUT—MURRAY GAP—MOUNT BIMBERI

On the border of New South Wales and the A.C.T. are a number of lovely mountain peaks which reach above the tree line and so provide panoramic views. Alpine vegetation is an additional attraction. Mount Bimberi, at 1912 metres, is the highest of the peaks and, because of its situation, it gives the best views of the district.

To reach the start of a very good walk, travel north for 37.3 kilometres along Tantangara Road, from the Snowy Mountains Highway, to a point on the east side of Currango Plain. The last 19.7 kilometres north of Tantangara Dam wall has a poor road but it is trafficable to the walk start at the Murray Gap jeep track turnoff. The spot is south-east of the Goodradigbee airstrip at a Survey Peg R1069. Murray Gap track is very rough and leads off uphill, just before the road swings down to and across Currango Plain.

Start the walk by heading 250 metres up the track to a bend at a small stream. Then follow the track to the range top, 1.15 kilometres away. At the top, ignore the minor left fork and descend 700 metres distance, to arrive at a small plain with Oldfields Hut on the north side of the trail. The hut is in reasonable condition and has a verandah with a view to Mount Bimberi. Continue east, forking left on the plain rather than taking Lone Pine Trail, then cross Murray Creek; then climb up to Murray Gap via Dunns Flat. Lunch could be either at the Flat where water is available or the Gap which is 6.0 kilometres from the walk start. At the Gap there is a gate and sign prohibiting vehicular traffic beyond. At Murray Gap, the trail must be left and a scrub bash north up steep slopes follows. There is a 400 metre rise in elevation so you should find the climb a bit tiring. The upper 100 metres is, however, through extremely beautiful alpine herb and grass fields and views become better and better as you rise. It is 2.5 kilometres from the gap to the peak but, once you reach the top, you won't want to leave as it is so magnificent. Views include virtually the whole of the route you have just walked, the Cooleman Plains,

Corin Dam, Mount Murray just to the south and many of the peaks of the Kosciusko National Park.

Be careful when you leave to descend, making sure that you initially head south east then due south so that you avoid Little Bimberi and do not end up in dense forest down the slopes east from Murray Gap. The route should be an exact retrace of the outward journey.

MAP REF: **Cooleman Caves map provided with this publication.** Map 50.

WALK DISTANCE: 17 km.

GRADING: One day, hard.

99 ROUND MOUNTAIN—MOUNT JAGUNGAL

The Snowy Mountains country has a wide variety of walking venues, but perhaps the two best spots are the main Range and the Mount Jagungal area. The former features exposed tops and views and the latter, rambling alpine country including alpine plains, lovely snow gums and a few majestic peaks, exposed like the Main Range, and giving excellent views. Mount Jagungal dominates everything else for a huge area and rises up to 2061 metres, about 500 metres higher than the surroundings. There are good camping possibilities in many places, but it is suggested that you try a two day walk, camping at the foot of mighty Jagungal—or Big Bogong as it is also known. The camp spot is in the extreme headwaters of the Tumut River.

To reach the walk area, travel along the Tooma Road between Kiandra and Khancoban. Some 19.0 kilometres west of Cabramurra is the start of signposted Round Mountain Trail. It leads off from the south side of the road as a jeep track, but there is a barrier about a kilometre south and the track is open to walkers only beyond that point. Round Mountain itself is just next to the turnoff.

Start off walking along the trail. There are very few problems with navigation as virtually no side tracks branch off. Farm Ridge Trail, initially, leads east past Round Mountain Hut and Thiess Village track leads west both within the first 2.5 kilometres. You should generally walk south-south-west across delightful alpine plains, streams and flowers, gradually rising up the Toolong Range. About 10.5 kilometres from the walk start, the track veers to the south east and 4.0 kilometres later approaches Jagungal.

Near the base of Jagungal Grey Mare Trail branches off east. It leads to O'Keefes Hut, Farm Ridge and on to the Far Bald Mountain area. Turn east and follow this track for about 300 to 400 metres to where you cross the small stream which is the extreme upper headwaters of the Tumut River. Several good camp spots exist near the stream, the best is about 400 metres uphill beyond the ford.

Once settled into camp, the ascent of Jagungal will be a must. The top is 2.0 kilometres away and scrub is thick around the base but soon gives way to grassy slopes and flowers. There is no defined route but many parties go south-east to a spur then turn north-east for the main climb. The top is a mass of granite boulders and is quite impressive. Views from the top would surely be some of the best in New South Wales.

On the second day, follow the Grey Mare Trail in a north-easterly direction through snow gum country. After two kilometres, a guaging station should be passed near a creek which has a reliable water supply and a further 1.8 kilometres along the trail, O'Keefe's Hut should be reached. It lies to the right of the track in a large natural clearing, is in good condition and has a creek water supply close to the doorway.

The jeep track should then be followed northwards along a ridge for 1.5 kilometres, then down across Bogong Creek and up steeply to Farm Ridge a further 1.5 kilometres away.

Farm Ridge is the site of an old alpine grazing property and abandoned stockyards and ruined buildings can still be seen. Farm Ridge Trail forks off left from Grey Mare Trail at this spot. It should be followed north-west uphill. The ridge becomes quite lightly timbered and there are many very pleasant alpine clearings along the way. About three kilometres from Grey Mare Trail the headwaters of a south flowing stream could provide water for a meal break at an idyllic lunch spot on an alpine meadow with a superb view of Mount Jagungal.

After lunch, continue north-west one kilometre then north 1.4 kilometres. The trail then leaves the ridge and turns west, descending gradually for about a kilometre then again turns north to descend steeply down a well defined spur for 1.5 kilometres to the treeless Tumut River flats. A normally easily negotiated ford should be reached after 500 metres of walking across the flats, northwards. The spot is not very good for lunch or camping. A steep climb northwards follows to attain a spur crest within 600 metres distance. At this point the trail doubles back south-west and climbs for 1.3 kilometres to Round Mountain Hut. Midway between these points is a creek with a reliable water supply. Round Mountain Hut is in good condition with camp areas around it. Water lies 100 metres north in a creek.

Continue uphill for a further 500 metres amidst snow gums to rejoin the Round Mountain Trail. Turn north and retrace the previous day's walk route for 1.5 kilometres to the Tooma Road and the end of the walk.

MAP REF: **Jagungal Map provided with this publication.** Maps 51 and Map 51B.

WALK DISTANCE: 38.5 km.

GRADING: Two days, medium.

100 KOSCIUSKO NATIONAL PARK—MAIN RANGE.

Undoubtedly the Main Range of the Snowy Mountains would rank as one of the best walking venues in New South Wales or, for that matter, in Australia. Every Australian peak over 2000 metres high, except three, are situated in the range and the other three are all nearby. The tops are exposed and treeless with expansive views and there is a fair amount of interest caused by glacial action in the past. Apart from those in Tasmania, Australia's only tarns are here and the range is also renowned for displays of alpine flowers in summer.

A truly memorable two day walk circuit is possible, starting and finishing at Thredbo Ski Village on the Alpine Way, with an overnight camp beside Blue Lake, one of the tarns which is backed by 2196-metre-high Mount Twynam. The route includes the seven highest summits in Australia. The walk grading, however, is not hard as the circuit remains high and each peak does not involve long climbs.

Use the Crackenback Chairlift from Thredbo Village to save a 600 metre rise in elevation. (On the return it is suggested that you walk down the grassy ski slopes near the Chairlift.) The only major cause for concern is the weather, which can become quite foul and is apt to change dramatically. Should foggy conditions occur, extreme care should be exercised and compasses must be used. In a number of places snowpole lines can be used for guidance. The best time to visit the area is in mid-summer.

From the top station of the Crackenback Chairlift, at 1965 metres, set off north-west following a trail and snowpoles up through alpine meadow for about 1.3 kilometres, to a point east of the peak of North Ramshead — the first of a number of boulder-strewn summits to be climbed. The peak is 800 metres distant across snow grass and is 2177 metres high. To the north you can see Mount Kosciusko and all the main peaks along the range. To the south-west, 1.3 kilometres away, is Ramshead Itself. It is your next goal; however, you should first descend the western slopes of North Ramshead, drop packs, then head off to the peak. It is 2190 metres high and permits really good views, especially to the south and west.

Return to the packs, then sidle north along a minor pad on the western slopes of a ridge for 1.5 kilometres to Lake Cootapatamba. This tarn is in an exceptionally pretty setting, renowned for alpine flowers and it is suggested that lunch be by the shore. Next, head north north east 700 metres on a minor pad up to Rawsons Pass where there is a road. Follow the minor continuation of the road up north-west for 500 metres until you are near the main north spur of Mount Kosciusko where a good foot pad branches off north. Drop packs again and continue up the road to Kosciusko summit 2228 metres, so that you can finally say you have reached the top of Australia. There is a superb 360° view. Again, return to the packs and descend north-north-east near the crest of the range. At the first saddle, Hannels Spur Track enters from the left but should be ignored. Climb up to the top of Muellers Peak next which requires veering left off the main trail. Muellers provides more wonderful views down on to Lake Albina from its northern side. Go north-north-west from the top, then drop packs again down the slopes a bit then head off north-west to scale Mount Townsend, Australia's second highest at 2210 metres. It is only 2.0 kilometres from Muellers Peak, and views are best to the north-west. Go back to the packs and pick a route down the very steep slopes to Lake Albina. The descent is short but time consuming. There is still some 6.0 kilometres to walk for the day so, depending upon time available, have a rest by this lovely tarn. About 100 metres up the west side of its outlet is a good place for views of Watsons Crags and Lady Northcote's Canyon.

Ascend the steep slopes east from Lake Albina's northern end to rejoin the Main Range Track on the tops, 600 metres away. The climb is hard but, once on the tops, walking for the rest of the day is far easier. Turn left and walk over Mount Lee and Sharp Carruthers Peak before starting an easterly descent off the range to Blue Lake rather than forking left up the Mount Twynham jeep track. In the Carruthers Peak area you should see lovely Club Lake down to the right. It also is a glacial tarn. Fork left 600 metres short of Blue Lake after passing a locked hut then at Blue Lake you can be assured of an ideal campsite although there is no firewood so fuel stoves need to be carried if you wish to cook.

On the second day, packs should be left at the lake whilst an initial side trip is made—north to the top of Mount Wynam, the third highest in Australia at 2196 metres. It is noted for views to the north and down on to Blue Lake. The summit is about 1.5 kilometres from the lake's south-west shore which is the usual camping place. Access is best up the lake's west side to avoid cliffs.

Return to camp then retrace 600 metres of the previous day's walk, west up to a junction where you should fork left and walk basically down south-east for 2.5 kilometres to the Snowy River, via the Charlottes Pass jeep track. Have lunch by the Snowy ford then climb to Charlottes Pass, 500 metres away, and turn right to follow the now-virtually-disused road south-west for 4.0 kilometres. A snowpole line branches off south-south-west across the Snowy River plains to the Crackenback Chairlift top station, some 5.0 kilometres away and should be followed. The last 1.3 kilometres of the pole line is a retrace of the outward route of the previous day. From the top station, descend the grassy and flower-studded ski slopes to Thredbo Village to end what should have been a walk which will be remembered for life.

MAP REF: **_Koscuisko map provided with this publication._** Map 54.

WALK DISTANCE: 35.0 km.

GRADING: Two days, medium.

SELECTED REFERENCE WORKS

DISLEY, JOHN *Your Way with Map and Compass: Orienteering* (Teacher's Book) Canadian Orienteering Service.

PALLIN, PADDY *Bushwalking and Camping,* Paddy Pallin, Sydney.

BLACKSHAW, ALAN *Mountaineering,* Penguin, London, 1966.

PLATE, M. W. *Australian Bushcraft* (Periwinkle) Lansdowne, Melbourne, 1971.

KEEN, T. G. *Understanding Weather in Australia,* Rigby, Adelaide, 1972.

First Aid, The St John Ambulance Association.

Instant First Aid, Rigby, Adelaide, 1969.

Safety in the Bush, Hobart Walking Club.

MORCOMBE, MICHAEL *Australian National Parks, 'The East',* (Periwinkle) Lansdowne, Melbourne, 1969.

CHILD, JOHN *Australian Alpine Life* (Periwinkle) Lansdowne, Melbourne, 1969.

MILLET; MERVYN *Australian Eucalypts* (Periwinkle) Lansdowne, Melbourne, 1969.

CAYLEY, N. W. *What bird is That?*, Angus and Robertson, Sydney, 1966.

GOODE, JOHN *Guide to Australian Insects,* Cassells, Melbourne.

GARNET, J. ROS. *Venomous Australian Animals Dangerous to Man,* Commonwealth Serum Laboratories.

Bushwalking Near Canberra, Canberra Bushwalking Club.

Snowy Mountains Walks, The Geehi Club.